CRISIS
ON MULTIPLE EARTHS
THE TEAM-UPS

Gardner Fox
John Broome
WRITERS

Murphy Anderson
Dick Dillin
Carmine Infantino
Gil Kane
PENCILLERS

Murphy Anderson
Joe Giella
Sid Greene
INKERS

Carmine Infantino & Murphy Anderson
Gil Kane & Murphy Anderson
Murphy Anderson
ORIGINAL SERIES COVERS

V O L U M E   O N E

Dan DiDio VP-Executive Editor **Julius Schwartz** Editor-original series **Robert Greenberger** Senior Editor-collected edition
Robbin Brosterman Senior Art Director **Paul Levitz** President & Publisher **Georg Brewer** VP-Design & DC Direct Creative
Richard Bruning Senior VP-Creative Director **Patrick Caldon** Senior VP-Finance & Operations
Chris Caramalis VP-Finance **Terri Cunningham** VP-Managing Editor **Stephanie Fierman** Senior VP-Sales & Marketing
Alison Gill VP-Manufacturing **Rich Johnson** VP-Book Trade Sales **Hank Kanalz** VP-General Manager, WildStorm
Lillian Laserson Senior VP & General Counsel **Jim Lee** Editorial Director-WildStorm **Paula Lowitt** Senior VP-Business & Legal Affairs
David McKillips VP-Advertising & Custom Publishing **John Nee** VP-Business Development **Gregory Noveck** Senior VP-Creative Affairs
Cheryl Rubin Senior VP-Brand Management **Jeff Trojan** VP-Business Development, DC Direct **Bob Wayne** VP-Sales

TABLE OF CONTENTS

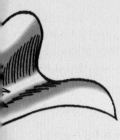

CRISIS ON MULTIPLE EARTHS THE TEAM-UPS VOLUME 1
Published by DC Comics. Cover, introduction, and compilation copyright © 2005 DC Comics. All Rights Reserved.
Originally published in single magazine form in THE BRAVE & THE BOLD 61, FLASH 123, 129, 137, 151, GREEN LANTERN 40,
SHOWCASE 55-56, THE SPECTRE 7. Copyright © 1961, 1962, 1963, 1964, 1965, 1968 DC Comics. All Rights Reserved.
All characters, their distinctive likenesses and related elements featured in this publication are trademarks of DC Comics.
The stories, characters and incidents featured in this publication are entirely fictional.
DC Comics does not read or accept unsolicited submissions of ideas, stories or artwork.
DC Comics, 1700 Broadway, New York, NY 10019 • A Warner Bros. Entertainment Company • Printed in Canada. First Printing.
ISBN: 1-4012-0470-8 • Cover illustration by Jerry Ordway • Publication design by Murphy Fogelnest

Much has been written about how editor Julius Schwartz and writer Gardner Fox introduced the parallel worlds concept to comics with the now-classic FLASH #123. The science fiction plot device had never before been done in comics in this way, and readers lapped it up and demanded more.

It took less than a year, but the two Flashes met once more and this time the question was raised: What about the older Flash's colleagues, the members of the fabled Justice Society of America?

The answer came yet another year later as it took two Flashes to rescue the captured JSAers from old-time foe Vandal Savage. With the original team of heroes free, it was only a matter of time before the mightiest collection of heroes ever assembled, the Justice League of America, got to meet their counterparts.

Truth be told, though, based on cover dates, the story in FLASH #137 was actually a setup for "Crisis on Earth-One" in JLA #21.

Still, regular meetings between the teams was a natural, and interest in the Golden Age heroes was increasing. This encouraged Schwartz to literally showcase more of them as seen in the pairings of Dr. Fate with Hourman and Starman with Black Canary. Had sales warranted, Schwartz was ready for more, and was ready to pair Dr. Mid-Nite and the Sandman, but it became clear that the readers preferred seeing heroes from the two different generations combine their talents.

Readers clamored for more one-on-one meetings between the like-named heroes and when the Green Lanterns paired up for the first time, the story created concepts that have continued to fuel the DC Universe to this day, as witnessed first in CRISIS ON INFINITE EARTHS in 1985 and in 2005, the sequel event INFINITE CRISIS.

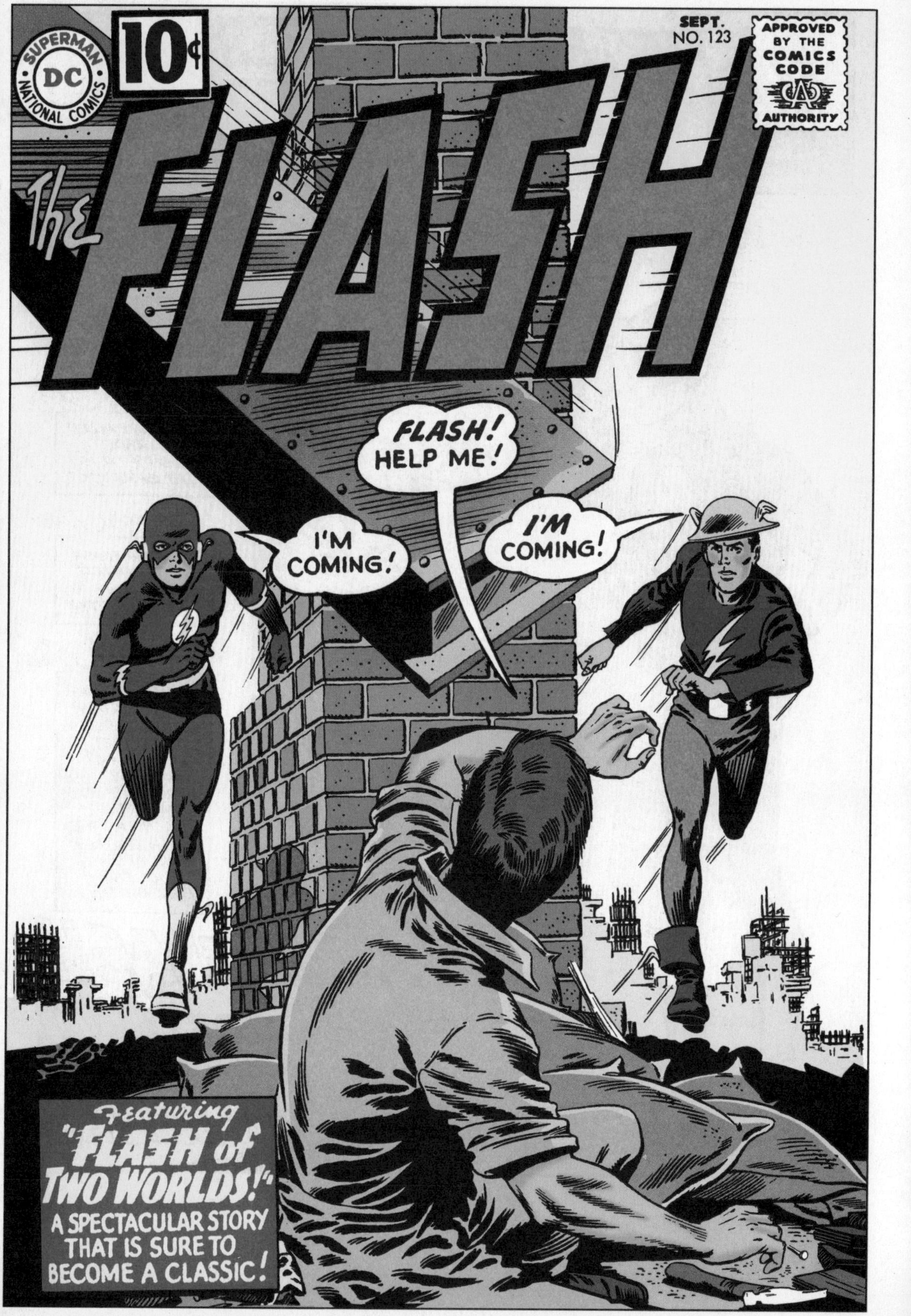
SUPERMAN DC NATIONAL COMICS
10¢
SEPT. NO. 123
APPROVED BY THE COMICS CODE AUTHORITY
THE FLASH
FLASH! HELP ME!
I'M COMING!
I'M COMING!
Featuring "FLASH of TWO WORLDS!" A SPECTACULAR STORY THAT IS SURE TO BECOME A CLASSIC!

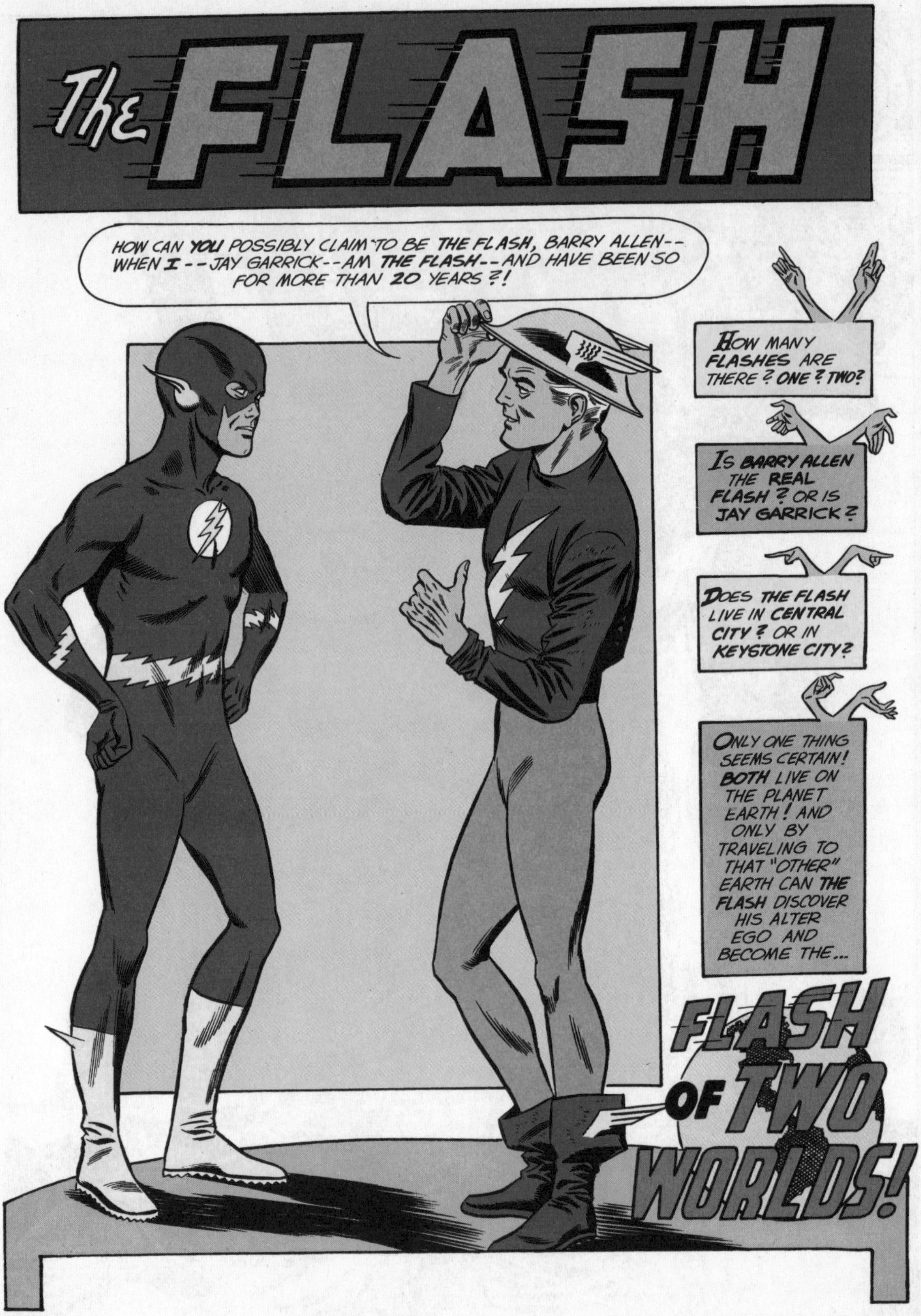
The FLASH
HOW CAN YOU POSSIBLY CLAIM TO BE THE FLASH, BARRY ALLEN-- WHEN I--JAY GARRICK--AM THE FLASH--AND HAVE BEEN SO FOR MORE THAN 20 YEARS?!
HOW MANY FLASHES ARE THERE? ONE? TWO?
IS BARRY ALLEN THE REAL FLASH? OR IS JAY GARRICK?
DOES THE FLASH LIVE IN CENTRAL CITY? OR IN KEYSTONE CITY?
ONLY ONE THING SEEMS CERTAIN! BOTH LIVE ON THE PLANET EARTH! AND ONLY BY TRAVELING TO THAT "OTHER" EARTH CAN THE FLASH DISCOVER HIS ALTER EGO AND BECOME THE...
FLASH OF TWO WORLDS!

AT ONE O'CLOCK IN THE AFTERNOON, BARRY ALLEN HURRIES TOWARD THE CENTRAL CITY COMMUNITY CENTER...

GOSH, I'VE GOT A DATE TO MEET IRIS-- AND I'M LATE AS USUAL! SHE'LL BE FURIOUS!

POLICE WORK TIED ME UP-- BUT ALL SHE'LL CONSIDER IS THE FACT I WAS SUPPOSED TO BE THERE AT TWELVE! SHE'S CHAIRLADY OF THE PICTURE NEWS ORPHAN FUND GROUP-- ONE OF HER PET PROJECTS...

HE'S LATE! OHHH-- THIS IS JUST TOO MUCH! I'LL NEVER HAVE ANYTHING TO DO WITH HIM AGAIN!

OH, BOY! IT'S EVEN WORSE THAN I THOUGHT!

IRIS... I JUST COULDN'T HELP IT! I WAS BUSY AT HEADQUARTERS!

I'M NOT TALKING ABOUT YOU, BARRY! IT'S THAT MAGICIAN WHO WAS SUPPOSED TO BE HERE TO ENTERTAIN THE ORPHANS! HE HASN'T SHOWN UP! THEY'LL BE TERRIBLY DISAPPOINTED!

Hmm-- I CAN'T STAY, IRIS, BUT TO MAKE AMENDS-- SUPPOSE I PHONE FLASH AND ASK HIM TO COME OVER AND FILL IN? I JUST LEFT HIM AT POLICE HEADQUARTERS!

THE FLASH? OH, BARRY-- YOU'RE AN ABSOLUTE DARLING!

MOMENTS LATER IN THE SHADOW OF A BUILDING OVERHANG, A RING EJECTS A SCARLET COSTUME THAT INSTANTLY EXPANDS ON CONTACT WITH AIR...

I TOLD IRIS FLASH HAD BEEN AT POLICE HEADQUARTERS, WHICH WAS TRUE ENOUGH SINCE I AM THE FLASH... AND THAT HE'D BE RIGHT OVER, WHICH IS-- ALSO TRUE!

MEANWHILE, IN THE **COMMUNITY CENTER**...

BOYS AND GIRLS-- I HAVE WONDERFUL NEWS! INSTEAD OF A MAGICIAN TO ENTERTAIN YOU, I'VE ARRANGED A SPECIAL SURPRISE VISIT FROM...

--THE WORLD-FAMOUS **FLASH**-- WHO WILL DEMONSTRATE SOME OF HIS SPECTACULAR SPEED STUNTS-- SEE? HE'S HERE NOW!

WHEE! LOOK AT HIM GO!

WHOOSH!

ON STAGE, AN INSTANT LATER, APPEARS THE **SCARLET SPEEDSTER**-- IN PERSON...

WHY DON'T YOU JOIN THE KIDS, IRIS? I'M GOING TO NEED THE WHOLE STAGE FOR MY DEMONSTRATION--WHICH INVOLVES PLAYING A GAME OF TENNIS WITH MYSELF!

AT EYE-BLURRING SPEED, THE **FASTEST MAN ALIVE** SERVES A BALL--THEN BEFORE HIS IMAGE CAN FADE FROM THE RETINA OF THE EYE HE IS ON THE OTHER SIDE OF THE NET-- DRIVING IT BACK...

KIDS, I'M THE FIRST MAN IN HISTORY WHO CAN WIN...

...AND LOSE THE SAME GAME!

AFTER AN HOUR OF LISTENING TO THE OOHS AND AAHS OF HAPPY CHILDREN, *THE FLASH* PREPARES TO MAKE THE MOST SENSATIONAL EXIT IN STAGE HISTORY...

IN INDIA, FAKIRS PERFORM A ROPE TRICK, USING HYPNOSIS! I'M GOING TO GO THEM ONE BETTER! WATCH CAREFULLY NOW...

HIS HAND--ROTATING SO SWIFTLY IT CANNOT BE SEEN--KEEPS THE ROPE UPRIGHT IN THE AIR...

NOT ONLY AM I GOING TO CLIMB THE ROPE AND DISAPPEAR--BUT THE ROPE ITSELF WILL VANISH, TOO!

THE ENTHRALLED AUDIENCE WATCHES *THE FLASH* CLIMB UP THE ROPE...

AND WHEN HE REACHES THE TOP...

HE'S GONE!

POP!

WOW! WHAT A TRICK!

SLOWLY THE MINUTES PASS, AND A FROWN OF WORRY CREASES IRIS WEST'S FOREHEAD AS THE CHILDREN CLAMOR AROUND HER...

WHY DOESN'T *FLASH* COME BACK?

WHERE IS HE, MISS WEST?

IT ISN'T LIKE *FLASH* TO DISAPPEAR AND NOT RETURN! WHAT COULD HAVE HAPPENED TO HIM?

WHAT *HAS* HAPPENED TO THE *SCARLET SPEEDSTER?* BY VIBRATING HIS BODY AND TWIRLING THE ROPE AT SUPER--SPEED, HE DISAPPEARED FROM SIGHT--*BUT WHERE TO?!*

4.

ONE SPLIT-SECOND AFTER HE VANISHES FROM THE STAGE, *FLASH* REAPPEARS ON A LONELY ROAD, STARING ABOUT IN ASTONISHMENT...

WHERE IS EVERY-BODY? WHAT AM I DOING HERE? AND-- *WHERE* IS *HERE?*

I COULD HAVE VIBRATED SO SWIFTLY THAT I PASSED THROUGH SOME SORT OF SPACE-WARP! I'M OUTSIDE *CENTRAL CITY*, I GUESS! BUT IT WON'T TAKE ME LONG TO GET BACK TO THE *COMMUNITY CENTER* STAGE!

AS HE RACES THROUGH THE CITY, A VAGUE UNEASINESS STIRS IN HIM...

STRANGE! I DON'T SEE THE *MEMORIAL TOWER*--OR THE *SPORTS STADIUM!* I JUST HOPE I HAVEN'T GONE THROUGH SOME SORT OF *TIME-WARP*-- AND THAT I'LL ENTER *CENTRAL CITY* BEFORE THEY WERE BUILT!

AS HE DASHES INTO THE *COMMUNITY CENTER*, HE FINDS IT DARK AND EMPTY...

WHERE IS EVERYBODY? THIS IS THE *COMMUNITY BUILD-ING*-- BUT IT'S DUSTY--LONG UNUSED...

NOW DEFINITELY WORRIED, THE *FASTEST MAN ALIVE* RACES CROSSTOWN...

I'LL STOP BY AND SEE IRIS-- FIND OUT WHAT HAPPENED...

A FURTHER SHOCK AWAITS HIM AS...

HUH? THIS ISN'T THE *PICTURE NEWS* BUILDING! INSTEAD--THE *KEYSTONE CITY HERALD* BUILDING IS WHERE IT OUGHT TO BE! WHAT'S GOING ON? WHERE AM I? WHAT--WHAT DAY IS IT?

KEYSTONE CITY HERALD

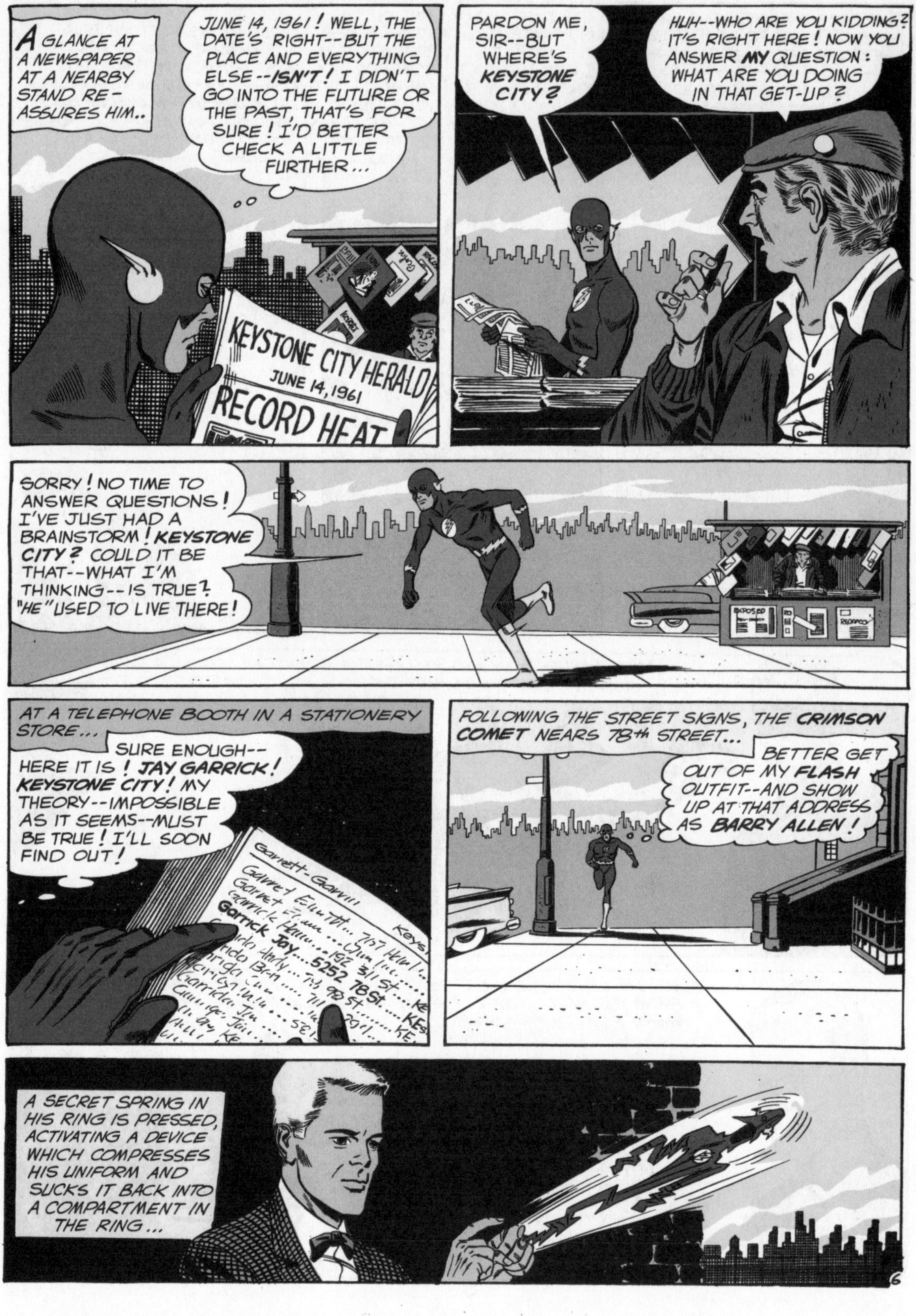
A GLANCE AT A NEWSPAPER AT A NEARBY STAND RE-ASSURES HIM..
JUNE 14, 1961! WELL, THE DATE'S RIGHT--BUT THE PLACE AND EVERYTHING ELSE--ISN'T! I DIDN'T GO INTO THE FUTURE OR THE PAST, THAT'S FOR SURE! I'D BETTER CHECK A LITTLE FURTHER...
KEYSTONE CITY HERALD
JUNE 14, 1961
RECORD HEAT
PARDON ME, SIR--BUT WHERE'S KEYSTONE CITY?
HUH--WHO ARE YOU KIDDING? IT'S RIGHT HERE! NOW YOU ANSWER MY QUESTION: WHAT ARE YOU DOING IN THAT GET-UP?
SORRY! NO TIME TO ANSWER QUESTIONS! I'VE JUST HAD A BRAINSTORM! KEYSTONE CITY? COULD IT BE THAT--WHAT I'M THINKING--IS TRUE? "HE" USED TO LIVE THERE!
AT A TELEPHONE BOOTH IN A STATIONERY STORE...
SURE ENOUGH--HERE IT IS! JAY GARRICK! KEYSTONE CITY! MY THEORY--IMPOSSIBLE AS IT SEEMS--MUST BE TRUE! I'LL SOON FIND OUT!
Garrett-Garvin
Keys
Garrick Jay...5252 78 St.
FOLLOWING THE STREET SIGNS, THE CRIMSON COMET NEARS 78th STREET...
BETTER GET OUT OF MY FLASH OUTFIT--AND SHOW UP AT THAT ADDRESS AS BARRY ALLEN!
A SECRET SPRING IN HIS RING IS PRESSED, ACTIVATING A DEVICE WHICH COMPRESSES HIS UNIFORM AND SUCKS IT BACK INTO A COMPARTMENT IN THE RING...
6

THEN BARRY'S FOREFINGER RINGS THE BELL AT 5252 78th STREET! THE DOOR OPENS AND...

YES--YOU'RE JAY GARRICK! A BIT OLDER--

YOU SEEM TO KNOW ME--BUT I DON'T RECALL EVER MEETING YOU!

MAY I SEE YOU IN PRIVATE, PLEASE? I SHARE A SECRET KNOWN ONLY TO YOU AND YOUR GIRL FRIEND--JOAN WILLIAMS!

COME IN! THIS IS THE FORMER JOAN WILLIAMS--NOW MRS. JAY GARRICK! BUT WHAT DEEP SECRET ARE YOU TALKING ABOUT?

BEFORE YOU ASK ME ANY QUESTIONS--LET ME TELL YOU WHAT I KNOW ABOUT YOU! BACK IN 1940, JAY GARRICK--YOU WERE A STUDENT AT MIDWESTERN UNIVERSITY! WHILE WORKING ON AN EXPERIMENT IN THE COLLEGE LABORATORY...

"YOU ACCIDENTALLY KNOCKED OVER A RETORT FILLED WITH HARD WATER! YOU INHALED ITS FUMES..."

WHEW! THAT GAS IS POWERFUL STUFF! IT'S--TOO MUCH FOR ME...

"YOU LAY UNCONSCIOUS ALL NIGHT LONG, BREATHING IN THE GASES EMANATING FROM THE HARD WATER! WHEN PROFESSOR HUGHES FOUND YOU, YOU WERE PRETTY FAR GONE..."

JAY, MY BOY-- HELP! SOMEBODY--HELP ME!

"AFTER SPENDING SOME WEEKS IN THE HOSPITAL RECOVERING, YOU EMERGED IN PERFECT HEALTH TO BECOME--*THE FLASH!* YOU FOUGHT CRIME AND CRIMINALS--AND OVER-CAME INJUSTICE...:"

AS HE CONCLUDES HIS NARRATIVE, BARRY SEES A STRANGE LOOK PASS BETWEEN JAY GARRICK AND HIS WIFE...

HOW COULD HE POSSIBLY KNOW ALL THAT?

WE WERE SURE WE'D KEPT THAT SECRET SO WELL! HOW DID HE FIND OUT?

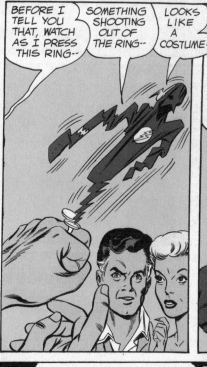

BEFORE I TELL YOU THAT, WATCH AS I PRESS THIS RING--

SOMETHING SHOOTING OUT OF THE RING--

LOOKS LIKE A COSTUME--

DONNING HIS UNIFORM, BARRY ALLEN BECOMES *THE FLASH*...

YOU SEE, ON *MY* EARTH, I AM ALSO-- *THE FLASH!* JUST AS YOU ARE-- ON *YOURS!*

TWO EARTHS? WHAT ARE YOU TALK-ING ABOUT?

RAPIDLY, BARRY (*FLASH*) ALLEN RELATES HIS RECENT EX-PERIENCE ON THE STAGE OF THE *COMMUNITY CENTER,* THEN...

THE WAY I SEE IT, I VIBRATED SO FAST--I TORE A GAP IN THE VIBRATORY SHIELDS SEPARATING OUR WORLDS! AS YOU KNOW--TWO OBJECTS CAN OCCUPY THE SAME SPACE AND TIME-- IF THEY VIBRATE AT DIFFERENT SPEEDS!

8

MY THEORY IS, BOTH EARTHS WERE CREATED AT THE SAME TIME IN TWO QUITE SIMILAR UNIVERSES! THEY VIBRATE DIFFERENTLY-- WHICH KEEPS THEM APART! LIFE, CUSTOMS-- EVEN LANGUAGES--EVOLVED ON YOUR EARTH ALMOST EXACTLY AS THEY DID ON MY EARTH! DESTINY MUST HAVE DECREED THERE'D BE A *FLASH*-- ON EACH EARTH!

MY NAME IS BARRY ALLEN! I'M A POLICE SCIENTIST! I LIVE IN *CENTRAL CITY*, WHICH IS ALMOST THE IDENTICAL TWIN OF YOUR *KEYSTONE CITY*, EXCEPT FOR A FEW DETAILS! ONE NIGHT, I, TOO, WAS WORKING ON AN EXPERIMENT...

"SUDDENLY A LIGHTNING FLASH HIT MY EQUIP-MENT, SMASHING VIALS OF CHEMICALS, BATHING ME IN THEM..."

CRAACK!

"DAZED--I CROUCHED AMID THE WRECKAGE OF THOSE VIALS AND CONTAINERS, DRIPPING FROM THE STRANGE BATH I'D BEEN COMPELLED TO TAKE..."

LIGHTNING...CERTAINLY IS--UNPREDICTABLE! IT KNOCKED ME OVER-- BUT DIDN'T SCRATCH THE CABINET--BROKE ONLY CERTAIN CHEMICALS AND BATHED ME IN THEM!

"SLIGHTLY WOOZY, I STARTED HOMEWARD ONLY TO DISCOVER I COULD OUTRUN A TAXICAB..."

WH--WHAT'S HAPPENING TO ME?

SO YOU SEE, I BECAME THE SUPER-FAST *FLASH* ON MY EARTH MUCH AS YOU BECAME *THE FLASH* ON YOURS! INDEED, READING OF *YOUR* FLASH ADVENTURES INSPIRED ME TO ASSUME THE SECRET IDENTITY OF *THE FLASH!*

WHAT?! HOW DID YOU EVER READ ABOUT *ME?*

YOU WERE ONCE WELL-KNOWN IN MY WORLD--AS A FICTIONAL CHARACTER APPEARING IN A MAGAZINE CALLED *FLASH COMICS!* WHEN I WAS A YOUNGSTER--YOU WERE MY FAVORITE HERO! A WRITER NAMED *GARDNER FOX* WROTE ABOUT YOUR ADVENTURES--WHICH HE CLAIMED CAME TO HIM IN DREAMS!

OBVIOUSLY WHEN *FOX* WAS ASLEEP, HIS MIND WAS "TUNED IN" ON YOUR VIBRATORY EARTH! THAT EXPLAINS HOW HE "DREAMED UP" *THE FLASH!* THE MAGAZINE WAS DISCONTINUED IN 1949!

AMAZING! THAT'S THE VERY YEAR I--*THE FLASH*--RETIRED...

YOU KNOW, I HAD NO SUCH INGENIOUS WAY OF GETTING IN AND OUT OF MY OUTFIT AS YOU DO! I SIMPLY TOSSED MY GARMENTS ASIDE AND KEPT MY *FLASH* COSTUME ON UNDER THEM! ODD, THAT YOU SHOULD APPEAR JUST NOW, BARRY-- WHEN I'VE BEEN THINKING OF COMING OUT OF RETIREMENT!

I'VE KEPT MYSELF IN GOOD SHAPE SO THERE'LL BE NO TROUBLE GETTING INTO MY OUTFIT! I'M STILL AS FAST AS EVER--THOUGH I NO LONGER HAVE MY FORMER ENDURANCE! NOW TO THE REASON WHY I'M MAKING A COMEBACK...

"YESTERDAY, THE FIRST OF A SERIES OF UNUSUAL THEFTS OCCURRED IN BROAD DAYLIGHT, WHEN IN THE *KEYSTONE CITY* BANK, MONEY LEAPED FROM THE TELLER'S CASH DRAWERS--TO DISAPPEAR!"

Ohhh--THE MONEY.. FADING AWAY...!

10

"THE SECOND STRANGE ROBBERY TOOK PLACE AT NOON IN CARMODY'S JEWEL SALON -- WHEN AN ODD BLACKNESS DESCENDED OVER EVERYTHING..."
I LIT A MATCH AND AM HOLDING IT IN FRONT OF ME--YET CAN'T SEE THE FLAME!
WHAT'S WRONG?
"WHEN THE PALL LIFTED, THE MOST VALUABLE GEMS IN THE STORE WERE MISSING!"
WE'VE BEEN ROBBED! SOUND THE ALARM!
"THE THIRD CRIME WAS COMMITTED WHEN STRANGE, EERIE MUSIC WAS HEARD-- AND SECONDS AFTERWARD, AN ARMORED BANK CAR CRASHED INTO A STONE WALL..."
WHILE WE WERE UNCONSCIOUS FROM THE CRASH-- SOMEBODY BROKE INTO THE CAR AND LOOTED IT!
THE POLICE ARE COMPLETELY BAFFLED! I'VE BEEN THINKING THAT THE FLASH MIGHT GIVE THEM A HAND..
AND I'D LIKE TO GIVE YOU A HAND, JAY! AS LONG AS I'M HERE, I'LL JOIN FORCES WITH YOU-- AND HELP SOLVE THE CRIMES!
GLAD TO HAVE YOU, FLASH!
WHOEVER THOSE CROOKS ARE-- THEY'RE IN FOR DOUBLE FLASH TROUBLE!

CRISIS ON MULTIPLE EARTHS
THE TEAM UPS

CHAPTER 2
FLASH of TWO WORLDS!

UNKNOWN TO EITHER OF THE TWO *FLASHES*, IN A MAGNIFICENT ROOM FITTED OUT WITH STOLEN TREASURES SIT THREE MEN--THE THINKER-- THE FIDDLER--THE SHADE--EACH A MASTER CRIMINAL, AN AVOWED FOE OF THE *FASTEST MAN ALIVE*! ALREADY, EACH HAS COMMITTED A ROBBERY! NOW THEY PLAN MORE...

EACH OF US HAS RECENTLY ESCAPED FROM THE PRISON WHERE *THE FLASH* PUT US!

THAT'S WHY WE'VE RETURNED TO *KEYSTONE CITY* AND JOINED FORCES, *THINKER*!

RIGHT YOU ARE, *FIDDLER*! TO CARRY ON WHERE WE LEFT OFF--TO ROB AND LOOT! AND IF LUCK'S WITH US, TO DESTROY OUR ARCH-ENEMY, *THE FLASH*!

THE THINKER CLASPS HIS HANDS OVER AN ODD METAL HAT...

YES, IT'S JUST POSSIBLE *THE FLASH* WILL COME OUT OF RETIREMENT TO TRY AND STOP US! BUT WITH THIS *THINKING CAP*-- WHICH CAN CAUSE ANYTHING I THINK OF TO HAPPEN WITHIN FIFTY YARDS OF ME--I'M WELL-ARMED TO DEFEAT HIM!

THE FIDDLER LIFTS HIS STRADIVARIUS VIOLIN...

MORE THAN A DOZEN YEARS HAVE PASSED SINCE WE SAW *THE FLASH*! NOW THAT I'VE IMPROVED MY FIDDLE, I'LL MAKE MYSELF RICH AND OVERCOME *FLASH* AT THE SAME TIME! WHILE IN JAIL WE HEARD NOTHING ABOUT *HIM*--BUT I HOPE NOW HE HEARS ABOUT *US*!

THE SHADE TOUCHES THE UNIQUE CANE WHICH IS HIS OWN INVENTION, AND CHUCKLES... I ALSO IMPROVED MY CANE HERE, WHICH MAKES ABSOLUTE DARKNESS FOR ME! I THINK, FELLOW CONSPIRATORS, WE ARE READY! FOR EVERY TRICK *THE FLASH* MIGHT HAVE, WE CAN GO HIM ONE BETTER!

⑫

ABRUPTLY *THE THINKER* CLAPS THE METAL CAP ON HIS HEAD...

I'M OFF NOW--TO STEAL THE PRICELESS *NEPTUNE CUP* FROM MILLIONAIRE EDWARD JARVIS!

LIKE THAT?! SURELY YOU'RE NOT GOING TO WEAR YOUR *THINKING CAP* IN PUBLIC?

YOU DON'T SEE THE *THINKING CAP* NOW, DO YOU? JUST AN ORDINARY FEDORA! THAT'S BECAUSE I'LL PLACE A MENTAL COMMAND ON WHOEVER NOTICES ME--TO SEE ONLY SUCH A HAT!

AMAZING, *THINKER*! AND WHILE YOU'RE OFF AFTER THE *NEPTUNE CUP*, I'LL BE ON MY WAY TO THE *KEYSTONE MUSEUM*!

THE EUROPEAN CROWN JEWELS ARE ON DISPLAY AT THE MUSEUM-- BUT WOULD LOOK MUCH BETTER IN OUR POSSESSION, AGREED?

AGREED, *FIDDLER!* AS FOR MYSELF I'M OFF TO THE WATERFRONT-- WHERE A COLLECTION OF HISTORICAL CURIOS WORTH MILLIONS OF DOLLARS LIES WAITING FOR MY FINGERS!

AT THIS MOMENT, IN THE GARRICK HOME, JAY SWITCHES TO *THE FLASH* IN HIS CUSTOMARY MANNER...

NOT AS SPECTACULAR AS YOUR RING, BARRY-- BUT EFFECTIVE ENOUGH IN ITS OWN WAY!

I CAN'T TELL YOU HOW EXCITED I AM TO BE GOING OFF ON A CASE WITH MY BOY-HOOD HERO!

SIDE BY SIDE THE TWO *SCARLET SPEEDSTERS* RACE ACROSS *KEYSTONE CITY*...

WE'D BETTER SPLIT UP HERE! APART, WE CAN COMPLETELY COVER THE CITY IN A MATTER OF MINUTES!

FINE! WE'LL MEET BACK AT YOUR HOUSE!

SOON AFTER, ON THE BROAD LAWNS OF THE JARVIS ESTATE...

I GAINED MY REPUTATION BY THINKING OUT MY CRIMES TO THE MINUTEST DETAIL! I EVEN PLANNED HOW TO USE THOSE WATCH-DOGS--TO HELP ME OVERCOME *THE FLASH!*

13

MENTALLY DOMINATING THE WATCHDOGS, *THE THINKER* PROJECTS AN IMAGE OF *THE FLASH* AND ISSUES A COMMAND...

WHEN AND IF THIS MAN APPEARS-- CALL OUT TO HIM-- TELL HIM WHAT'S HAPPENING INSIDE THE HOUSE!

PROCEEDING TO THE FRONT DOOR OF THE JARVIS MANSION...

PLEASE COME IN, SIR!

HA HA! I'M USING MY MENTAL POWERS WHICH THE *THINKING CAP* MULTIPLIES ENORMOUSLY-- TO HAVE THE BUTLER INVITE ME IN!

BY INCREASING THE ENERGY GIVEN OFF BY THE BRAIN TO ITS FULLEST CAPACITY, I CAN WORK SCIENTIFIC MIRACLES!

YOU'RE HERE TO STEAL THE *NEPTUNE CUP?* A PLEASURE, SIR, TO BE ROBBED BY YOU! ALLOW ME TO SHOW YOU WHERE THE CUP IS!

THERE! I'VE UNLOCKED THE CABINET IN WHICH I KEEP IT!

A BEAUTIFUL PIECE OF WORKMANSHIP! NOW-- LEAVE ME ALONE SO I MAY ADMIRE IT!

AT THIS MOMENT, SPEEDING PAST THE JARVIS ESTATE COMES THE "OLD" FLASH...

FLASH-- WAIT! THE THINKER IS INSIDE THE HOUSE-- STEALING THE NEPTUNE CUP!

HUH? AM I HEARING THINGS? THOSE DOGS-- TALKING! ESPECIALLY ABOUT-- THE THINKER?

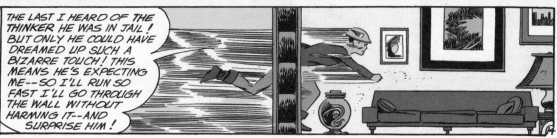

THE LAST I HEARD OF THE THINKER HE WAS IN JAIL! BUT ONLY HE COULD HAVE DREAMED UP SUCH A BIZARRE TOUCH! THIS MEANS HE'S EXPECTING ME-- SO I'LL RUN SO FAST I'LL GO THROUGH THE WALL WITHOUT HARMING IT-- AND SURPRISE HIM!

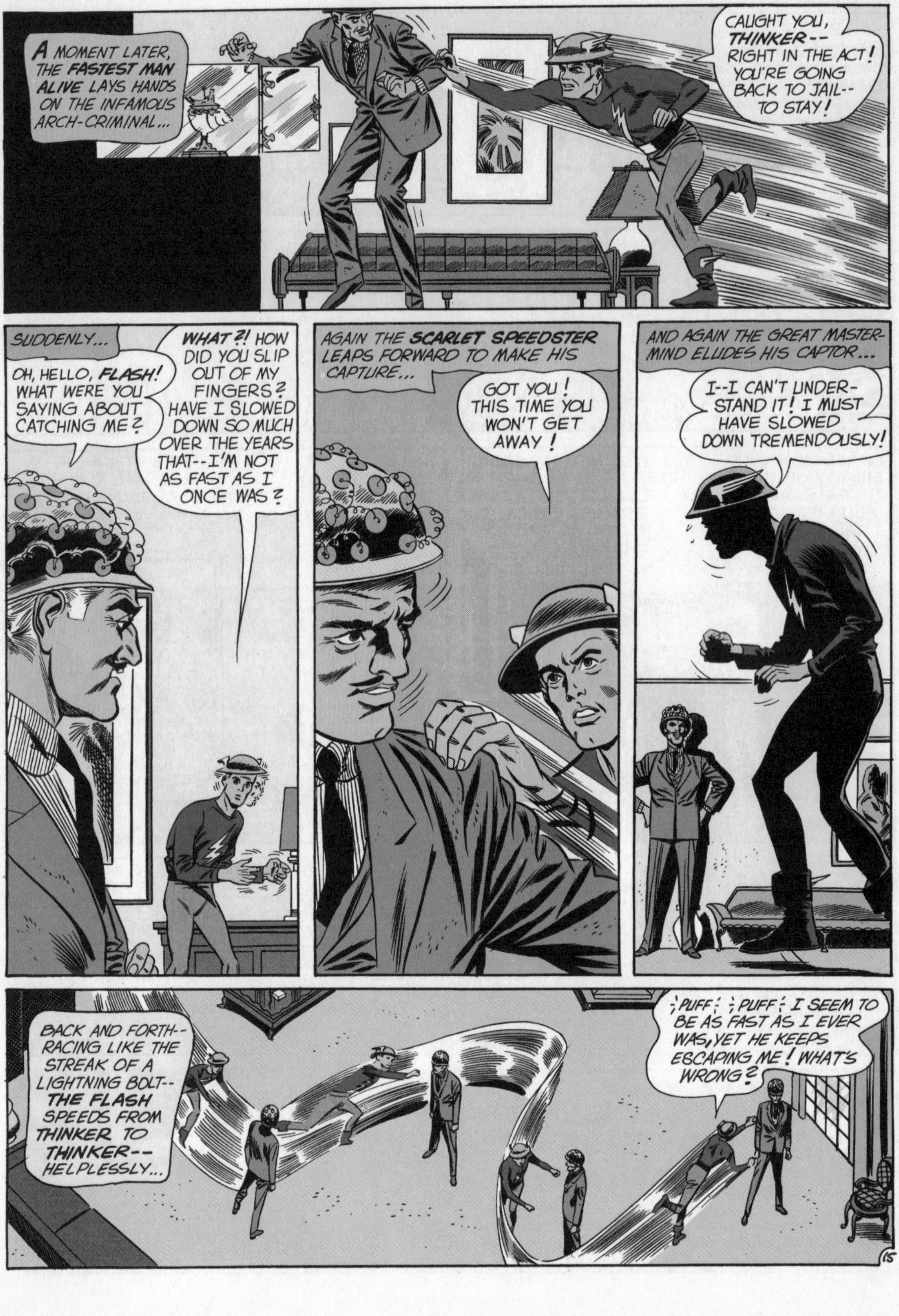
A MOMENT LATER, THE FASTEST MAN ALIVE LAYS HANDS ON THE INFAMOUS ARCH-CRIMINAL...
CAUGHT YOU, THINKER-- RIGHT IN THE ACT! YOU'RE GOING BACK TO JAIL-- TO STAY!
SUDDENLY...
OH, HELLO, FLASH! WHAT WERE YOU SAYING ABOUT CATCHING ME?
WHAT?! HOW DID YOU SLIP OUT OF MY FINGERS? HAVE I SLOWED DOWN SO MUCH OVER THE YEARS THAT--I'M NOT AS FAST AS I ONCE WAS?
AGAIN THE SCARLET SPEEDSTER LEAPS FORWARD TO MAKE HIS CAPTURE...
GOT YOU! THIS TIME YOU WON'T GET AWAY!
AND AGAIN THE GREAT MASTER-MIND ELUDES HIS CAPTOR...
I--I CAN'T UNDER-STAND IT! I MUST HAVE SLOWED DOWN TREMENDOUSLY!
BACK AND FORTH-- RACING LIKE THE STREAK OF A LIGHTNING BOLT-- THE FLASH SPEEDS FROM THINKER TO THINKER-- HELPLESSLY...
-PUFF- -PUFF- I SEEM TO BE AS FAST AS I EVER WAS, YET HE KEEPS ESCAPING ME! WHAT'S WRONG?
15

EXHAUSTED AND WEARY, *THE FLASH* LEANS AGAINST A CURIO CASE AS...

HE'S JUST TOO MUCH FOR ME! :, PUFF :, :, PUFF :,

SINCE YOU ADMIT IT, *FLASH*--I'LL MAKE MY *REAL* APPEARANCE FROM THIS CLOSET! THOSE OTHER *"THINKERS"* YOU SAW WERE ONLY MENTAL MIRAGES! IT WAS SO MUCH FUN TO SEE YOU KNOCK YOUR-- SELF OUT TRYING TO CATCH THEM!

I'VE DECIDED TO LET YOU LIVE-- SO YOU CAN FURNISH ME WITH MORE AMUSEMENT AT A LATER DATE! NOW THAT I'VE HAD MY FUN--*AND THE NEPTUNE CUP*-- I'LL BID YOU FAREWELL!

N-NO! YOU WON'T GET AWAY, *THINKER*...

AS HIS QUARRY LEAVES THE ROOM, THE *CRIMSON COMET* SPURTS FORWARD...

I'VE GOT TO SUMMON UP WHAT'S LEFT OF MY STRENGTH--OVER- TAKE HIM--

I'LL SLAM THE DOOR SHUT--WITH MENTAL ENERGY!

AND JUST AS *THE FLASH* REACHES THE DOOR- WAY...

TOOK ME BY SURPRISE...HAD NO CHANCE TO VIBRATE THROUGH-- I'M BLACKING OUT!

IN THE MEANTIME, ALONG THE WATER- FRONT WHERE A PRIVATE YACHT HAS DOCKED, A STRANGE BLACK CLOUD ENVELOPS THE SHIP...

WHAT IN THE WORLD IS THAT ODD BLACKNESS? IT'S SO DEEP AND THICK I CAN'T SEE ANY- THING INSIDE IT! I BETTER INVESTIGATE...

16

In the captain's cabin...

My special contact lenses enable me to see in this deep darkness! Ahh--this is the last of the historical curios which are valued at over five million dollars!

On the main deck, THE FLASH is stumbling along helplessly, blinded by the pitch-black fog...

I can't keep groping like this! I've got to get rid of this darkness so I'll know what's going on!

Around and around--faster and faster--spins the SCARLET SPEEDSTER--setting into rotation the darkness around him...

Gathering momentum, the darkness rotates more swiftly, until only a tornado-like funnel remains...

There! With the darkness concentrated all in one place, I can see what's going on!

Other eyes also see that ebony column and are stunned by it

Only FLASH could have done that! I've got to get away from here--fast!

22

WITHIN SPLIT-SECONDS, THE **SCARLET SPEEDSTER** HAS SEARCHED THE YACHT FROM PROW TO STERN AND...

THE HISTORICAL CURIOS TO BE EXHIBITED IN THIS COUNTRY ARE GONE AND--AH! THAT SPEED-BOAT HAS A MAN IN IT WHO LOOKS SUSPICIOUSLY LIKE A VILLAIN I ONCE READ ABOUT IN THE OLD **FLASH COMICS**--THE SHADE!

YES, **FLASH**--I'M HERE! **THE SHADE**! BUT-- YOU LOOK DIFFERENT THAN YOU USED TO! HOW COME?

YOU'LL FIND OUT--AFTER I CATCH YOU!

MY FIRST BLACKOUT TRICK DIDN'T STOP **FLASH**--BUT THIS ONE WILL!

FROM **THE SHADE'S CANE** THICK BLACK STREAMERS OF UTTER DARKNESS SHOOT FORTH ACROSS THE WATERS...

YOU DON'T THINK THAT BLACKOUT STUNT WILL WORK A SECOND TIME, DO YOU?

THERE'S MORE TO THIS DARKNESS THAN MEETS THE EYE, **FLASH**!

AS **FLASH** DASHES INTO THAT AWESOME BLACKNESS, HIS FEET SHOOT OUT FROM UNDER HIM AND...

OH! HE MIXED **OIL** WITH THE DARKNESS-- MAKING THE WATER SO **SLIPPERY** I-- CAN'T STAND UP! I'M FALLING! THE SHADE WILL-- GET AWAY!

18

SOME TIME LATER, IN THE GARRICK HOUSE...
THERE YOU ARE, JAY! I'M AFRAID I'VE GOT TO REPORT--FAILURE! I HAD THE SHADE AND--HE GOT AWAY!
MUCH AS I REGRET SAYING IT--THE SAME THING HAPPENED TO ME AGAINST THE THINKER!
THOSE ARCH-VILLAINS HAVE COME UP WITH IMPROVED TECHNIQUES! IT WON'T BE AS EASY TO STOP THEM AS I THOUGHT!
THEN WHY DON'T WE WORK TOGETHER--AS A TEAM? WE OUGHT TO BE TWICE AS EFFECTIVE THAT WAY!
TOGETHER, NEW FLASH AND OLD FLASH STREAK OUT TO TAKE UP THE CHALLENGES OF THE SUPER-CRIMINALS--UNITING AS A DUO FOR THE VERY FIRST TIME...
BUT, UNKNOWN TO THE FLASH PAIR, A STARTLING SURPRISE AWAITS THEM WHEN THEY COME TO GRIPS WITH THE LAST OF THE VILLAINOUS TRIO..
The FIDDLER!
THE WHIRLWIND ACTION STARTS ON THE FOURTH PAGE FOLLOWING...
19

CRISIS
ON MULTIPLE EARTHS
THE TEAM UPS

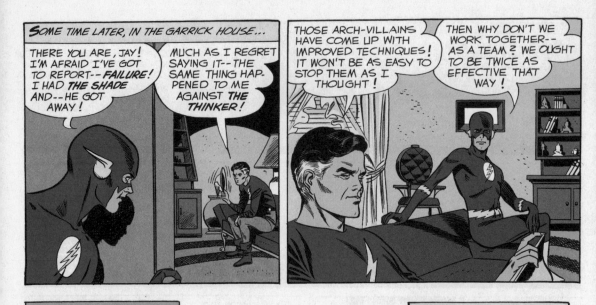

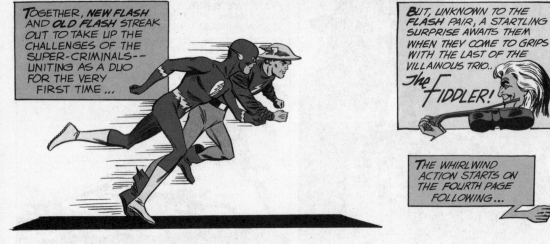

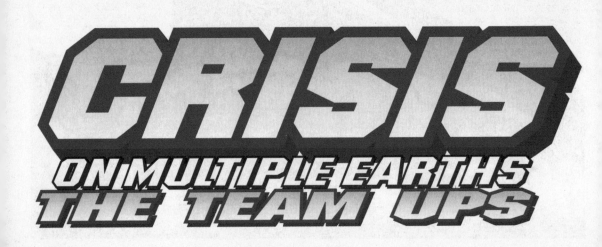

CHAPTER 3

FLASH of TWO WORLDS!

MY VIOLIN WILL CAUSE DISTRACTIONS TO OCCUR-- LIKE THAT SHOWER OF BROKEN WINDOWS WHICH CAUSES PEOPLE TO SCRAMBLE OUT OF THE WAY--SO NO ONE WILL PAY ME ANY ATTENTION!

AS *THE FIDDLER* MOVES THROUGH *KEYSTONE CITY* ON HIS WAY TO THE MUSEUM, HIS *FIDDLE CAR* UNDER AUTO-MATIC CONTROLS, THE EERIE MUSIC FROM HIS STRADI-VARIUS CAUSES ODD ACCIDENTS TO HAPPEN AHEAD OF HIM...

SHORTLY, AS THE TWO *FLASHES* BURST ONTO THE SCENE ...

HELP! HELP ME!

THAT CONSTRUCTION WORK UP AHEAD! SOMEONE'S IN TROUBLE!

ON EITHER SIDE OF A FALLING METAL GIRDER, THEY DASH TOWARD A MAN PINNED TO THE GROUND IN ITS PATH..

HELP ME, *FLASH! SAVE* ME!

I'M COMING!

I'M COMING!

MOVING AT SUPER-SPEED, ONE *FLASH* GRIPS THE FALLEN MAN...

GOT YOU!

20

WHILE THE OTHER *FLASH...*

BY CREATING A POWERFUL UPDRAFT, I'M CAUSING THE GIRDER TO RISE INTO THE AIR, BACK TO THE POSITION IT FELL FROM!

THE GIRDER FELL WHEN STRANGE MUSIC-- LIKE FROM A VIOLIN-- WAS HEARD! I SPRAINED MY ANKLE WHEN I RAN TO GET OUT OF ITS WAY! I COULDN'T MOVE!

STRANGE VIOLIN MUSIC? SOUNDS LIKE MY OLD FOE *THE FIDDLER!* HIS MUSIC CAN DO MIGHTY STRANGE TRICKS! COME ON, *FLASH* -- HE CAN'T BE FAR AWAY!

ONCE MORE THE TWIN THUNDER-BOLTS HURTLE INTO ACTION AS THEY TRAIL A SERIES OF ODD ACCIDENTS TO THE *KEYSTONE CITY MUSEUM...*

THERE'S HIS *FIDDLE CAR!* NOBODY'D NOTICE IT THERE, THE MUSEUM'S IN SUCH AN OUT OF THE WAY PLACE! HE MUST BE INSIDE!

VIBRATING IN UNISON, THE *SCARLET SPEEDSTERS* CATAPULT FORWARD...

WHAT'S HE UP TO--PLAYING HIS VIOLIN?

HE'S NOT JUST FIDDLING AROUND HERE FOR THE LOVE OF IT--THAT'S FOR SURE!

MEANWHILE, AT THE CROOKS' SECRET HIDE-AWAY...

HA! HA! YOU SHOULD HAVE SEEN *FLASH* TRYING TO CATCH THOSE MENTAL IMAGES OF ME! I NEVER LAUGHED SO MUCH IN MY LIFE!

ODD THAT HE SHOULD HAVE CHANGED SO MUCH SINCE WE LAST SAW HIM! HE LOOKED *YOUNGER*--WORE A DIFFERENT COSTUME!

21

DIFFERENT COSTUME? HE WORE THE SAME ONE! AND HE LOOKED THE SAME AS ALWAYS TO ME! A LITTLE SLOWER, SOMEWHAT OLDER--

WAIT--THERE'S ONLY ONE ANSWER! THERE MUST NOW BE TWO FLASHES! AND--IF THAT'S THE CASE, THE FIDDLER MAY BE IN DOUBLE TROUBLE!

WE BETTER SET OUT AT ONCE-- REACH THE MUSEUM BEFORE THOSE TWO FLASHES OVERCOME THE FIDDLER!

I HOPE WE'RE NOT TOO LATE!

SHORTLY, AT THE KEYSTONE CITY MUSEUM...

NO SIGN OF TROUBLE! WE'RE IN TIME!

FIDDLER--THERE ARE TWO FLASHES! COME ON, LET'S GET OUT OF HERE! WE CAN COPE WITH ONE--BUT TWO MAY BE TOO MUCH FOR US!

RELAX, MY FRIENDS! I CAN TAKE TWO FLASHES IN STRIDE AS EASILY AS ONE! JUST WATCH AS I PLAY MY VIOLIN...

IN STUNNED AMUSEMENT THE THINKER GASPS AND THE SHADE GAWKS AS...

THERE THEY ARE-- AND THEY'RE UNDER THE SPELL OF YOUR MUSIC!

THEY'RE DANCING-- LIKE PUPPETS!

22

27

BY EREBUS! THEY'RE NOT ONLY DANCING-- THEY'RE ACTUALLY STEALING THE JEWELS FOR YOU!

YES! YOU *TWO FLASHES*-- NEVER MIND THOSE *LITTLE* INDIVIDUAL GEMS! JUST BRING ME THE *BIG* JEWELED TREASURES --THE *CROWNS* AND *SCEPTRES*!

HELPLESS BEFORE THE OVERPOWERING MUSIC-- THE TWIN THUNDERBOLTS FILL THEIR HANDS WITH PRICELESS OBJECTS AND BRING THEM TO *THE FIDDLER*...

YOU SEE? THEY ARE POWERLESS TO RESIST MY MUSICAL COMMANDS!

ENOUGH OF THIS! I HAVE THE PRIZE JEWELS--AND WE'VE TAUGHT BOTH *FLASHES* OUR POWER! TO MAKE CERTAIN THEY DON'T BOTHER US FOR A WHILE-- I'LL FREEZE THEM SOLID FOR 24 HOURS!

AS THE EERIE STRAINS OF MUSIC FLOAT AROUND THEM, BOTH *FLASHES* GO RIGID...

THAT'LL HOLD THEM! NOW LET'S GET OUT OF HERE!

BUT AS *THE FIDDLER* AND HIS COHORTS TURN TO LEAVE THE MUSEUM...

HOLD ON, YOU CROOKS!

YOU AREN'T GOING ANY- WHERE!

THEY'RE FREE?! I BETTER GIVE THEM A HEAVIER DOSE--

AS THE "OLD" *FLASH* RACES PAST THE *SHADE*, HE SENDS HIM WHIRLING...

YOU'RE REALLY IN THE DARK NOW, *SHADE*! YOU'RE SPINNING SO FAST YOU CAN'T SEE A THING!

23

SIMULTANEOUSLY, THE OTHER **FLASH** GRASPS **THE FIDDLER'S** HANDS AND MOVES THEM SO SWIFTLY THAT...

THIS MAY BE THE FIRST **MUSICAL HANDCUFFS** IN THE LONG HISTORY OF CRIME!

WORKING AS ONE, FOUR HANDS DISASSEMBLE THE **THINKING CAP** BEFORE **THE THINKER** CAN GATHER HIS WITS FOR A SINGLE THOUGHT...

MINUTES LATER, THE THREE ARCH-CRIMINALS ARE BEING BOOKED AT THE LOCAL POLICE STATION...

I STILL CAN'T UNDERSTAND HOW YOU OVERCAME MY FIDDLE!

LIKE ALL CROOKS, YOU MADE A MISTAKE, **FIDDLER!** WE WERE FORCED TO OBEY YOU-- BUT YOU NEGLECTED TO ORDER US NOT TO TRY AND ESCAPE!

WHEN WE PICKED UP THOSE TINY GEMS WE PLACED THEM IN OUR EARS, RATHER THAN DISCARD THEM WHEN YOU SAID TO BRING YOU LARGER JEWELS!

THOUGH WE COULD STILL HEAR YOU, THE GEMS DISTORTED THE PITCH OF YOUR MUSIC JUST ENOUGH SO THAT IT NO LONGER HAD ANY EFFECT ON US!

LATER, AT A SPOT OUTSIDE **KEYSTONE CITY**...

THIS IS WHERE I VIBRATED INTO YOUR WORLD, JAY! IT'S TIME NOW TO RETURN TO MY OWN! I HOPE YOU CAN VISIT ME SOME DAY...

MAYBE I WILL, BARRY! NOW THAT I'VE COME OUT OF RETIREMENT, I THINK I'LL GO ON BEING **THE FLASH!**

THE "OLD" **FLASH** WATCHES THE "NEW" **FLASH** VIBRATE FASTER AND FASTER UNTIL HE BLURS OUT OF SIGHT...

SO THAT'S HOW HE DOES IT! I MUST REMEMBER-- SO I CAN VISIT HIS EARTH SOMETIME!

24.

IN THE NEXT SPLIT-SECOND THE FLASH STANDS ON THE EMPTY STAGE OF THE COMMUNITY CENTER...

IRIS AND THE KIDS HAVE GONE! NO WONDER! I WAS ON THAT OTHER EARTH FOR SEVERAL HOURS! I BETTER LOOK UP IRIS AND GIVE HER SOME SORT OF EXPLANATION FOR MY VANISHING ACT...

IT SURE IS SWELL TO SEE MEMORIAL TOWER AND THE SPORTS STADIUM--AND KNOW I'M HOME IN CENTRAL CITY! AH-- AND THERE'S THE PICTURE NEWS BUILDING UP AHEAD!

AND AFTER FLASH GIVES A HALF-HEARTED EXPLANATION OF HIS DISAPPEARANCE...

--AND THAT'S ALL YOU CAN TELL ME, FLASH? THAT YOU TOOK OFF ON A MOST UNUSUAL CASE? I'M SURE OUR READERS WOULD LIKE TO HEAR WHAT HAPPENED--

IRIS--HONESTLY--IF THEY READ IT IN YOUR NEWSPAPER, THEY'D SAY IT WAS PURE FICTION!

THE ONLY ONES WHO'D REALLY BELIEVE IT WOULD BE THE READERS OF FLASH COMICS! THAT'S WHY I'M GOING TO LOOK UP GARDNER FOX WHO WROTE THE ORIGINAL FLASH STORIES AND TELL IT TO HIM! HE CAN WRITE THE WHOLE THING UP--IN A COMIC BOOK!

The End

(25)

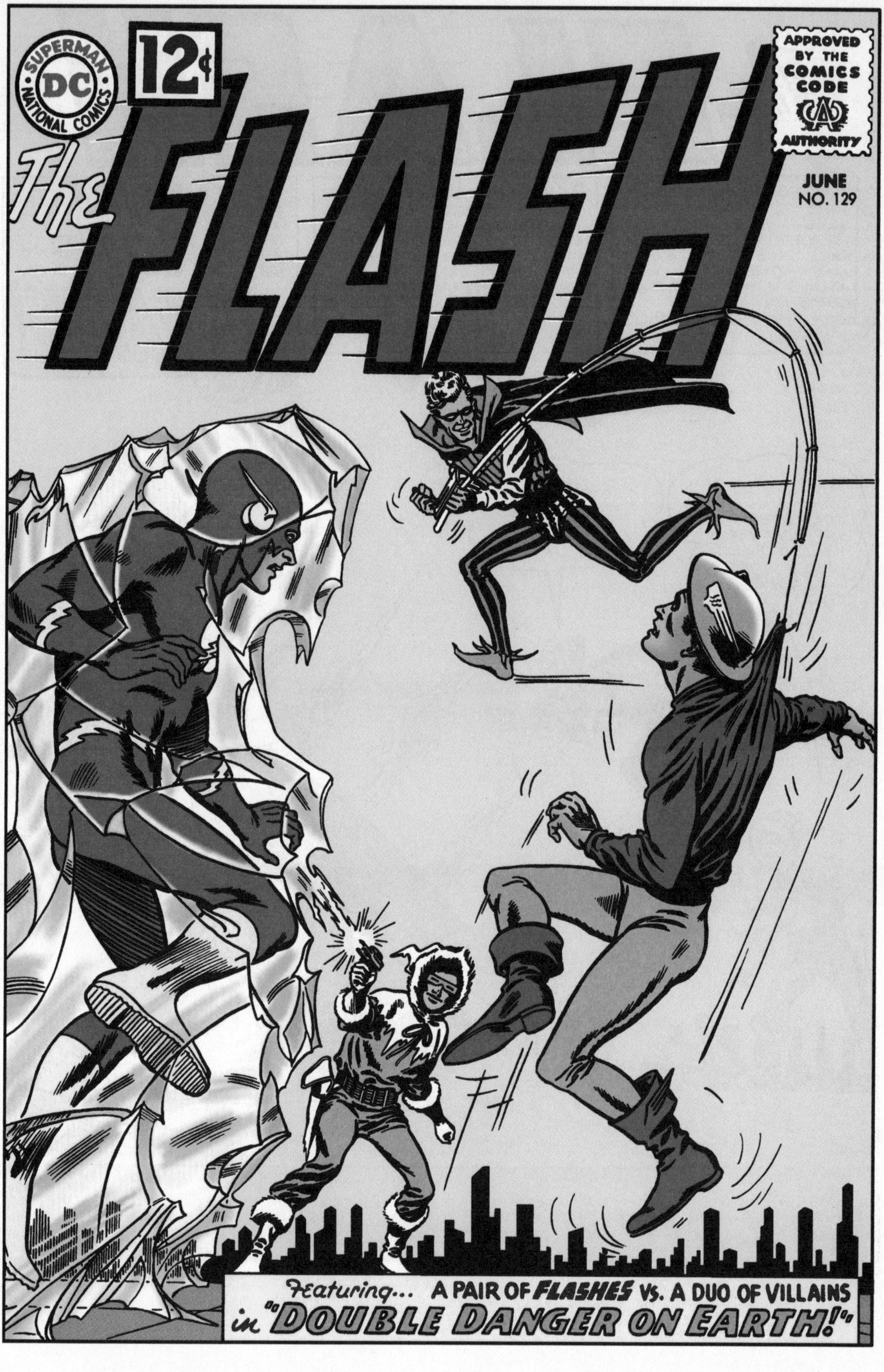

SUPERMAN
DC
NATIONAL COMICS
12¢
APPROVED BY THE COMICS CODE AUTHORITY
The FLASH
JUNE
NO. 129
Featuring... A PAIR OF FLASHES VS. A DUO OF VILLAINS
in "DOUBLE DANGER ON EARTH!"

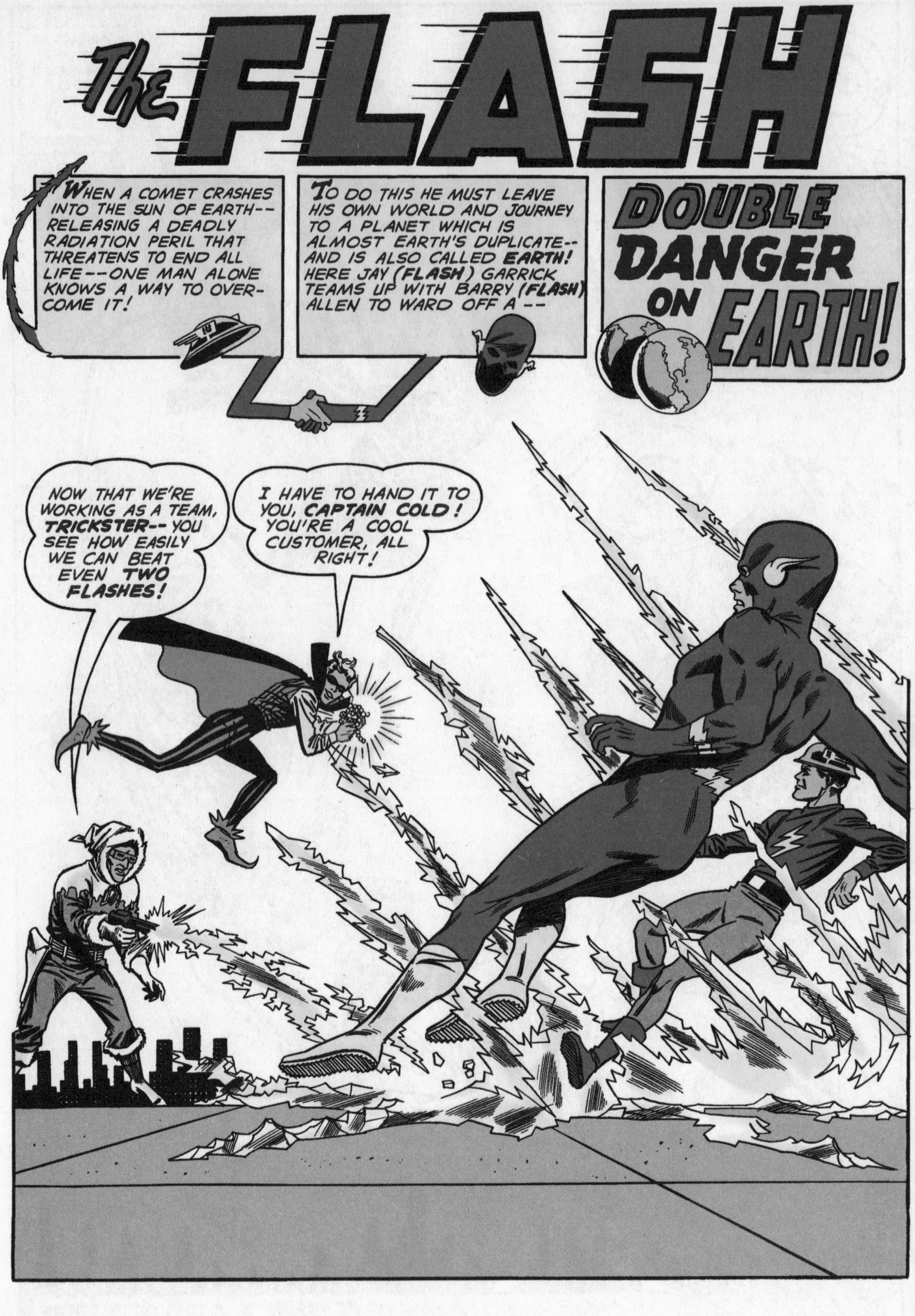

The FLASH
WHEN A COMET CRASHES INTO THE SUN OF EARTH-- RELEASING A DEADLY RADIATION PERIL THAT THREATENS TO END ALL LIFE--ONE MAN ALONE KNOWS A WAY TO OVER-COME IT!
TO DO THIS HE MUST LEAVE HIS OWN WORLD AND JOURNEY TO A PLANET WHICH IS ALMOST EARTH'S DUPLICATE-- AND IS ALSO CALLED EARTH! HERE JAY (FLASH) GARRICK TEAMS UP WITH BARRY (FLASH) ALLEN TO WARD OFF A --
DOUBLE DANGER ON EARTH!
NOW THAT WE'RE WORKING AS A TEAM, TRICKSTER-- YOU SEE HOW EASILY WE CAN BEAT EVEN TWO FLASHES!
I HAVE TO HAND IT TO YOU, CAPTAIN COLD! YOU'RE A COOL CUSTOMER, ALL RIGHT!

DURING LATE MARCH OF THE YEAR 1962, A MIGHTY COMET HURTLES THROUGH THE SOLAR SYSTEM-- BUT INSTEAD OF FOLLOWING AN ORBIT THAT WILL CARRY IT AROUND THE SUN, IT HEADS STRAIGHT FOR THE SOLAR BODY...

IT DRIVES DEEP INTO THE SUN ON APRIL 1, 1962 -- AND A GIGANTIC FLARE OF EPSILON RADIOACTIVITY RIPS OUTWARD FROM THE AWESOME COLLISION ...

THAT TYPE OF RADIOACTIVITY IS DEADLY TOWARD ALL LIFE ON EARTH!

IF WE CAN'T FIND A WAY TO STOP OR ABSORB IT IN TIME--MANKIND IS DOOMED!

WHAT'S THAT YOU SAY, READER? THERE'S NO RECORD OF A COMET HAVING HIT THE EARTH'S SUN ON APRIL 1, 1962? AH, BUT IT DID -- AND AS IT DID A WAVE OF TERRIBLE RADIATION MENACED EVERY LIVING THING ON EARTH! THIS IS NO APRIL FOOL'S JOKE-- NOR IS IT MERE FICTION! HOWEVER, THERE IS NO CAUSE FOR ALARM ...

FOR AS FLASH READERS KNOW, THERE IS ANOTHER EARTH -- ALMOST AN EXACT DUPLICATE OF OUR OWN-- WHERE THE FLASH IS NOT BARRY ALLEN BUT AN OLDER MAN NAMED JAY GARRICK...

HOW BAD IS IT, JAY?

PRETTY BAD, JOAN! IN FACT--IT'S MORTALLY DANGEROUS!

DEADLY RADIATION HITS EARTH FROM THE SUN!

YES, READER, IN THIS OTHER WORLD THE FLASH IS JAY GARRICK, WHO WAS MADE SUPER-SWIFT WHEN HE KNOCKED OVER A RETORT FILLED WITH HARD WATER AND INHALED THE FUMES...

IT IS THIS OTHER EARTH, THEN, THAT FACES THE GRIM RADIATION PERIL, NOT OUR OWN! FOR, AS JAY GARRICK EXPLAINS...

WHEN THE COMET CRASHED INTO THE SUN, IT WAS LIKE A MIGHTY ATOMIC BOMB EXPLODING-- ONLY ON A COSMIC SCALE!

EVERY ATOM BOMB EXPLOSION GIVES OFF HEAT AND A SHOCK-WAVE AND A RADIOACTIVE DUST CALLED "FALLOUT"! THE EXTENT OF THAT FALL-OUT IS MEASURED IN TERMS OF ROENTGENS! A CERTAIN AMOUNT OF THOSE ROENTGENS IS MORTALLY DANGEROUS!

"AS TIME GOES ON, THIS RADIOACTIVITY WILL BUILD UP IN OUR ATMOSPHERE, ITS ROENTGENS BECOMING MORE AND MORE DEADLY UNTIL EARTH TURNS INTO A LIFELESS PLANET..."

THE RADIATION IS LIKE A GIGANTIC ATOMIC BLAST TAKING PLACE IN THE SUN! IT WILL GET WORSE AND WORSE! PRELIMINARY CALCULATIONS SHOW THAT UNLESS THE RADIATION IS CHECKED--NONE OF US HAVE MORE THAN A FEW DAYS TO LIVE!

HOWEVER, MY BRANCH LABORATORY IN FLAGSTAFF, ARIZONA, HAS REPORTED THAT THERE IS VERY LIGHT RADIATION THERE--WHICH DISAPPEARS ENTIRELY IN THE VICINITY OF METEOR CRATER!

WHY SHOULD THAT BE?

I'M HOPING IT'S A SIGN THAT THE METEORITE BURIED IN THE CRATER *ABSORBS* THE RADIATION! MY JOB NOW IS TO CHECK INTO THE METEORITE, LEARN WHY IT ABSORBS THE RADIATION--AND TAKE STEPS TO PUT IT TO USE TO SAVE THE EARTH!

THE QUESTION IS--SHOULD I DO MY INVESTIGATING AS *JAY GARRICK,* WHOM THE PRESIDENT PUT IN OFFICIAL CHARGE OF THE RADIATION PERIL-- OR AS *THE FLASH,* SINCE I CAN WORK FASTER THAT WAY!

POOR DARLING! EVER SINCE BARRY ALLEN VISITED YOU * AND YOU DECIDED TO COME OUT OF RETIREMENT, THERE'S BEEN NO CALL FOR YOUR SERVICES AS *THE FLASH!*

I KNOW! I'M LIKE AN OLD FIRE HORSE WAITING FOR THE SOUND OF THE ALARM! THOSE WERE THE DAYS, JOAN! YOU WERE JOAN WILLIAMS THEN, NOT MRS. GARRICK...

*EDITOR'S NOTE: SEE THE FLASH #123: "FLASH OF TWO WORLDS!"

AS HE STARES WISTFULLY AT HIS UNIFORM, THE YEARS SEEM TO ROLL AWAY FOR THE FORMER *SCARLET SPEEDSTER...*

THE LAST TIME I WORE THAT BEFORE BARRY ALLEN VISITED US WAS ON THE *JUSTICE SOCIETY OF AMERICA* CASE "THE MYSTERY OF THE VANISHING DETECTIVES!" HOW WELL I REMEMBER THE LAST *JSA* ADVENTURE!

*EDITOR'S NOTE: ON JAY'S EARTH, THE *JUSTICE SOCIETY OF AMERICA* WAS A GROUP OF SUPER-HEROES WHO BANDED TOGETHER TO FIGHT CRIME AND INJUSTICE. ITS COUNTERPART ON OUR EARTH IS THE *JUSTICE LEAGUE OF AMERICA.*

"I CAN STILL SEE *WONDER WOMAN* LIFTING THAT SUBMARINE HIGH OUT OF THE WAVES--SHAKING OUT ITS VILLAINOUS CREW..."

"AND THE ATOM--AS HE BOWLED OVER HALF A DOZEN MEMBERS OF THE TURTLE-NECK GANG..."

"MY, YOU SHOULD HAVE SEEN THE WINGED WONDER, HAWKMAN--TWISTING WATER PIPES APART AND DELUGING THOSE CROOKS WITH TONS OF WATER..."

"AND GOOD OLD GREEN LANTERN--AS HE ENCASED HIS BODY IN EMERALD ARMOR SO BULLETS COULDN'T HARM HIM..."

BAM! BAM!

BAM!

"THEN THERE WAS DR. MID-NITE--UNDER COVER OF HIS BLACKOUT BOMB--WADING INTO A GANG OF CROOKS..."

"HOW ABOUT THE LOVELY BLACK CANARY? SHE WAS THERE, TOO..."

5

"WE WERE FIGHTING THE KEY, AS TOUGH AN OPPONENT AS WE EVER MET..."

SHAKING OFF HIS MEMORIES, JAY GARRICK COMPROMISES BY PUTTING ON HIS FLASH COSTUME AND COVERING IT WITH HIS REGULAR CLOTHES...

I DON'T KNOW WHEN I'LL BE BACK, HON! MAYBE NOT UNTIL THE RADIATION PERIL IS CONQUERED-- IF IT EVER IS!

I HAVE CONFIDENCE IN YOU, DEAR! YOU'VE NEVER FAILED ON A CASE YET...

IN HIS KEYSTONE CITY LABORATORY, AN HOUR LATER...

PLEASE WATCH, MR. GARRICK! THIS METAL CHUNK IS FROM THE CRATER METEORITE! WITH THIS LAMP WE'VE DUPLICATED THE DEADLY RADIATION...

AS THE EPSILON RADIATION STABS OUT--THE METEORITE GLOWS AND PULSES-- ABSORBING THE RADIATION AS A SPONGE DOES WATER...

THE GEIGER COUNTER DIDN'T EVEN CLICK! THAT MEANS WITH ENOUGH OF THIS METEORITE METAL-- WE CAN MAKE THE WORLD SAFE! I'LL BE ON MY WAY TO ARIZONA, NOW!

6

IN ARIZONIA, AT THE EDGE OF *METEOR CRATER*, HE MEETS OUTSTANDING SCIENTISTS AND HIGH-RANKING MILITARY OFFICALS WHO GIVE HIM A MESSAGE OF DOOM...

YOU DID EXCELLENT WORK, GARRICK--BUT IT WILL BE OF NO HELP...NO HELP AT ALL!

YOU SEE--THE METEORITE OF THE CRATER HAS MYSTERIOUSLY *VANISHED!*

*D*ISMAY SEIZES THE AUTHORITIES GROUPED ABOUT THE EMPTY CRATER...

WITHOUT THE METEORITE, WE'RE DONE FOR! AND THERE ISN'T ANOTHER SUCH TYPE OF METEORITE IN THE REST OF THE WORLD!

WHAT'LL WE DO? WHERE COULD IT HAVE GONE?

DEEP IN THOUGHT, JAY GARRICK SUDDENLY CRIES OUT HOPEFULLY...

WAIT, GENTLEMEN! THERE IS *ANOTHER* EARTH--EXISTING ALMOST SIMULTANEOUSLY WITH OUR OWN--PRACTICALLY A DUPLICATE OF OURS! OUR EARTH HAS A *METEOR CRATER*--SO MIGHT THAT OTHER EARTH!

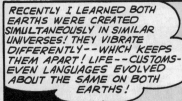

RECENTLY I LEARNED BOTH EARTHS WERE CREATED SIMULTANEOUSLY IN SIMILAR UNIVERSES! THEY VIBRATE DIFFERENTLY--WHICH KEEPS THEM APART! LIFE--CUSTOMS--EVEN LANGUAGES EVOLVED ABOUT THE SAME ON BOTH EARTHS!

IF WHAT YOU SAY IS TRUE--AND YOU CAN CONTACT THAT OTHER WORLD, DO SO!

IT'S OUR ONLY CHANCE TO STAY ALIVE, GARRICK! GET TO WORK ON IT!

OUT OF SIGHT OF THE OTHERS, JAY THROWS OFF HIS CIVILIAN GARB AND AS *THE FLASH*, RACES CROSS-COUNTRY TO A CERTAIN SPOT OUTSIDE *KEYSTONE CITY*...

FLASH OUTFIT ON! TIME IS MIGHTY IMPORTANT, NOW! I HAVE ABOUT THREE DAYS TO GET THAT METEOR, FOR AFTER THAT, THE EPSILON RADIATION WILL HAVE BUILT UP TO SUCH AN EXTENT THAT NOTHING WILL SAVE US!

*V*IBRATING AS HE HAD SEEN BARRY (FLASH) ALLEN DO, HE CARVES A PATHWAY BETWEEN WORLDS...

I HOPE THERE'S A *METEOR CRATER* IN BARRY ALLEN'S WORLD--WAITING FOR ME...

STORY CONTINUED ON THE PAGE FOLLOWING!

7

DOUBLE DANGER on EARTH!

Chapter 2

NOW LET US LOOK IN ON OUR OWN EARTH, WHERE THERE IS NO DANGER AT ALL-- EXCEPT PERHAPS TO BARRY (*FLASH*) ALLEN FROM IRIS WEST'S TEMPER-- FOR AS USUAL, HE IS LATE FOR A DATE WITH HIS GIRL FRIEND! TO SAVE TIME, HE TOUCHES THE SECRET SPRING ON HIS RING WHICH EJECTS HIS SCARLET COSTUME...

OH, BROTHER! IT'S EIGHT O'CLOCK-- AND I'M DUE RIGHT NOW AT IRIS'S APARTMENT! GOT TO HURRY, SO I'LL CHANGE INTO MY *FLASH* OUTFIT HERE...

AT SUPER-SPEED HE RIPS ACROSS TOWN TOWARD IRIS WEST'S APARTMENT, AND SOON ...

AT LAST-- THERE'S BARRY NOW! I JUST DON'T KNOW WHAT TO DO WITH HIM! HE'S ALWAYS LATE!

BRINNGG

BARRY ALLEN, I DECLARE! IF YOU WERE ANY SLOWER-- YOU'D STOP MOVING!

:PUFF!:-:PUFF!: I HURRIED, FAST AS I COULD...

GOT TO REMEMBER TO USE *BARRY'S* VOICE-- NOT *FLASH'S* VOICE!

HOLD ON, NOW!

IRIS WEST DOESN'T KNOW BARRY IS **THE FLASH**-- SO HOW COULD SHE ADDRESS THE FLASH AS-- *BARRY ALLEN*? IS IT POSSIBLE SHE HAS DISCOVERED HIS SECRET IDENTITY?

YOU KNOW, BARRY-- IN YOUR **COSTUME** FOR THE HEADLINE MAKERS BALL, YOU LOOK ALMOST LIKE THE **FLASH**! TOO BAD YOU AREN'T AS **FAST** AS HE IS!

THAT'S A PRETTY KEEN OUTFIT YOU HAVE YOURSELF, IRIS!

39

BY TAXI, THEY TRAVEL TO THE **HOTEL CENTRAL** WHERE SOCIETY IS GATHERING TO DONATE CASH FOR CHARITY AT THE ANNUAL **PICTURE NEWS** COSTUME BALL...

BEFORE THE NIGHT IS OVER, WE HOPE TO HIT THE $100,000 MARK!

I RECOGNIZE THE TELLERS AS MEMBERS OF THE **CENTRAL CITY** POLICE FORCE! GOOD! I KNOW THE CHARITY MONEY WILL BE SAFE!

THEY PROCEED INTO THE GRAND BALLROOM WHERE...

PEOPLE MASQUERADING AS SUCH HEADLINE MAKERS AS THE **MIRROR MASTER! TRICKSTER! CAPTAIN COLD! THE TOP!** *WHEW!* IF I DIDN'T KNOW THOSE VILLAINS WERE REALLY IN JAIL, I'D BE SUSPICIOUS!

AS THE ORCHESTRA PLAYS AND MOST OF THE PEOPLE ARE DANCING, A GUEST MOVES OUT INTO THE LOBBY...

THE THERMOMETER'S REACHED $100,000! I BROKE OUT OF JAIL TODAY WITH ONE OF MY COLD TRICKS-- IN TIME TO MAKE MYSELF RICH!

WHIPPING OUT HIS **COLD-GUN,** CAPTAIN COLD SENDS A PIERCING BEAM OF FROST THROUGH THE TELLERS' CAGES...

SUCH INTENSE COLD "QUICK-FREEZES" THEM SO THEY CAN'T MOVE!

AT THE SAME TIME, THE COLDNESS MAKES METAL AS BRITTLE AS GLASS! A SINGLE BLOW WITH MY HAND SMASHES THE METAL BARS OF THE CAGE!

CRASH!

9

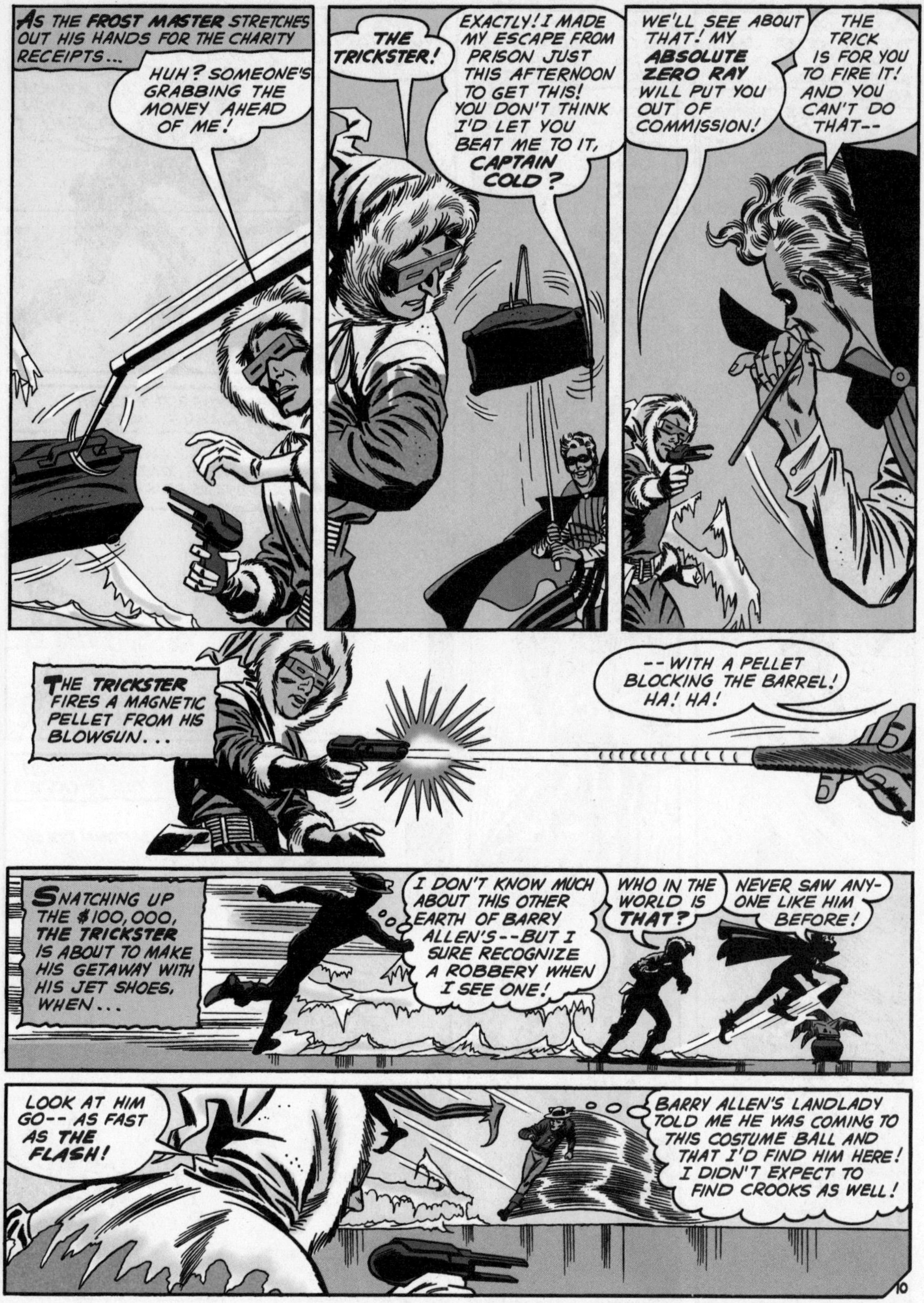
AS THE FROST MASTER STRETCHES OUT HIS HANDS FOR THE CHARITY RECEIPTS...
HUH? SOMEONE'S GRABBING THE MONEY AHEAD OF ME!
THE TRICKSTER!
EXACTLY! I MADE MY ESCAPE FROM PRISON JUST THIS AFTERNOON TO GET THIS! YOU DON'T THINK I'D LET YOU BEAT ME TO IT, CAPTAIN COLD?
WE'LL SEE ABOUT THAT! MY ABSOLUTE ZERO RAY WILL PUT YOU OUT OF COMMISSION!
THE TRICK IS FOR YOU TO FIRE IT! AND YOU CAN'T DO THAT--
THE TRICKSTER FIRES A MAGNETIC PELLET FROM HIS BLOWGUN...
--WITH A PELLET BLOCKING THE BARREL! HA! HA!
SNATCHING UP THE $100,000, THE TRICKSTER IS ABOUT TO MAKE HIS GETAWAY WITH HIS JET SHOES, WHEN...
I DON'T KNOW MUCH ABOUT THIS OTHER EARTH OF BARRY ALLEN'S--BUT I SURE RECOGNIZE A ROBBERY WHEN I SEE ONE!
WHO IN THE WORLD IS THAT?
NEVER SAW ANY-ONE LIKE HIM BEFORE!
LOOK AT HIM GO-- AS FAST AS THE FLASH!
BARRY ALLEN'S LANDLADY TOLD ME HE WAS COMING TO THIS COSTUME BALL AND THAT I'D FIND HIM HERE! I DIDN'T EXPECT TO FIND CROOKS AS WELL!
10

RACING DIRECTLY BELOW THE *TRICKSTER*, JAY (FLASH) GARRICK SPEEDS AROUND AND ROUND...

HE'S CREATED A DOWN-DRAFT WHICH IS CATCHING ME--MAKING ME FALL!

DOWNWARD PLUNGES THE CRIMINAL, CAUGHT BY THE AIR WHIRL-POOL...

I CAN'T STOP MYSELF! I'M GOING TO CRASH!

I'LL TAKE THAT MONEY AND RETURN IT TO THE AUTHORITIES!

AH--FINALLY WRENCHED THE MAGNETIC PELLET FROM MY COLD-GUN!

OH, NO YOU WON'T, YOU IMITATION *FLASH*!

THE VERY AIR FREEZES UNDER THE FLASH'S CHURNING FEET, MAKING HIM SLIP AND SLIDE, LOSING HIS BALANCE...

IF I DIDN'T KNOW BETTER, I'D THINK YOU WERE *THE FLASH* HIMSELF! YOU'RE AS FAST AS HE IS--BUT THAT COSTUME IS FROM *SQUARESVILLE*!

MY FEET-- SLIDING EVERY-WHICH-WAY!

HELPLESS BEFORE THE ICE WHICH CAUSES HIM TO CRASH HEAVILY, THE FLASH SEES THE TRICKSTER STIR AND BEGIN HIS MOVE...

THANKS, *CAPTAIN COLD!* I APPRECIATE YOUR SAVING ME FROM THIS "OTHER FLASH"! IF I WEREN'T DETERMINED TO KEEP ALL THIS MONEY, I'D SHARE IT WITH YOU!

11

MOCKING LAUGHTER TRAILS BEHIND THE RUNNING **TRICKSTER** AS HE RACES UPWARD ON HIS JET SHOES...

HEY, COME BACK HERE!

SORRY, I'VE GOT PLACES TO GO-- AND THINGS TO DO!

AS HE CIRCLES THE DANCE FLOOR WITH IRIS WEST, BARRY (**FLASH**) ALLEN FROWNS IN PUZZLEMENT...

THAT'S ODD! BY THIS TIME THEY WERE SUPPOSED TO ANNOUNCE WHETHER WE MADE THE $100,000 WE WERE AIMING FOR!

IT'S ALMOST MIDNIGHT, TOO!

I'LL HAVE A LOOK AROUND, IRIS! I'LL HURRY BACK--

--AT LEAST BEFORE THEY PLAY THE LAST NUMBER, BARRY! YOU KNOW HOW SLOW YOU ARE!

BUT ALL SLOWNESS DISAPPEARS AS **THE FLASH** HURTLES PAST THE FROZEN POLICE OFFICERS IN THE BROKEN TELLERS' CAGE...

THE POLICE TELLERS-- FROZEN SOLID! THE CHARITY MONEY-- GONE! THIS HAS ALL THE EARMARKS OF A JOB BY **CAPTAIN COLD!** SOMEHOW, HE MUST HAVE BROKEN OUT OF JAIL!

A LITTLE FURTHER ON...

HUH? AM I SEEING THINGS? JAY GARR-- I MEAN, **THE FLASH!**

¿WHEW!¿ I JUST HAD A RUN-IN WITH A COUPLE OF CROOKS! THEY ESCAPED ME BUT THEY COULDN'T HAVE GONE VERY FAR! LET'S GO AFTER THEM!

THERE'S ONE OF THEM NOW!

THE TRICKSTER!

12

43

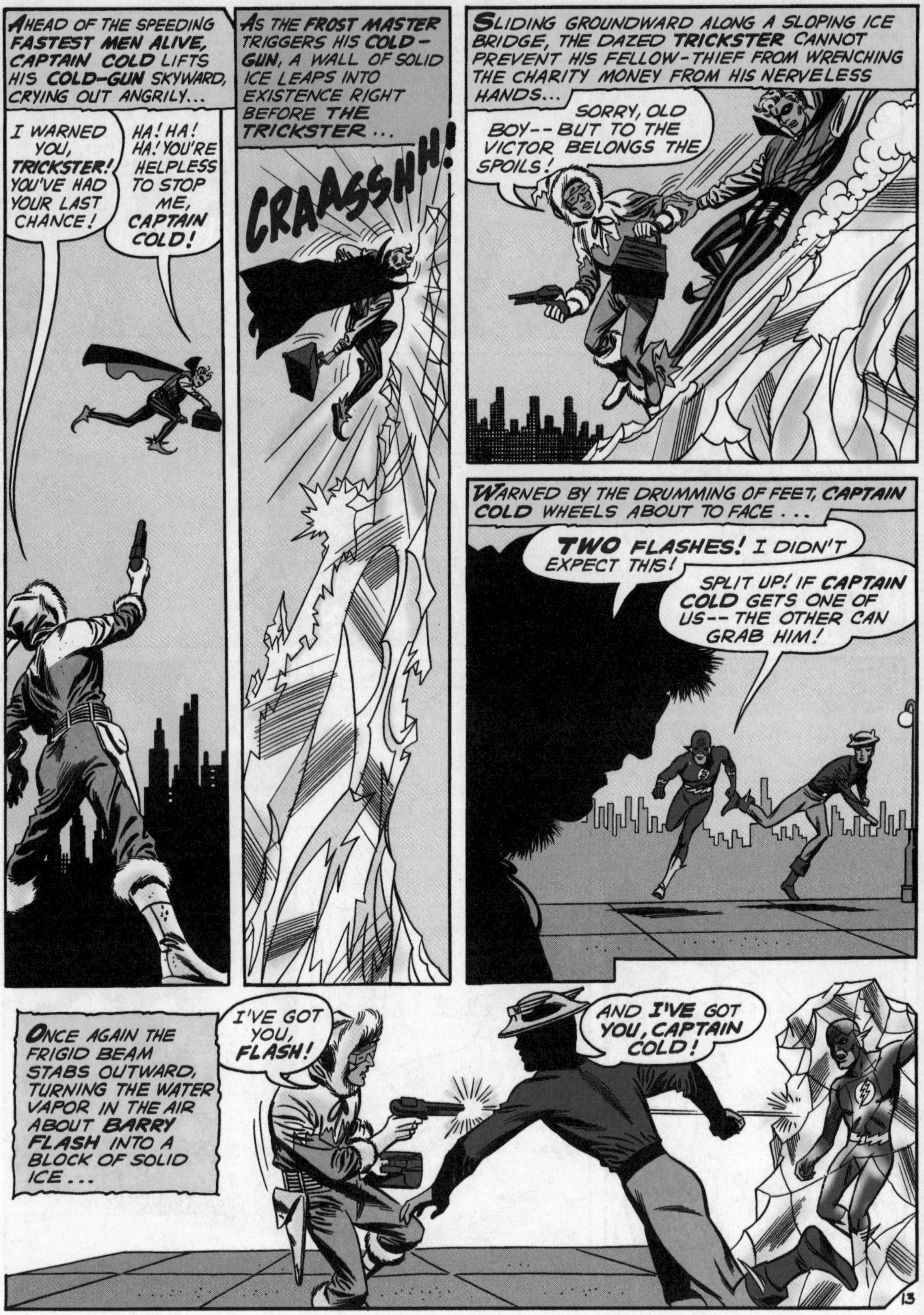

AHEAD OF THE SPEEDING FASTEST MEN ALIVE, CAPTAIN COLD LIFTS HIS COLD-GUN SKYWARD, CRYING OUT ANGRILY...
I WARNED YOU, TRICKSTER! YOU'VE HAD YOUR LAST CHANCE!
HA! HA! HA! YOU'RE HELPLESS TO STOP ME, CAPTAIN COLD!
AS THE FROST MASTER TRIGGERS HIS COLD-GUN, A WALL OF SOLID ICE LEAPS INTO EXISTENCE RIGHT BEFORE THE TRICKSTER...
CRAASSHH!
SLIDING GROUNDWARD ALONG A SLOPING ICE BRIDGE, THE DAZED TRICKSTER CANNOT PREVENT HIS FELLOW-THIEF FROM WRENCHING THE CHARITY MONEY FROM HIS NERVELESS HANDS...
SORRY, OLD BOY-- BUT TO THE VICTOR BELONGS THE SPOILS!
WARNED BY THE DRUMMING OF FEET, CAPTAIN COLD WHEELS ABOUT TO FACE...
TWO FLASHES! I DIDN'T EXPECT THIS!
SPLIT UP! IF CAPTAIN COLD GETS ONE OF US-- THE OTHER CAN GRAB HIM!
ONCE AGAIN THE FRIGID BEAM STABS OUTWARD, TURNING THE WATER VAPOR IN THE AIR ABOUT BARRY FLASH INTO A BLOCK OF SOLID ICE...
I'VE GOT YOU, FLASH!
AND I'VE GOT YOU, CAPTAIN COLD!
13

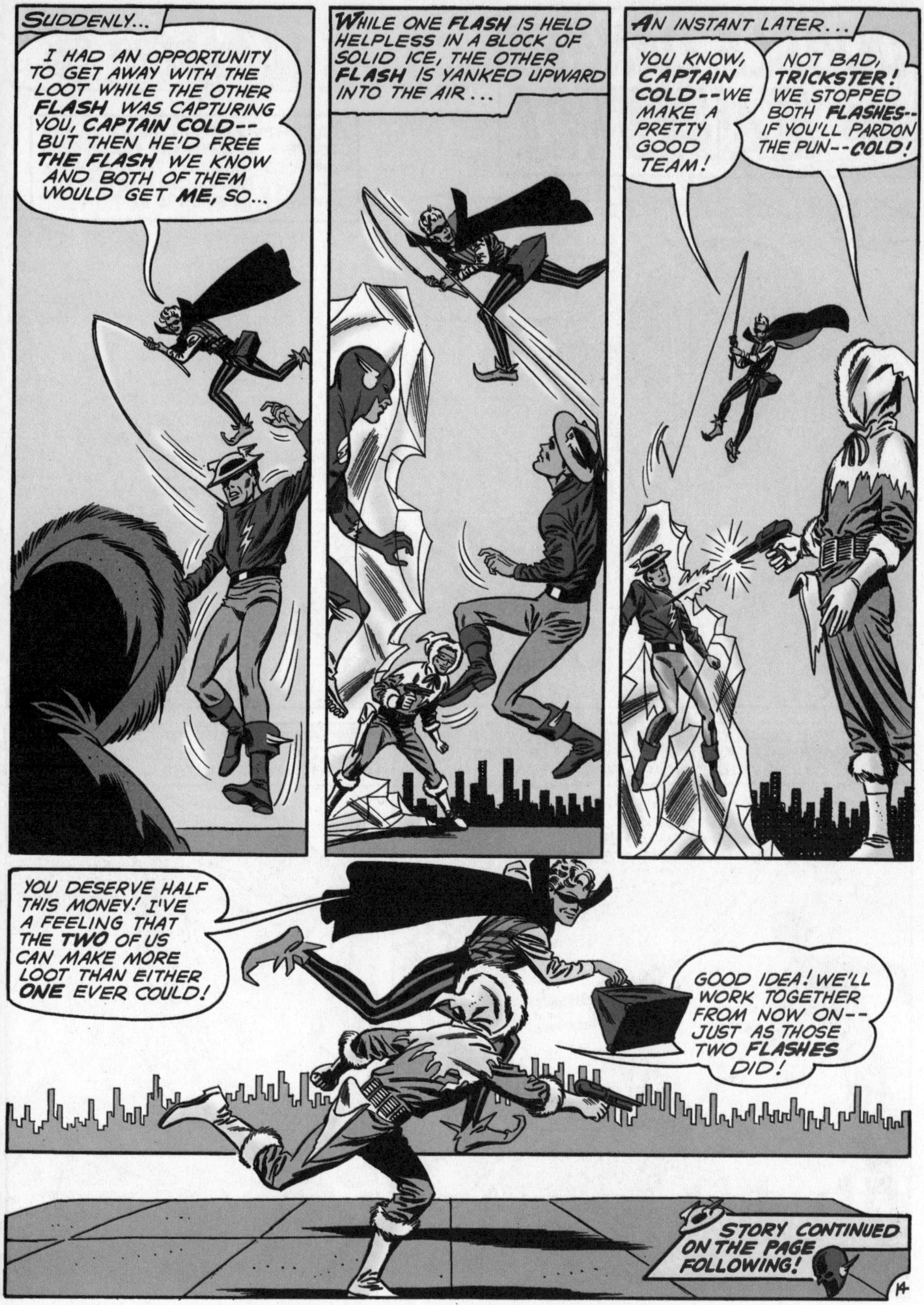
SUDDENLY...
I HAD AN OPPORTUNITY TO GET AWAY WITH THE LOOT WHILE THE OTHER FLASH WAS CAPTURING YOU, CAPTAIN COLD-- BUT THEN HE'D FREE THE FLASH WE KNOW AND BOTH OF THEM WOULD GET ME, SO...
WHILE ONE FLASH IS HELD HELPLESS IN A BLOCK OF SOLID ICE, THE OTHER FLASH IS YANKED UPWARD INTO THE AIR...
AN INSTANT LATER...
YOU KNOW, CAPTAIN COLD--WE MAKE A PRETTY GOOD TEAM!
NOT BAD, TRICKSTER! WE STOPPED BOTH FLASHES-- IF YOU'LL PARDON THE PUN--COLD!
YOU DESERVE HALF THIS MONEY! I'VE A FEELING THAT THE TWO OF US CAN MAKE MORE LOOT THAN EITHER ONE EVER COULD!
GOOD IDEA! WE'LL WORK TOGETHER FROM NOW ON-- JUST AS THOSE TWO FLASHES DID!
STORY CONTINUED ON THE PAGE FOLLOWING!
14

DOUBLE DANGER ON EARTH!

CHAPTER 3

HELD PRISONERS IN THE ICE BLOCKS CREATED BY *CAPTAIN COLD*, BOTH *FLASHES* REALIZE THEIR DEADLY DANGER! BUT--CAN THEY DO ANYTHING TO ESCAPE IT?

I'VE GOT TO FIND SOME WAY OUT--OR *CAPTAIN COLD* AND *THE TRICKSTER* WILL ROB AT WILL!

UNLESS I GET OUT OF HERE--EVERYONE ON MY WORLD WILL PERISH FROM THE *EPSILON RADIOACTIVITY!*

LET US TEMPORARILY TURN OUR ATTENTION FROM THE ICE-TRAPPED *FLASHES* TO THOSE MOMENTS JUST BEFORE *CAPTAIN COLD* CAPTURED THEM...

GOT TO TAKE-- A DEEP BREATH!

MUST BREATHE IN DEEPLY-- SO AS TO LEAVE A *GAP* BETWEEN MY BODY AND THE *ICE!*

THE SPACE BETWEEN THEIR BODIES AND THE ICE ENABLES THE SPEEDSTERS TO VIBRATE ...FASTER... FASTER...

15

SUDDENLY, THE SUPER-HEATED AIR GENERATED BY THE SUPER-SWIFT VIBRATIONS CAUSES THE ICE-BLOCKS TO SPLIT OPEN...

LOOKS AS IF WE HAD THE SAME IDEA--

--AT THE SAME TIME!

THEY SCOUR THE CITY AT WHIRLWIND SPEEDS, BUT FIND NO TRACE OF THE TRICKSTER AND CAPTAIN COLD...

WE'VE LOST THE TRAIL FOR NOW-- BUT THEY'LL SHOW UP AGAIN!

MEANWHILE, I HAVE A JOB TO DO HERE ON YOUR EARTH...

QUICKLY, JAY-FLASH RELATES THE TERRIBLE PROBLEM OF THE DEADLY EPSILON RADIATION THREATENING HIS WORLD...

SO I'VE GOT TO GET YOUR WORLD'S METEOR CRATER AT ONCE! IT'S THE ONLY HOPE OF SAVING MY WORLD!

I'D LIKE TO GIVE YOU A HAND BUT I BETTER STAY AROUND HERE AND WAIT FOR CAPTAIN COLD AND THE TRICKSTER TO STRIKE AGAIN! ANYHOW --GOOD LUCK! I'LL ALERT THE AUTHORITIES ABOUT YOUR MISSION HERE!

AS JAY (FLASH) GARRICK SPEEDS WESTWARD, BARRY (FLASH) ALLEN HURTLES EASTWARD, BUT ONLY A FEW BLOCKS...

:WHEW!: GOOD THING I SLOWED DOWN BEFORE IRIS TURNED TO LOOK AT ME! OTHERWISE, SHE MIGHT HAVE REALIZED THAT I REALLY AM THE FLASH!

WELL, MR. SLOWPOKE, WHERE HAVE YOU BEEN? I'M THE LAST PERSON LEFT AT THE BALL!

THERE WAS A ROBBERY, IRIS! AND AFTER ALL-- I AM A POLICEMAN, YOU KNOW!

A ROBBERY? TELL ME ALL ABOUT IT! AFTER ALL-- I AM A REPORTER, YOU KNOW!

BEFORE BARRY ALLEN CAN TAXI IRIS TO HER APARTMENT, JAY GARRICK IS ACROSS THE CONTINENT, AT METEOR CRATER...

I CAN'T DO THIS BY MYSELF! I NEED HELP-- SO I'LL ASK FOR IT AT THE CRATER MUSEUM!

16

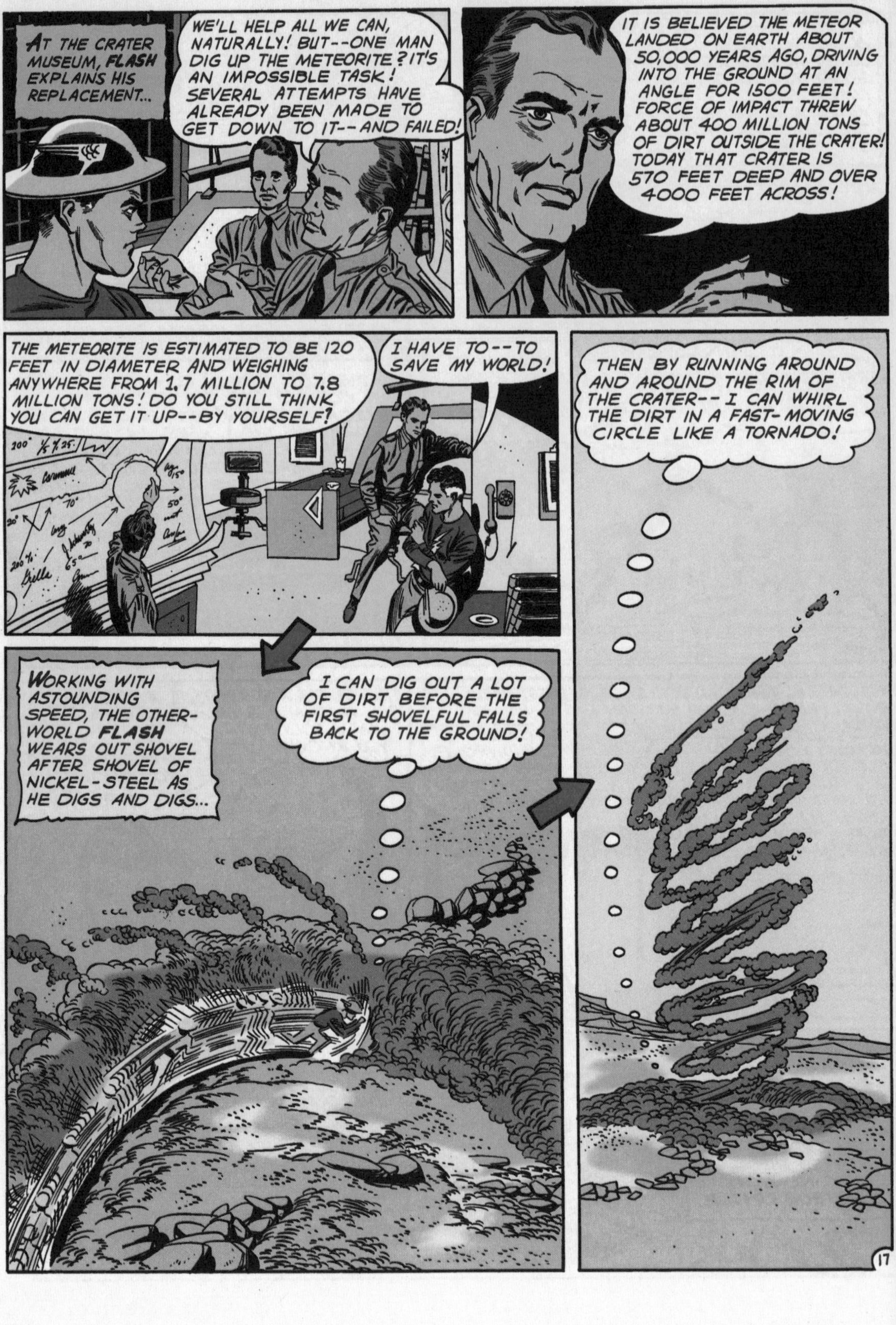
AT THE CRATER MUSEUM, FLASH EXPLAINS HIS REPLACEMENT...
WE'LL HELP ALL WE CAN, NATURALLY! BUT--ONE MAN DIG UP THE METEORITE? IT'S AN IMPOSSIBLE TASK! SEVERAL ATTEMPTS HAVE ALREADY BEEN MADE TO GET DOWN TO IT--AND FAILED!
IT IS BELIEVED THE METEOR LANDED ON EARTH ABOUT 50,000 YEARS AGO, DRIVING INTO THE GROUND AT AN ANGLE FOR 1500 FEET! FORCE OF IMPACT THREW ABOUT 400 MILLION TONS OF DIRT OUTSIDE THE CRATER! TODAY THAT CRATER IS 570 FEET DEEP AND OVER 4000 FEET ACROSS!
THE METEORITE IS ESTIMATED TO BE 120 FEET IN DIAMETER AND WEIGHING ANYWHERE FROM 1.7 MILLION TO 7.8 MILLION TONS! DO YOU STILL THINK YOU CAN GET IT UP--BY YOURSELF?
I HAVE TO--TO SAVE MY WORLD!
WORKING WITH ASTOUNDING SPEED, THE OTHER-WORLD FLASH WEARS OUT SHOVEL AFTER SHOVEL OF NICKEL-STEEL AS HE DIGS AND DIGS...
I CAN DIG OUT A LOT OF DIRT BEFORE THE FIRST SHOVELFUL FALLS BACK TO THE GROUND!
THEN BY RUNNING AROUND AND AROUND THE RIM OF THE CRATER--I CAN WHIRL THE DIRT IN A FAST-MOVING CIRCLE LIKE A TORNADO!
17

WITHIN MOMENTS A MIGHTY GUSHER OF DIRT, MUD AND WATER ERUPTS FROM THE IMPACT TUNNEL OF **METEOR CRATER**...

I'VE FORMED A SUCTION CUP WITH ROTATING WINDS-- WHICH DRAWS UP EVERYTHING BENEATH IT NOT FASTENED SECURELY...

AS THE DEBRIS SUBSIDES TO THE GROUND BEYOND THE CRATER RIM, FOR THE FIRST TIME IN RECORDED HISTORY, MEN'S EYES STARE DOWN AT THE FAMOUS METEORITE...

DESCENDING INTO THE CRATER, THE **SCARLET SPEEDSTER** USES HIS STUPENDOUS SPEED TO "CUT" THE METEORITE INTO SECTIONS...

SOON AN IMPOSING MOUNTAIN OF METEORIC INGOTS IS STACKED BY THE CRATER MUSEUM, AWAITING SHIPMENT...

AMAZING! BUT NOW THAT YOU'VE UNCOVERED IT-- HOW CAN YOU POSSIBLY TRANSPORT IT BACK TO YOUR WORLD?

NOT ALL IN ONE PIECE, THAT'S FOR SURE!

JUST AS A STRAW CAN PENETRATE A TREE WHEN BLOWN BY HURRICANE WINDS-- JUST AS I CAN VIBRATE THROUGH SOLID WALLS-- SO MY HANDS, BY MOVING AT SUPER-SPEED-- CAN SLICE THE METAL OF THE METEORITE!

I FIGURE ANOTHER HALF HOUR AND I'LL HAVE THE WHOLE METEORITE DISMANTLED AND READY TO GO!

IN THE MEANTIME, HIS FRIEND BARRY (**FLASH**) ALLEN HAS ARRANGED TO HAVE THESE METEORIC INGOTS BROUGHT TO **CENTRAL CITY** BY AIR TRANSPORT...

I'LL GIVE THEM AN HOUR'S START, THEN TAKE OFF MYSELF!

IN **CENTRAL CITY**, THE NEWSPAPERS HAVE SEIZED ON THE VISIT BY THE OTHER-EARTH **FLASH** WITH BANNER HEADLINES...

ISN'T THIS EXCITING, BARRY? ANOTHER **FLASH**! MY GOODNESS! AND TO THINK I HAVE THE EXCLUSIVE STORY ABOUT HIM!

JAY'S WORK IS ALMOST FINISHED HERE! WISH I COULD SAY THE SAME-- BUT I STILL HAVEN'T CAUGHT UP WITH **CAPTAIN COLD** AND THE **TRICKSTER** YET!

PICTURE NEWS

FLASH FROM OTHER EARTH HERE TO SAVE HIS OWN!

STORY BY IRIS WEST

FLASH

18

WHEN THE TWO **FLASHES** NEXT MEET, THE INGOTS ARE READY FOR SHIPMENT INTO JAY GARRICK'S WORLD...

HI, **FLASH!** I'M BUILDING THIS VIBRATOR-TRANSPORTER TO CARRY THESE INGOTS FROM YOUR WORLD TO MINE!

I'LL GIVE YOU A HAND WITH THEM!

THIS ASSEMBLY LINE BELT WILL FEED INGOTS INTO THE VIBRATOR, WHICH WILL SHIFT THEM TO MY WORLD! BY THE WAY-- WHAT ABOUT **CAPTAIN COLD** AND THE **TRICKSTER?**

THEY'RE STILL AT LARGE-- BUT THESE METEORITE INGOTS MIGHT HELP US TRAP THEM! LISTEN...

NEXT DAY, **PICTURE NEWS** IS FILLED WITH THE STORY OF A "BIG FIND"...

I WANT TO THANK YOU BOTH FOR THIS SCOOP!

WE WANT TO THANK YOU TOO, IRIS-- BUT WE CAN'T WITHOUT GIVING AWAY OUR PLAN TO CATCH **CAPTAIN COLD** AND THE **TRICKSTER!**

ARIZONA METEORITE CONTAINS DIAMOND FORTUNE!

OTHER WORLD FLASH RETURNS BILLION DOLLARS IN JEWELS!

"HAS NO USE FOR THEM," HE SAYS!

NEXT DAY, AS THE VIBRATOR-TRANSPORTER BEGINS TO FUNCTION, **CAPTAIN COLD** AND THE **TRICKSTER** ARRIVE IN ANSWER TO THOSE HEADLINES...

WITH THIS NEW FAN ATTACHMENT ON MY COLD-GUN, I CAN BLANKET THE CITY WITH AN IMPULSE OF ABSOLUTE COLD EVEN FASTER THAN I COULD BEFORE!

PRETTY COOL TRICK, **CAPTAIN COLD!**

MOMENTS LATER...

YOU FROZE BOTH **FLASHES** STIFF, TOO! NOW I CAN SCOOP UP THOSE DIAMONDS THEY REMOVED FROM THE METEORITE WITHOUT WORRYING ABOUT THEM!

YOU WERE RIGHT, **TRICKSTER!** WE **DO** MAKE AN UNBEATABLE CRIME TEAM!

19

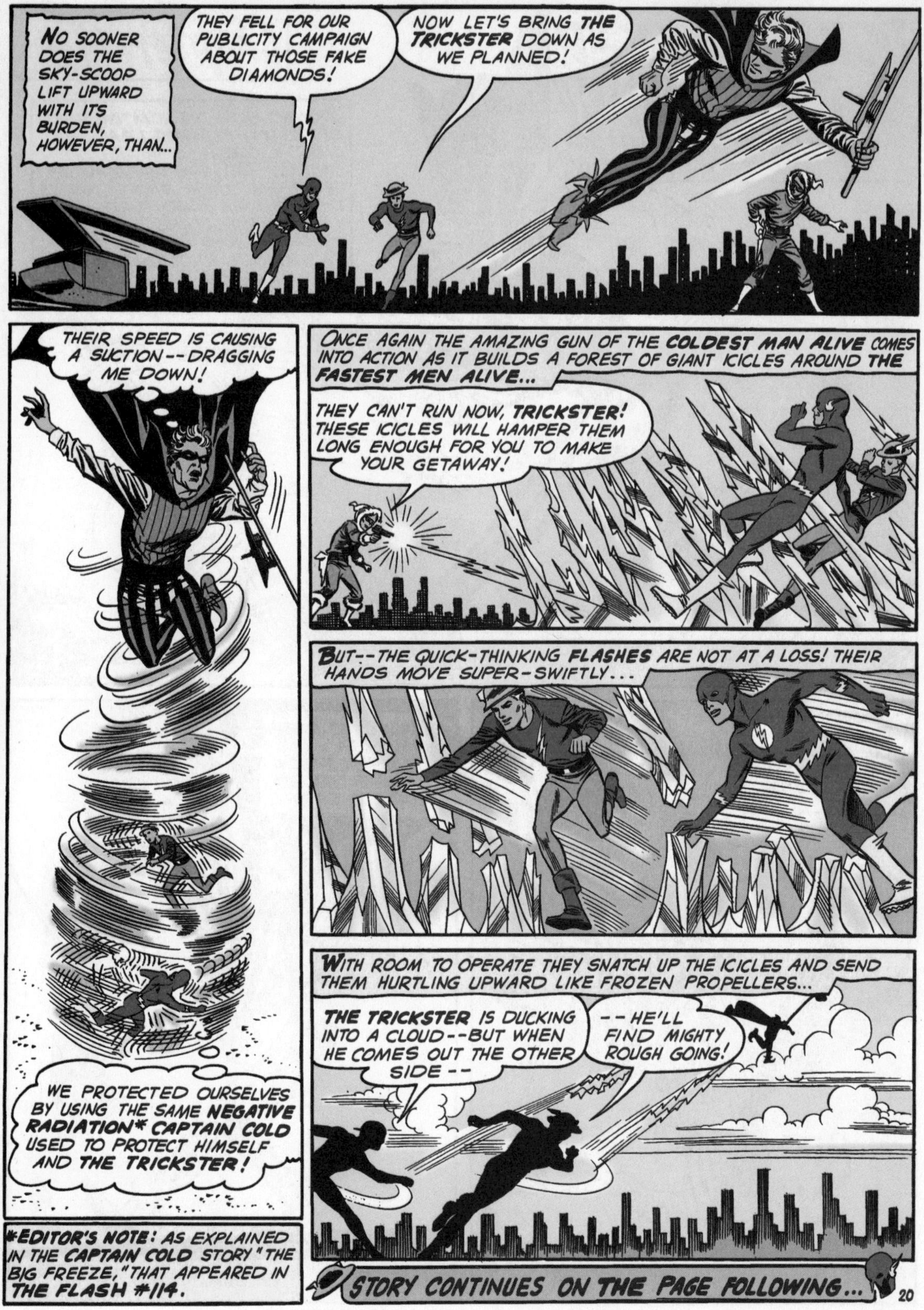
NO SOONER DOES THE SKY-SCOOP LIFT UPWARD WITH ITS BURDEN, HOWEVER, THAN...
THEY FELL FOR OUR PUBLICITY CAMPAIGN ABOUT THOSE FAKE DIAMONDS!
NOW LET'S BRING THE TRICKSTER DOWN AS WE PLANNED!
THEIR SPEED IS CAUSING A SUCTION--DRAGGING ME DOWN!
WE PROTECTED OURSELVES BY USING THE SAME NEGATIVE RADIATION* CAPTAIN COLD USED TO PROTECT HIMSELF AND THE TRICKSTER!
*EDITOR'S NOTE: AS EXPLAINED IN THE CAPTAIN COLD STORY "THE BIG FREEZE," THAT APPEARED IN THE FLASH #114.
ONCE AGAIN THE AMAZING GUN OF THE COLDEST MAN ALIVE COMES INTO ACTION AS IT BUILDS A FOREST OF GIANT ICICLES AROUND THE FASTEST MEN ALIVE...
THEY CAN'T RUN NOW, TRICKSTER! THESE ICICLES WILL HAMPER THEM LONG ENOUGH FOR YOU TO MAKE YOUR GETAWAY!
BUT--THE QUICK-THINKING FLASHES ARE NOT AT A LOSS! THEIR HANDS MOVE SUPER-SWIFTLY...
WITH ROOM TO OPERATE THEY SNATCH UP THE ICICLES AND SEND THEM HURTLING UPWARD LIKE FROZEN PROPELLERS...
THE TRICKSTER IS DUCKING INTO A CLOUD--BUT WHEN HE COMES OUT THE OTHER SIDE--
--HE'LL FIND MIGHTY ROUGH GOING!
STORY CONTINUES ON THE PAGE FOLLOWING...
20

DOUBLE DANGER ON EARTH!

Chapter 4

UPWARD FROM THE ROTATING HANDS OF THE TWO *FLASHES* LEAP THE GIANT ICICLES -- SPINNING SO SWIFTLY THE EYE CAN SCARCELY SEE THEM! THEIR SWIFT CIRCLING DISTURBS THE WIND CURRENTS -- SETS UP MINIATURE HURRICANES WHICH HIT AND BATTER *THE TRICKSTER,* KNOCKING HIM OFF BALANCE!

DOWN COME THE DIAMONDS, SCOOP-SHOVEL AND *TRICKSTER...*

RACING TO MEET HIM IS JAY *(FLASH)* GARRICK, ARMS EXTENDED FOR THE CATCH...

21

AND THEN-- BEFORE THE STUNNED EYES OF THE SCARLET SPEEDSTER...

HUH? HE'S -- DISAPPEARING!

AT THAT MOMENT, HALF A MILE AWAY...

I FIGURED CAPTAIN COLD MIGHT CAUSE A MIRAGE WITH HIS COLD-GUN AS HE'S DONE BEFORE*-- BUT I COULDN'T BE SURE!

*EDITOR'S NOTE! SEE SHOWCASE #8: IN WHICH FLASH FIRST MET "THE COLDEST MAN ON EARTH"!

I LET JAY GO AFTER THE TRICKSTER--JUST IN CASE IT WASN'T A MIRAGE, WHILE I FOLLOWED CAPTAIN COLD! SINCE HE DID USE A MIRAGE AND HELPED THE TRICKSTER ESCAPE, CAPTAIN COLD WILL BE ON HIS WAY TO MEET HIM! I'LL FOLLOW!

AS I DO, I'LL LEAVE A TRAIL FOR JAY TO FOLLOW! WHEN HE SEES HE'S BEEN FOOLED BY THAT MIRAGE, HE'LL START LOOKING FOR ME-- AND I WANT HIM TO KNOW WHICH WAY I'M GOING!

AS HE RUNS, THE FLASH MOVES HIS FINGER AT SUPER-SPEED, SLICING OFF THIN SLIVERS OF THE METEORITE WHICH HE CARRIES...

THESE METAL SHAVINGS ARE JUST AS GOOD AS AN ARROW POINTING OUT THE WAY!

22

CAPTAIN COLD LEADS FLASH TO A CAVE HIGH IN THE NEARBY MOUNTAINS...

THERE'S *THE TRICKSTER*, TOO-- WHO PROBABLY HID IN THE CLOUD AS THE WINDS BLEW IT ALONG UNTIL HE THOUGHT IT SAFE TO EMERGE AND HEAD FOR THE CAVE!

INSIDE THE CAVE, THE THIEVES ARE DIVIDING THEIR LOOT AS...

ANOTHER FOR YOU, ANOTHER FOR ME!

YOU KNOW-- THESE DIAMONDS LOOK A LITTLE ODD--

THAT'S BECAUSE THEY AREN'T *REAL* DIAMONDS-- BUT GLASS CHUNKS! THE OTHER-EARTH *FLASH* AND I DOCTORED THEM TO RESEMBLE REAL GEMS!

WE WERE TRICKED!

WE WALKED INTO YOUR TRAP, FLASH-- BUT IT WON'T DO YOU ANY GOOD!

I HAVE A NEW ATTACHMENT FOR MY *COLD-GUN*-- JUST FOR YOU, FLASH!

I HAVE A TRICK GADGET THAT WILL AMUSE YOU, TOO!

SAVE YOUR TRICKS AND GADGETS, FELLOWS! YOU WON'T BE ABLE TO USE THEM ON ME! YOU SEE, ALL I HAVE TO DO TO STOP YOU BOTH IS-- *SNAP MY FINGERS!*

HAVE YOU LOST YOUR SENSES?

NO ONE-- BUT NO ONE--OUT- TRICKS THE TRICKSTER!

TRUE TO HIS WORD--FLASH SNAPS HIS FINGERS...

SNAP!

23

AS THOSE FINGERS SNAP-- CAPTAIN COLD WHIRLS TO FACE THE TRICKSTER WHO ALSO TURNS AROUND TO FACE HIM-- AND BOTH FIRE...

TRICKSTER-- I SHOT YOU! HOW--?

AND I-- SHOT YOU! HOW--?

THEN-- SLOWING DOWN SO THAT HE BECOMES VISIBLE, THE OTHER WORLD FLASH REVEALS HIS PRESENCE...

IT WAS I WHO GRABBED YOUR "GUN-HANDS" AND SWUNG YOU AROUND-- AT THE SIGNAL OF THE FLASH'S SNAPPING FINGERS!

WITH MY SPEED-GEARED EYE-SIGHT I SAW THE OTHER FLASH RUN INTO THE CAVE SO FAST YOU COULDN'T SEE HIM! HE UNDERSTOOD MY SNAPPING FINGERS TO MEAN-- PUT YOU BOTH OUT OF ACTION!

LATER, AFTER THE TWO CRIMINALS HAVE BEEN TURNED OVER TO THE POLICE-- AND THE PEOPLE OF CENTRAL CITY REMOVED FROM THE COLD PALL THAT HELD THEM MOTIONLESS-- THE TWO FLASHES FOLLOW THE METEORIC INGOTS INTO JAY GARRICK'S EARTH...

THE INGOTS HAVE ALREADY BEEN VIBRATED INTO MY WORLD, BARRY!

LET'S SEE HOW THEY'RE BEING USED!

AFTER BEING GROUND TO POWDER, THE METEORIC METAL IS PLACED IN SPECIAL SPRAY ATTACHMENTS FITTED TO ROCKET-SATELLITES AND SHOT INTO THE STRATOSPHERE...

I STILL CAN'T UNDERSTAND WHAT HAPPENED TO YOUR METEORITE, JAY!

I THINK I'VE SOLVED THAT MYSTERY!

WHEN THE EPSILON RADIATION HIT OUR EARTH, OUR METEORITE ABSORBED IT! WE THOUGHT IT ABSORBED ONLY THE RADIATION AROUND THE CRATER BUT IT MUST HAVE ABSORBED FAR MORE -- ENOUGH ACTUALLY TO SAVE ALL OUR LIVES! BUT ITS EFFECTIVENESS LASTED ONLY 24 HOURS...

24

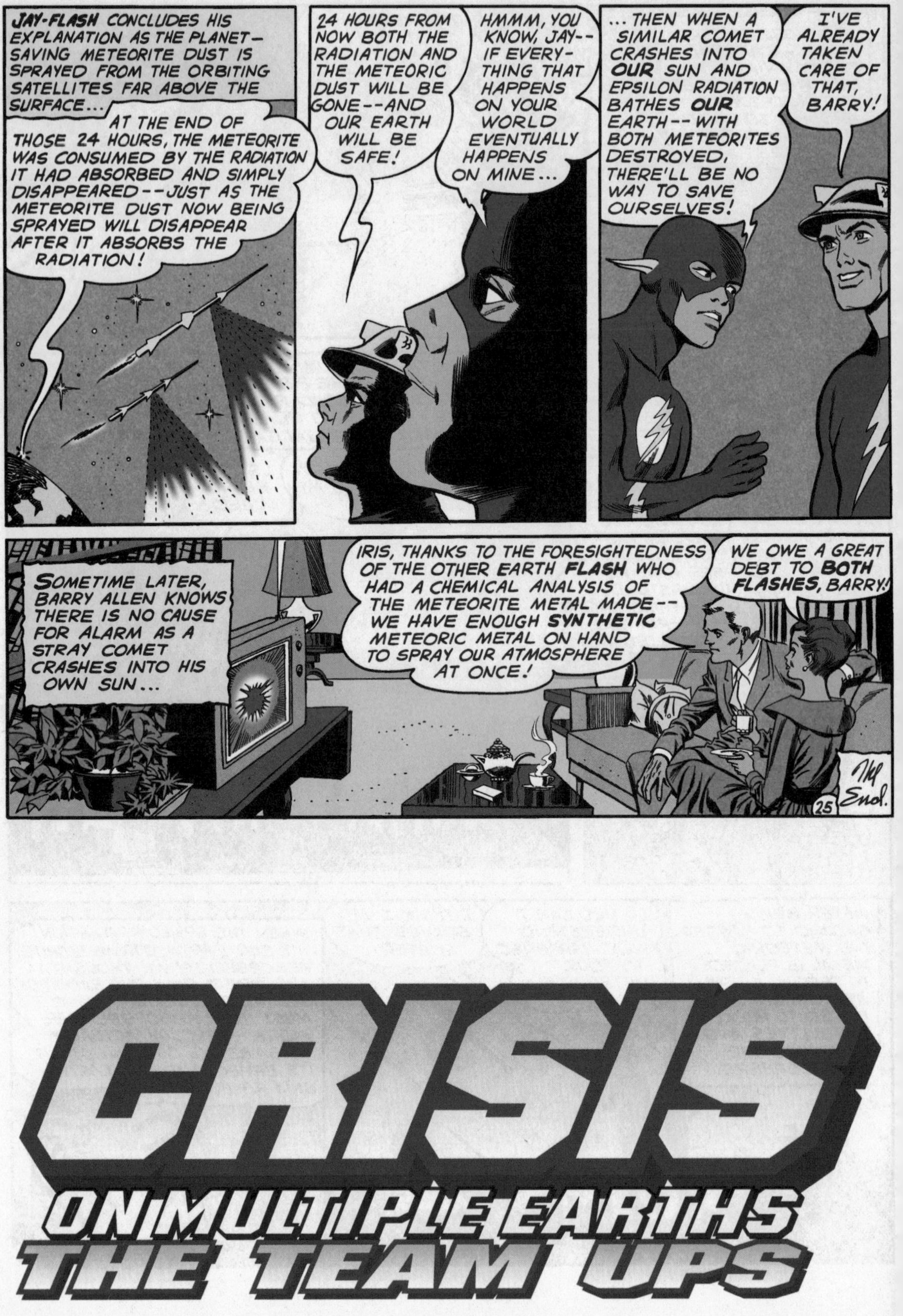
JAY-FLASH CONCLUDES HIS EXPLANATION AS THE PLANET-SAVING METEORITE DUST IS SPRAYED FROM THE ORBITING SATELLITES FAR ABOVE THE SURFACE...
AT THE END OF THOSE 24 HOURS, THE METEORITE WAS CONSUMED BY THE RADIATION IT HAD ABSORBED AND SIMPLY DISAPPEARED--JUST AS THE METEORITE DUST NOW BEING SPRAYED WILL DISAPPEAR AFTER IT ABSORBS THE RADIATION!
24 HOURS FROM NOW BOTH THE RADIATION AND THE METEORIC DUST WILL BE GONE--AND OUR EARTH WILL BE SAFE!
HMMM, YOU KNOW, JAY--IF EVERYTHING THAT HAPPENS ON YOUR WORLD EVENTUALLY HAPPENS ON MINE...
...THEN WHEN A SIMILAR COMET CRASHES INTO OUR SUN AND EPSILON RADIATION BATHES OUR EARTH--WITH BOTH METEORITES DESTROYED, THERE'LL BE NO WAY TO SAVE OURSELVES!
I'VE ALREADY TAKEN CARE OF THAT, BARRY!
SOMETIME LATER, BARRY ALLEN KNOWS THERE IS NO CAUSE FOR ALARM AS A STRAY COMET CRASHES INTO HIS OWN SUN...
IRIS, THANKS TO THE FORESIGHTEDNESS OF THE OTHER EARTH FLASH WHO HAD A CHEMICAL ANALYSIS OF THE METEORITE METAL MADE--WE HAVE ENOUGH SYNTHETIC METEORIC METAL ON HAND TO SPRAY OUR ATMOSPHERE AT ONCE!
WE OWE A GREAT DEBT TO BOTH FLASHES, BARRY!
25

CRISIS ON MULTIPLE EARTHS
THE TEAM UPS

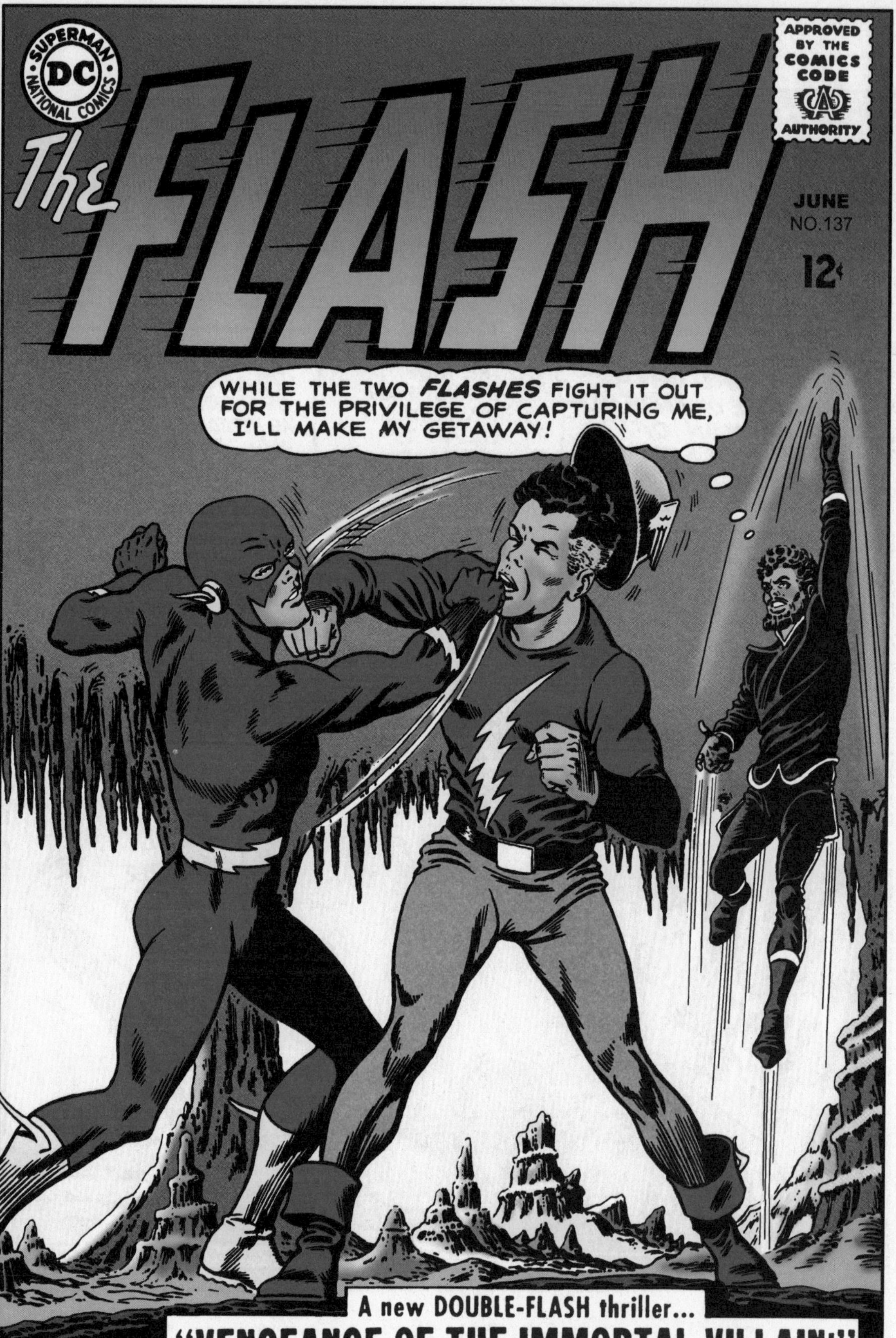
SUPERMAN DC NATIONAL COMICS
APPROVED BY THE COMICS CODE AUTHORITY
The FLASH
JUNE
NO.137
12¢
WHILE THE TWO FLASHES FIGHT IT OUT FOR THE PRIVILEGE OF CAPTURING ME, I'LL MAKE MY GETAWAY!
A new DOUBLE-FLASH thriller...
"VENGEANCE OF THE IMMORTAL VILLAIN!"

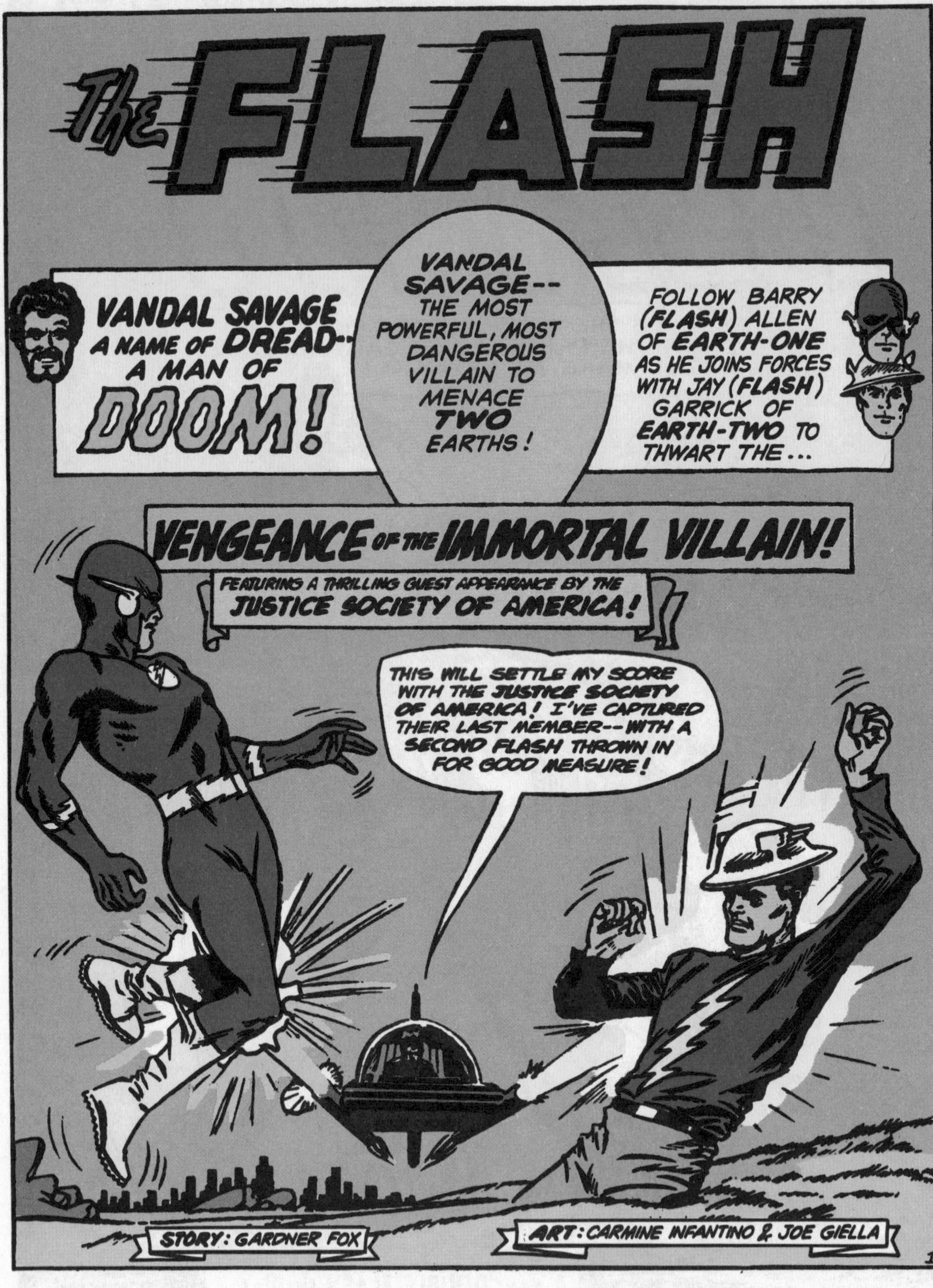

THE FLASH
VANDAL SAVAGE A NAME OF DREAD-- A MAN OF DOOM!
VANDAL SAVAGE-- THE MOST POWERFUL, MOST DANGEROUS VILLAIN TO MENACE TWO EARTHS!
FOLLOW BARRY (FLASH) ALLEN OF EARTH-ONE AS HE JOINS FORCES WITH JAY (FLASH) GARRICK OF EARTH-TWO TO THWART THE...
VENGEANCE OF THE IMMORTAL VILLAIN!
FEATURING A THRILLING GUEST APPEARANCE BY THE JUSTICE SOCIETY OF AMERICA!
THIS WILL SETTLE MY SCORE WITH THE JUSTICE SOCIETY OF AMERICA! I'VE CAPTURED THEIR LAST MEMBER-- WITH A SECOND FLASH THROWN IN FOR GOOD MEASURE!
STORY: GARDNER FOX
ART: CARMINE INFANTINO & JOE GIELLA
1

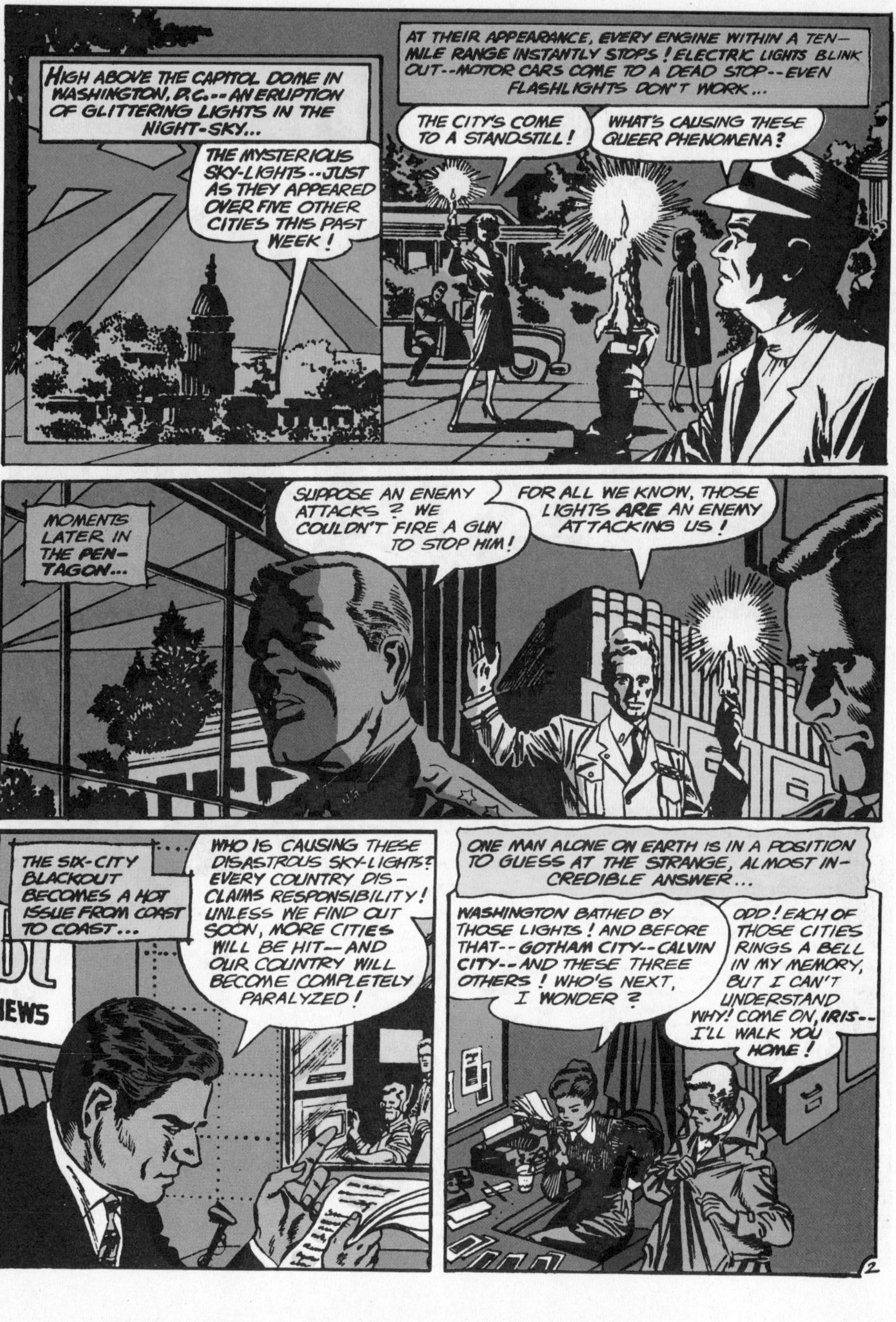
HIGH ABOVE THE CAPITOL DOME IN WASHINGTON, D.C.--AN ERUPTION OF GLITTERING LIGHTS IN THE NIGHT-SKY...
THE MYSTERIOUS SKY-LIGHTS--JUST AS THEY APPEARED OVER FIVE OTHER CITIES THIS PAST WEEK!
AT THEIR APPEARANCE, EVERY ENGINE WITHIN A TEN-MILE RANGE INSTANTLY STOPS! ELECTRIC LIGHTS BLINK OUT--MOTOR CARS COME TO A DEAD STOP--EVEN FLASHLIGHTS DON'T WORK...
THE CITY'S COME TO A STANDSTILL!
WHAT'S CAUSING THESE QUEER PHENOMENA?
MOMENTS LATER IN THE PENTAGON...
SUPPOSE AN ENEMY ATTACKS? WE COULDN'T FIRE A GUN TO STOP HIM!
FOR ALL WE KNOW, THOSE LIGHTS ARE AN ENEMY ATTACKING US!
THE SIX-CITY BLACKOUT BECOMES A HOT ISSUE FROM COAST TO COAST...
WHO IS CAUSING THESE DISASTROUS SKY-LIGHTS? EVERY COUNTRY DISCLAIMS RESPONSIBILITY! UNLESS WE FIND OUT SOON, MORE CITIES WILL BE HIT--AND OUR COUNTRY WILL BECOME COMPLETELY PARALYZED!
NEWS
ONE MAN ALONE ON EARTH IS IN A POSITION TO GUESS AT THE STRANGE, ALMOST INCREDIBLE ANSWER...
WASHINGTON BATHED BY THOSE LIGHTS! AND BEFORE THAT--GOTHAM CITY--CALVIN CITY--AND THESE THREE OTHERS! WHO'S NEXT, I WONDER?
ODD! EACH OF THOSE CITIES RINGS A BELL IN MY MEMORY, BUT I CAN'T UNDERSTAND WHY! COME ON, IRIS--I'LL WALK YOU HOME!
2

ALL THE WAY HOME FROM IRIS WEST'S APARTMENT, BARRY (FLASH) ALLEN PONDERS THE FAINT MEMORY OF THE CITY NAMES...

CALVIN CITY... WASHINGTON... GOTHAM CITY... WHAT HAVE THEY IN COMMON...?

THEN AS HE PUTS HIS KEY IN HIS DOOR LOCK...

OF COURSE! I JUST REMEMBERED IT STRUCK ME--LIKE A "FLASH"!

TURNING TO A WALL CABINET IN HIS ROOM, HE BRINGS OUT A MAP OF WHAT APPEARS TO BE THE EARTH...

I'M THE ONLY PERSON IN MY WORLD WHO'S EVER SEEN THIS MAP OF EARTH!

THIS IS THE EARTH OF MY GOOD FRIEND JAY (FLASH) GARRICK, WHERE THERE'S A KEYSTONE CITY IN THE PLACE OF CENTRAL CITY WHERE I LIVE! Hmmm-- I WAS RIGHT! THE CITIES WHERE THE SKY-LIGHTS APPEARED--ARE CITIES ON THE OTHER EARTH WHERE THE MEMBERS OF THE FORMER JUSTICE SOCIETY OF AMERICA RESIDED!

HOW WELL I REMEMBER THOSE COLORFUL HEROES FROM MY BOYHOOD READING OF ALL-STAR COMICS! HAWK-MAN! DOCTOR MID-NITE! THE ATOM FROM CALVIN COLLEGE AND CALVIN CITY! WONDER WOMAN WORKED IN WASHINGTON IN THOSE DAYS! GREEN LANTERN WAS IN GOTHAM CITY! AND GOOD OLD JOHNNY THUNDER...

SINCE EACH OF THE CITIES WHERE THE SKY-LIGHTS HAVE APPEARED CORRESPOND TO THE CITIES WHERE THOSE JUSTICE SOCIETY MEMBERS LIVED, THOSE LIGHTS MIGHT BE CONNECTED WITH THEM! IT'S A LONG CHANCE--BUT IT'S WORTH INVESTIGATING...!

AN INSTANT LATER, HE TOUCHES A SECRET SPRING IN HIS RING, EXPOSING HIS *FLASH* COSTUME TO INFLATING OXYGEN...

VROOOSH!

THEN HE IS SPEEDING THROUGH CENTRAL CITY ALONG A WIDE CITY THOROUGH--FARE...

ANY POSSIBLE HOPE OF STOPPING THOSE SKY-LIGHTS MAKES THIS TRIP TO THAT "OTHER" EARTH OF JAY GARRICK WELL WORTH-WHILE! PRACTICALLY EVERY-THING THAT HAPPENS IN HIS WORLD ALSO HAPPENS IN MINE!

AT A FOCAL POINT BETWEEN THESE WORLDS--THE *CENTRAL CITY COMMUNITY CENTER*--FLASH VIBRATES AS HE DID IN HIS *FIRST* ADVENTURE ON *EARTH-TWO**--

BY VIBRATING AT A CERTAIN SPEED I'M SURE TO CROSS OVER THE SPATIAL HELIX LINKING MY EARTH WITH THAT OF JAY GARRICK!

* EDITOR'S NOTE: THE FLASH # 123: "FLASH OF TWO WORLDS!"

MOMENTS LATER HE IS RACING THROUGH KEY-STONE CITY...

SINCE I KNOW WHERE MY *FLASH* COUNTERPART ON THIS EARTH LIVES, I'LL MAKE HIS HOME MY FIRST STOP!

WITHIN SPLIT-SECONDS AT THE HOME OF JAY GARRICK, 5252 78 STREET, KEYSTONE CITY, U.S.A. ...

OHHH--BARRY ALLEN! COME IN, COME IN! JAY WILL BE SO GLAD TO SEE YOU--AS SOON AS HE RETURNS!

HE'S NOT HOME, JOAN?

HE'S OUT ON A CASE AT THE MOMENT BUT HE'LL BE BACK SHORTLY! PLEASE SIT DOWN--AND TELL ME WHAT BRINGS THE FLASH TO THIS EARTH...

4

BUT BEFORE BARRY-FLASH CAN EXPLAIN HIS MISSION, JAY-FLASH RETURNS HOME...

YOU BOYS ARE IN FOR A LONG GABFEST--SO HERE ARE SOME SANDWICHES TO MUNCH ON!

JAY, IN MY WORLD THERE ARE MYSTERIOUS LIGHTS IN THE SKY THAT...

WHAT ?! THOSE SAME LIGHTS ARE HERE IN MY WORLD! LISTEN...

AFTER EACH SUPER-HERO TELLS HIS STORY...

WHAT YOU TELL ME IS MOST INTERESTING, JAY! I'VE JUST RETURNED FROM THOSE SIX CITIES YOU MENTIONED...

AND WHEN I CHECKED UP IN EACH OF THESE CITIES I FOUND OUT THAT MY OLD JUSTICE SOCIETY BUDDIES--HAVE DISAPPEARED!

THAT SEEMS TO BE THE CLINCHER, ALL RIGHT! THERE MUST BE A CON-NECTION BETWEEN THE APPEARANCE OF THE SKY-LIGHTS AND THE DISAPPEARANCE OF THOSE JSA MEMBERS!

IF WE'RE RIGHT--THE NEXT APPEAR-ANCE OF THE SKY-LIGHTS MAY VERY WELL BE OVER MY HOME TOWN--KEYSTONE CITY!

POSSIBLY TO DRAW YOUR ATTENTION TO IT--SO YOU'LL DISAPPEAR TOO!

AND THEN--BEFORE THEIR STARING EYES...

THERE IT IS--EXACTLY AS THE LIGHTS APPEARED OVER THE OTHER SIX CITIES!

CORRESPONDING TO THE SKY-LIGHTS IN MY OWN WORLD. BUT WHOEVER OR WHATEVER IS CAUSING THEM, IS IN FOR A SURPRISE!

5

THROUGH A CITY BLANKETED BY DARKNESS RACE THE TWO FASTEST MEN ALIVE...

OUR UNKNOWN MENACE PLANS ON CAPTURING *THE FLASH*--

---BUT HE CAN'T ANTICIPATE THAT THERE WILL BE TWO FLASHES ON HAND TO FIGHT HIM!

THEIR KEEN EYES SEARCH EVERY-WHERE FOR THE DEVICE CAUSING THE STRANGE SKY-LIGHTS...

SINCE EACH SKY-LIGHT APPEARED OVER DIFFERENT CITIES, THERE MUST BE SOME KIND OF GADGET AROUND HERE CREATING IT!

IT SHOULDN'T TAKE LONG TO FIND IT AT THE RATE WE'RE TRAVELING!

THEN--ON A SIDE ROAD SOME MILES OUTSIDE THE CITY...

THERE IT IS! I'LL SHUT IT OFF-- RESTORING EVERYTHING BACK TO NORMAL IN KEYSTONE CITY!

BUT--AS THE SCARLET SPEEDSTER REACHES FOR THE STRANGE ENGINE, ANOTHER MACHINE NEARBY SUDDENLY SHOOTS OUT A BEAM OF LIGHT...

OHHH! A CUBE OF SOME SORT FORMING ABOUT ME--HOLDING ME RIGID!

AFTER THE CUBE FORMS SOLIDLY ABOUT HIM, IT LIFTS UPWARD INTO THE AIR, CARRY-ING THE HELPLESS JAY-FLASH INSIDE IT...

NO CHANCE OF BARRY RESCUING ME-- HE CAN'T FLY THROUGH THE AIR! IT LOOKS LIKE WE'VE LOST OUR FIGHT WITH THE SKY-LIGHT MENACE!

6.

MOMENTARILY STUNNED BY SURPRISE AT WHAT HAS HAPPENED, THE SCARLET SPEEDSTER LEAPS FORWARD--

MISSED! IT'S MOVING JUST BEYOND MY REACH!

BY CAUSING A SUCTION WHIRL-POOL--I MIGHT BE ABLE TO DRAW IT DOWN SO I CAN GRAB HOLD OF IT!

THE DOWNDRAFT JUST WASN'T STRONG ENOUGH! WHATEVER FORCE HAS THE CUBE IN ITS POWER IS TOO POWERFUL TO BUDGE!

OVER KEYSTONE CITY MOVES THE ODD CUBE--AND RACING UP A BUILDING WALL TO INTERCEPT IT SPEEDS BARRY-FLASH...

WHATEVER HOPE I HAVE OF STOPPING THOSE SKY-LIGHTS IN MY WORLD--WILL INVOLVE SAVING FLASH FIRST!

BUT AGAIN HIS STRAINING FINGERS TOUCH ONLY EMPTY AIR...

HE'S JUST A FOOT AWAY-- BUT IT MIGHT AS WELL BE A MILE!

7

DOWN ONE BUILDING AND UP ANOTHER-- ONLY TO FAIL AGAIN AND AGAIN!

THIS IS MY LAST CHANCE! THERE ARE NO MORE BUILDINGS AFTER THIS TO GO UP WITHIN REACHING DISTANCE OF THE CUBE!

TOO LATE! IT'S MOVING BEYOND THE ROOF-EDGE--

WITH A WILD DESPAIRING BROAD JUMP, HE FLINGS HIMSELF OUT INTO EMPTY AIR...

GOT TO RISK EVERYTHING ON THIS FINAL TRY!

I REACHED IT-- BUT CAN'T KEEP MY FOOTING!

QUICKLY, HE BEGINS TO ROTATE HIS ARMS LIKE PROPELLERS--AND THEIR FRANTIC POUNDING OF THE AIR LIFTS HIM SLOWLY UPRIGHT...

GAINING MY BALANCE--!

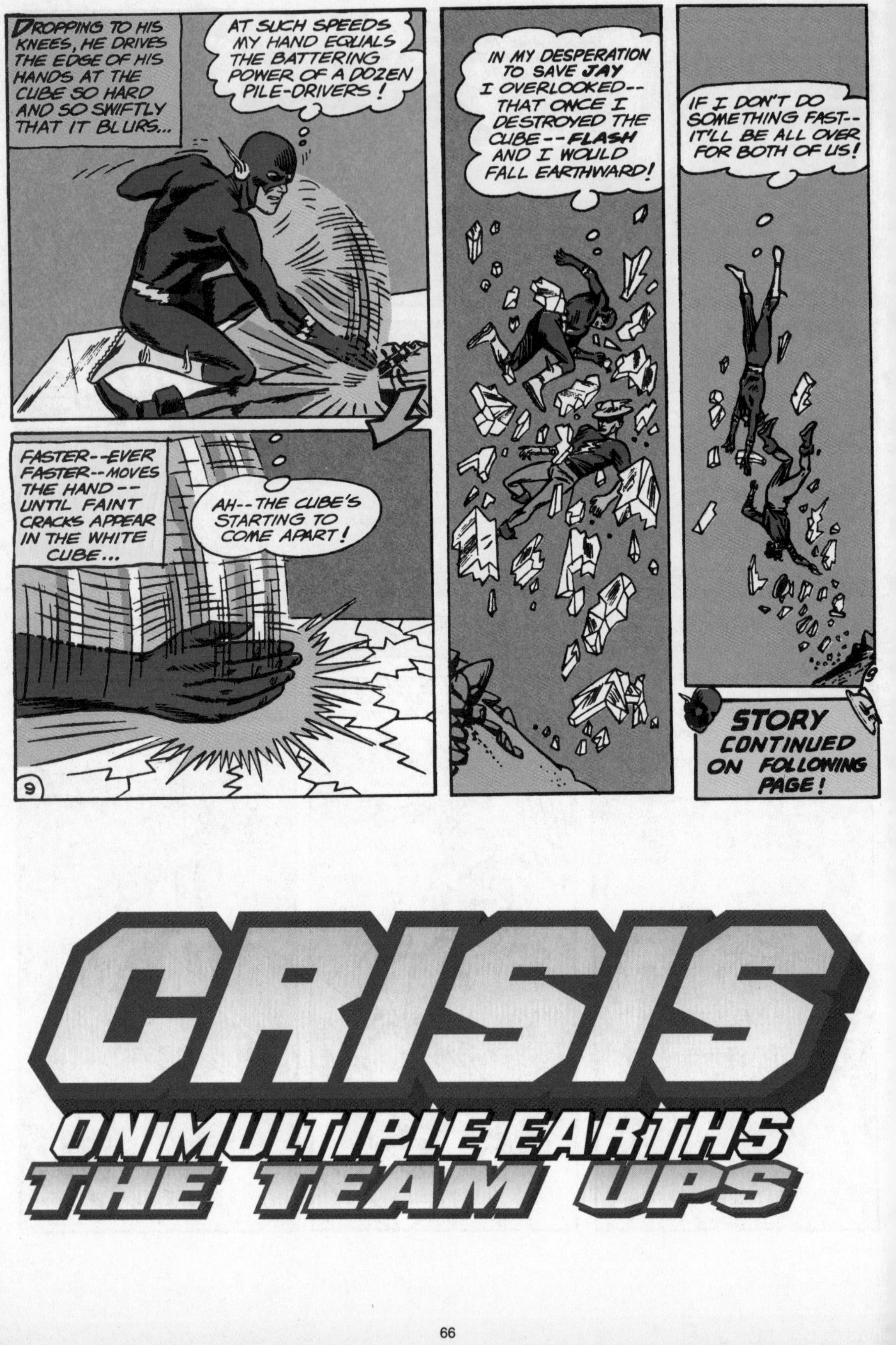
DROPPING TO HIS KNEES, HE DRIVES THE EDGE OF HIS HANDS AT THE CUBE SO HARD AND SO SWIFTLY THAT IT BLURS...
AT SUCH SPEEDS MY HAND EQUALS THE BATTERING POWER OF A DOZEN PILE-DRIVERS!
FASTER--EVER FASTER--MOVES THE HAND--UNTIL FAINT CRACKS APPEAR IN THE WHITE CUBE...
AH--THE CUBE'S STARTING TO COME APART!
9
IN MY DESPERATION TO SAVE JAY I OVERLOOKED--THAT ONCE I DESTROYED THE CUBE--FLASH AND I WOULD FALL EARTHWARD!
IF I DON'T DO SOMETHING FAST--IT'LL BE ALL OVER FOR BOTH OF US!
9
STORY CONTINUED ON FOLLOWING PAGE!

CRISIS ON MULTIPLE EARTHS THE TEAM UPS

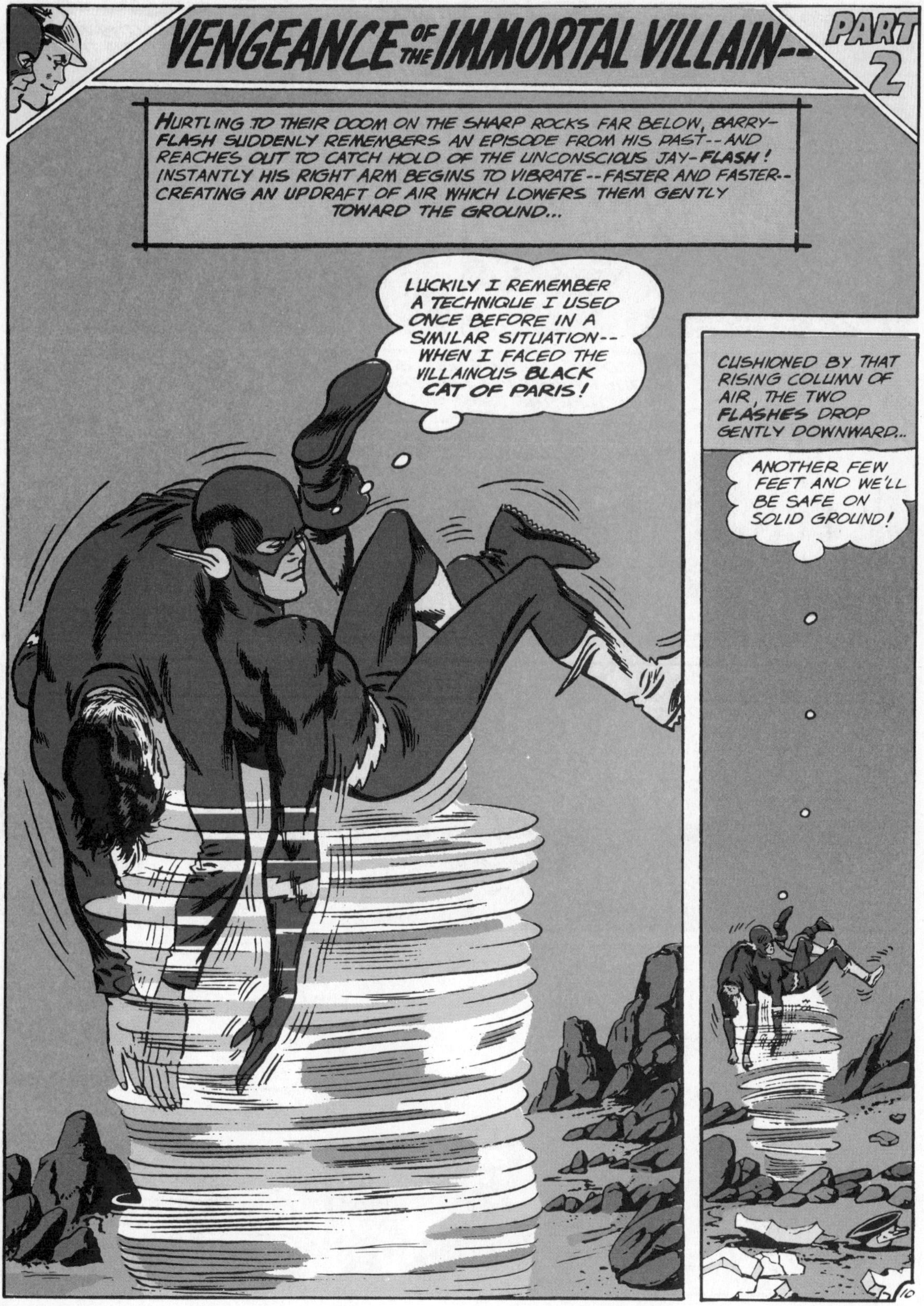

VENGEANCE OF THE IMMORTAL VILLAIN--
PART 2
HURTLING TO THEIR DOOM ON THE SHARP ROCKS FAR BELOW, BARRY-FLASH SUDDENLY REMEMBERS AN EPISODE FROM HIS PAST--AND REACHES OUT TO CATCH HOLD OF THE UNCONSCIOUS JAY-FLASH! INSTANTLY HIS RIGHT ARM BEGINS TO VIBRATE--FASTER AND FASTER--CREATING AN UPDRAFT OF AIR WHICH LOWERS THEM GENTLY TOWARD THE GROUND...
LUCKILY I REMEMBER A TECHNIQUE I USED ONCE BEFORE IN A SIMILAR SITUATION--WHEN I FACED THE VILLAINOUS BLACK CAT OF PARIS!
CUSHIONED BY THAT RISING COLUMN OF AIR, THE TWO FLASHES DROP GENTLY DOWNWARD...
ANOTHER FEW FEET AND WE'LL BE SAFE ON SOLID GROUND!
10

PROTECTED BY THE ROTATING RIGHT ARM OF BARRY-FLASH, THE DUO SOON TOUCHES TERRA FIRMA...

Whew! I'M STILL WOOZY FROM BEING IN THAT CUBE!

TAKE A BREATHER, JAY-- AND THEN WE'LL GO BACK TO THE SKY-LIGHTS MACHINE AND MAKE ANOTHER TRY AT TURN- ING IT OFF!

MEANWHILE, MANY MILES TO THE SOUTH, IN A SCIENTIFICALLY EQUIPPED HIDEOUT UNDER MAMMOTH CAVES...

WHAT COULD HAVE HAPPENED TO THE FINAL CUBE-- AND THE FLASH INSIDE IT?

SO FAR, EVERYTHING'S GONE JUST RIGHT! IT WAS EASY TO CAPTURE THE FIRST SIX JUSTICE SOCIETY MEMBERS. I KNEW THE TERRIBLE MENACE OF THE SKY-LIGHTS I CREATED WOULD BRING THEM OUT OF RETIREMENT!

AS THEY WERE ABOUT TO TOUCH THE MACHINES, THEY UNWITTINGLY TRIPPED AN ELECTRIC EYE BEAM THAT ENCASED THEM IN A CUBE INVENTED BY ONE OF MY OLD INJUSTICE SOCIETY* PALS, BRAIN WAVE! NO ONE COULD HAVE ESCAPED FROM INSIDE IT!

* EDITOR'S NOTE: THE INJUSTICE SOCIETY OF THE WORLD-- AN ORGANIZATION OF THE GREATEST CRIMINALS OF EARTH-- APPEARED IN ALL-STAR COMICS # 37, OCT-NOV 1947.

MANY YEARS AGO YOU JUSTICE SOCIETY MEMBERS CAPTURED THE INJUSTICE SOCIETY AND PUT US AWAY IN PRISON! BUT WHAT ARE A FEW YEARS TO A MAN LIKE ME-- WHO IS IMMORTAL!

NOW-- SHORT YEARS LATER-- I HAVE ESCAPED JAIL AND HAVE BEGUN TO AVENGE MY DEFEAT AT YOUR HANDS!

GREEN LANTERN AND HIS POWER RING WERE HELPLESS ONCE THE CUBE CLOSED IN ON HIM! JOHNNY THUNDER COULDN'T SPEAK THE WORDS *CEI-U* WHICH WOULD ACTIVATE HIS FANTASTIC *THUNDERBOLT!* ATOM'S *"ATOMIC PUNCH"* WAS OF NO AVAIL AGAINST MY CUBE-PRISON!

DOCTOR MID-NITE COULDN'T REACH HIS *BLACKOUT BOMB* IN TIME TO HELP HIM! HAWKMAN'S ANTI-GRAVITY *"NINTH METAL"* FAILED! AND THE *AMAZON* POWERS OF *WONDER WOMAN* ARE ENCASED FOREVER IN THE CUBE FROM WHICH THERE IS NO ESCAPE!

OR *IS* THERE A WAY OF ESCAPE-- UNKNOWN TO ME? MY INSTRUMENTS SHOW THE CUBE THAT HELD THE *FLASH* HAS BEEN DESTROYED! IF *FLASH* COULD DO IT-- PERHAPS HIS FELLOW MEMBERS CAN, TOO!

IN A SENSE I MADE THEM ALL *IMMORTAL* WHEN I PLACED THEM IN THE CUBES! THEY WILL WITNESS MY TAKING OVER THE WORLD, SEE MY WICKED TRIUMPHS-- BUT COMPLETELY HELPLESS TO STOP ME! TO HONOR THE OCCASION, I EVEN DESIGNED THIS NEW UNIFORM I AM WEARING!

12

WHO IS THIS MAN WHO WIELDS SUCH AWESOME POWERS?
TO UNDERSTAND, WE MUST GO BACK IN TIME 50,000 YEARS TO THE AGE OF THE CAVEMEN, WHERE VANDAR ADG WAS CHIEF OF A BAND OF CRO-MAGNONS...

A MIGHTY HUNTER, A GREAT FIGHTER, THIS CHIEF WAS LEADING HIS WARRIORS TO THE ATTACK ONE DAY WHEN OUT OF THE SKIES CAME A SCREAMING FIREBALL...

WITH A TITANIC EXPLOSION, THE FLAMING METEOR BURST OVER VANDAR ADG'S HEAD...

UNCONSCIOUS, HE WAS CARRIED TO HIS CAVE. WHEN HE WOKE--HE HAD BECOME IMMORTAL!

HE LIVED ON WHILE THE CRO-MAGNONS DIED OUT--

LIVED TO WALK THE STREETS OF ANCIENT SUMER AS ITS KING...

LATER, HE WAS KNOWN AS THE EGYPTIAN PHARAOH CHEOPS, BUILDER OF THE PYRAMIDS...

THEN GENGHIS KHAN...

LATER, HE BECAME A POWER BEHIND HISTORY'S SCENES-- HE WAS THE ADVISOR TO NAPOLEON ...

YOU MUST ATTACK, SIRE! THE AUSTRIANS, THE PRUSSIANS AND THE ENGLISH CANNOT WITHSTAND YOUR POWER!

VERY WELL, MARSHAL SAUVAGE! I WILL GIVE THE NECESSARY ORDERS!

TO BISMARCK...

THIS IS A GREAT TRIUMPH FOR YOUR ARMIES, PRINCE BISMARCK!

JA! A GREATER ONE FOR YOUR DIPLOMACY, BARON VON SAVAGE!

UNTIL TODAY-- HAVING TURNED HIS GREAT TALENTS TO A QUEST FOR EARTH DOMINATION-- VANDAL SAVAGE HAS BEGUN HIS PROGRAM BY CAPTURING SIX OF THE JUSTICE SOCIETY MEMBERS WHO HAD IMPRISONED HIM ...

ONLY THE FLASH IS STILL AT LARGE TO GIVE ME TROUBLE! SINCE I FAILED TO CAPTURE HIM BY REMOTE-CONTROL, I SHALL GO OUT AND DO SO PERSONALLY!

SOON HE IS HURTLING IN HIS FLYING LABORATORY TOWARD THE SKY-LIGHTS MACHINE OUTSIDE KEYSTONE CITY...

IF I KNOW FLASH, HE WON'T GIVE UP-- BUT WILL ATTEMPT TO SHUT OFF THE SKY-LIGHTS ENGINE AGAIN!

AS HE APPROACHES THE HIDDEN MACHINE, HE SEES...

I MUSTN'T GET TOO CLOSE TO IT--OR I'LL BE CAUGHT IN ANOTHER CUBE!

THERE HE IS-- RIGHT IN MY LINE OF FIRE!

INSTANTLY A BEAM OF BRIGHT LIGHT BATHES ONE OF THE SCARLET SPEEDSTERS...

MY FEET--SINKING INTO THE GROUND! WHO-- OOOOH! DESPITE HIS NEW UNIFORM-- I RECOGNIZE HIM! IT'S VANDAL SAVAGE-- THE IMMORTAL VILLAIN!

14

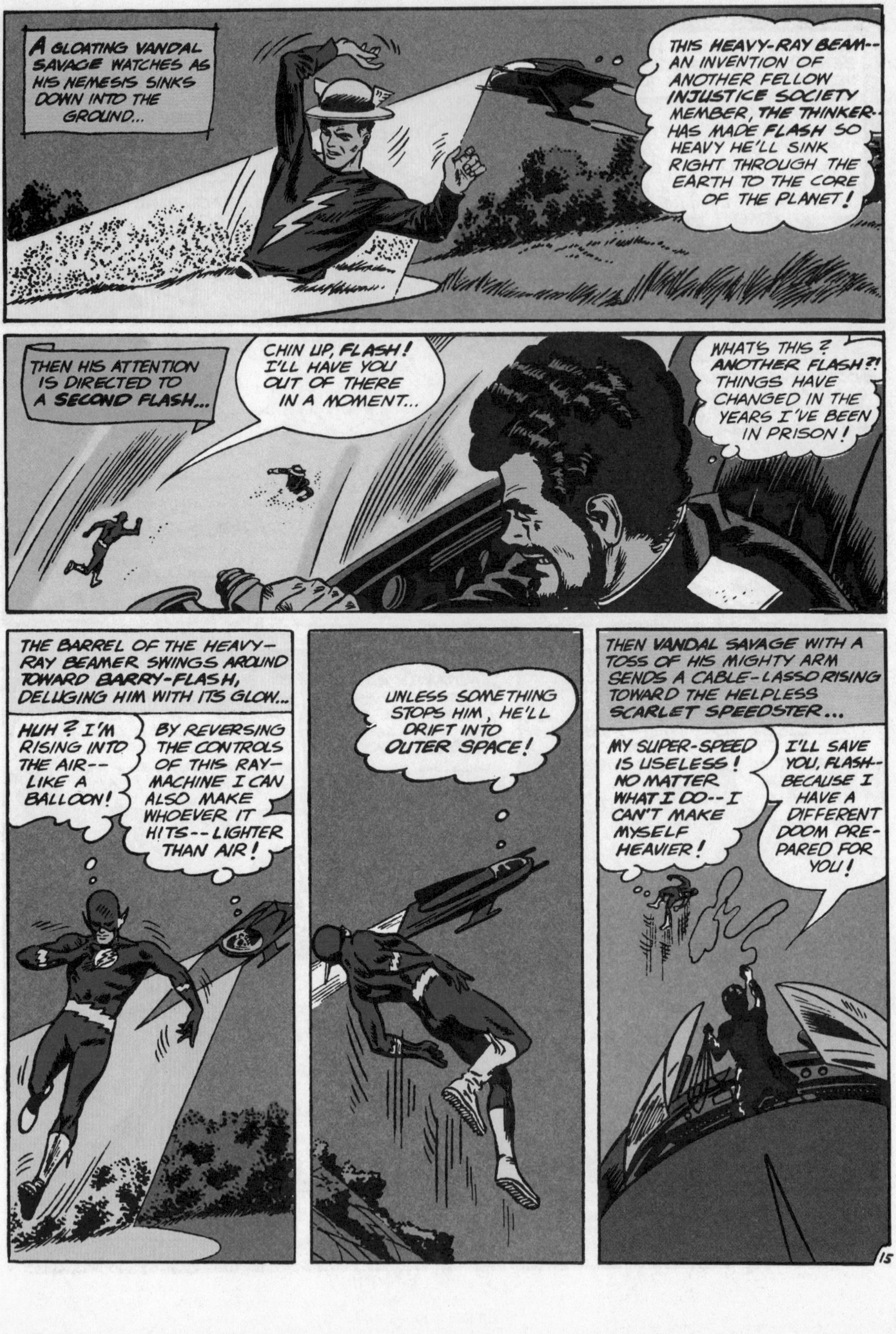
A GLOATING VANDAL SAVAGE WATCHES AS HIS NEMESIS SINKS DOWN INTO THE GROUND...
THIS HEAVY-RAY BEAM-- AN INVENTION OF ANOTHER FELLOW INJUSTICE SOCIETY MEMBER, THE THINKER- HAS MADE FLASH SO HEAVY HE'LL SINK RIGHT THROUGH THE EARTH TO THE CORE OF THE PLANET!
THEN HIS ATTENTION IS DIRECTED TO A SECOND FLASH...
CHIN UP, FLASH! I'LL HAVE YOU OUT OF THERE IN A MOMENT...
WHAT'S THIS? ANOTHER FLASH?! THINGS HAVE CHANGED IN THE YEARS I'VE BEEN IN PRISON!
THE BARREL OF THE HEAVY-RAY BEAMER SWINGS AROUND TOWARD BARRY-FLASH, DELUGING HIM WITH ITS GLOW...
HUH? I'M RISING INTO THE AIR-- LIKE A BALLOON!
BY REVERSING THE CONTROLS OF THIS RAY-MACHINE I CAN ALSO MAKE WHOEVER IT HITS--LIGHTER THAN AIR!
UNLESS SOMETHING STOPS HIM, HE'LL DRIFT INTO OUTER SPACE!
THEN VANDAL SAVAGE WITH A TOSS OF HIS MIGHTY ARM SENDS A CABLE-LASSO RISING TOWARD THE HELPLESS SCARLET SPEEDSTER...
MY SUPER-SPEED IS USELESS! NO MATTER WHAT I DO--I CAN'T MAKE MYSELF HEAVIER!
I'LL SAVE YOU, FLASH-- BECAUSE I HAVE A DIFFERENT DOOM PREPARED FOR YOU!
15

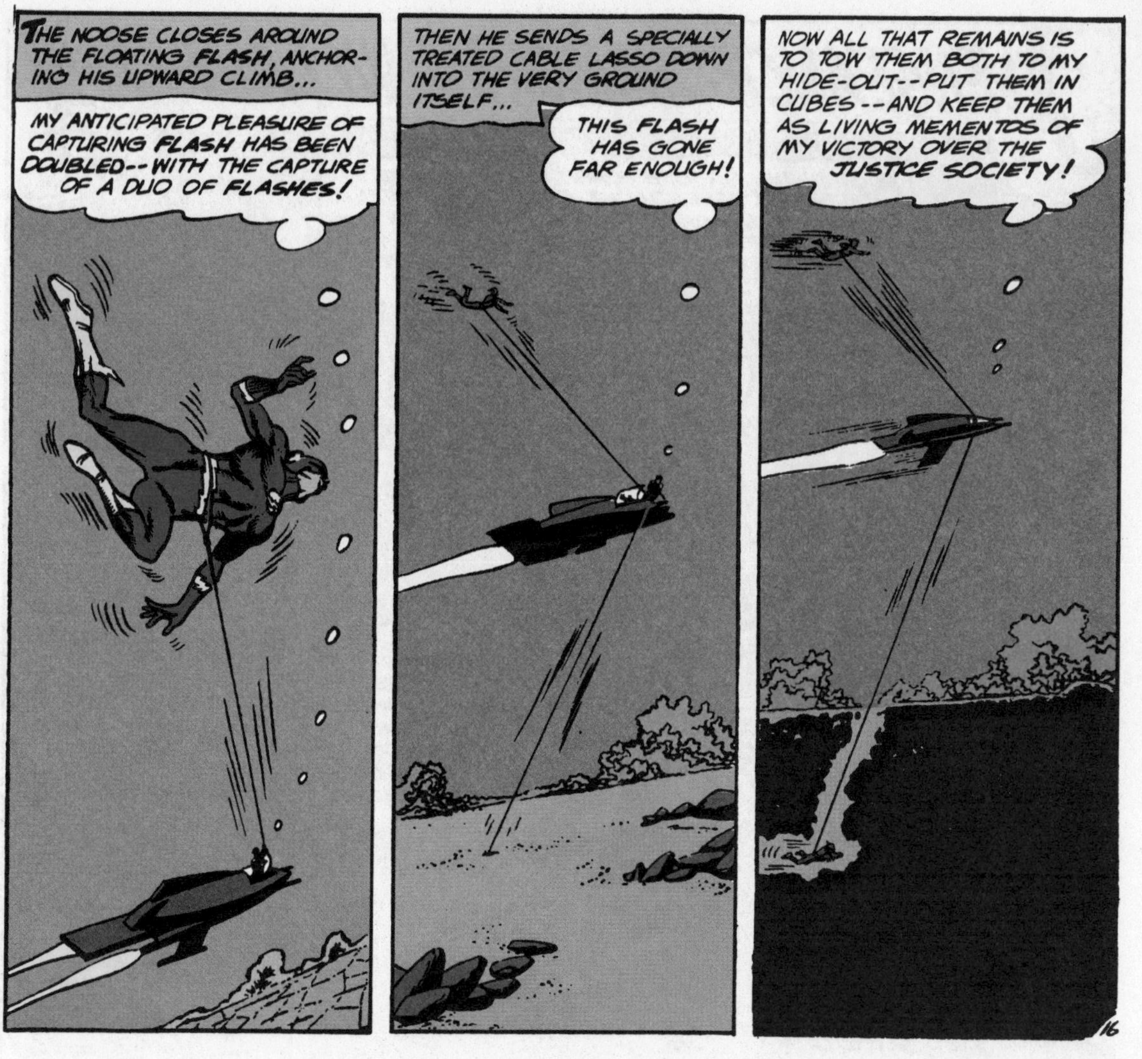
THE NOOSE CLOSES AROUND THE FLOATING FLASH, ANCHORING HIS UPWARD CLIMB...
MY ANTICIPATED PLEASURE OF CAPTURING FLASH HAS BEEN DOUBLED--WITH THE CAPTURE OF A DUO OF FLASHES!
THEN HE SENDS A SPECIALLY TREATED CABLE LASSO DOWN INTO THE VERY GROUND ITSELF...
THIS FLASH HAS GONE FAR ENOUGH!
NOW ALL THAT REMAINS IS TO TOW THEM BOTH TO MY HIDE-OUT--PUT THEM IN CUBES--AND KEEP THEM AS LIVING MEMENTOS OF MY VICTORY OVER THE JUSTICE SOCIETY!
16

CRISIS ON MULTIPLE EARTHS THE TEAM UPS

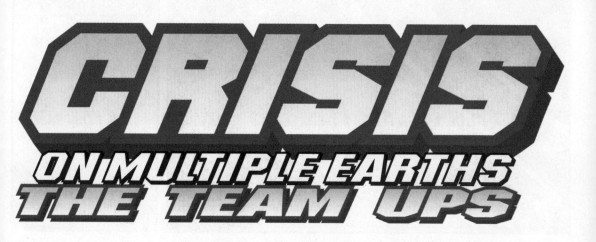

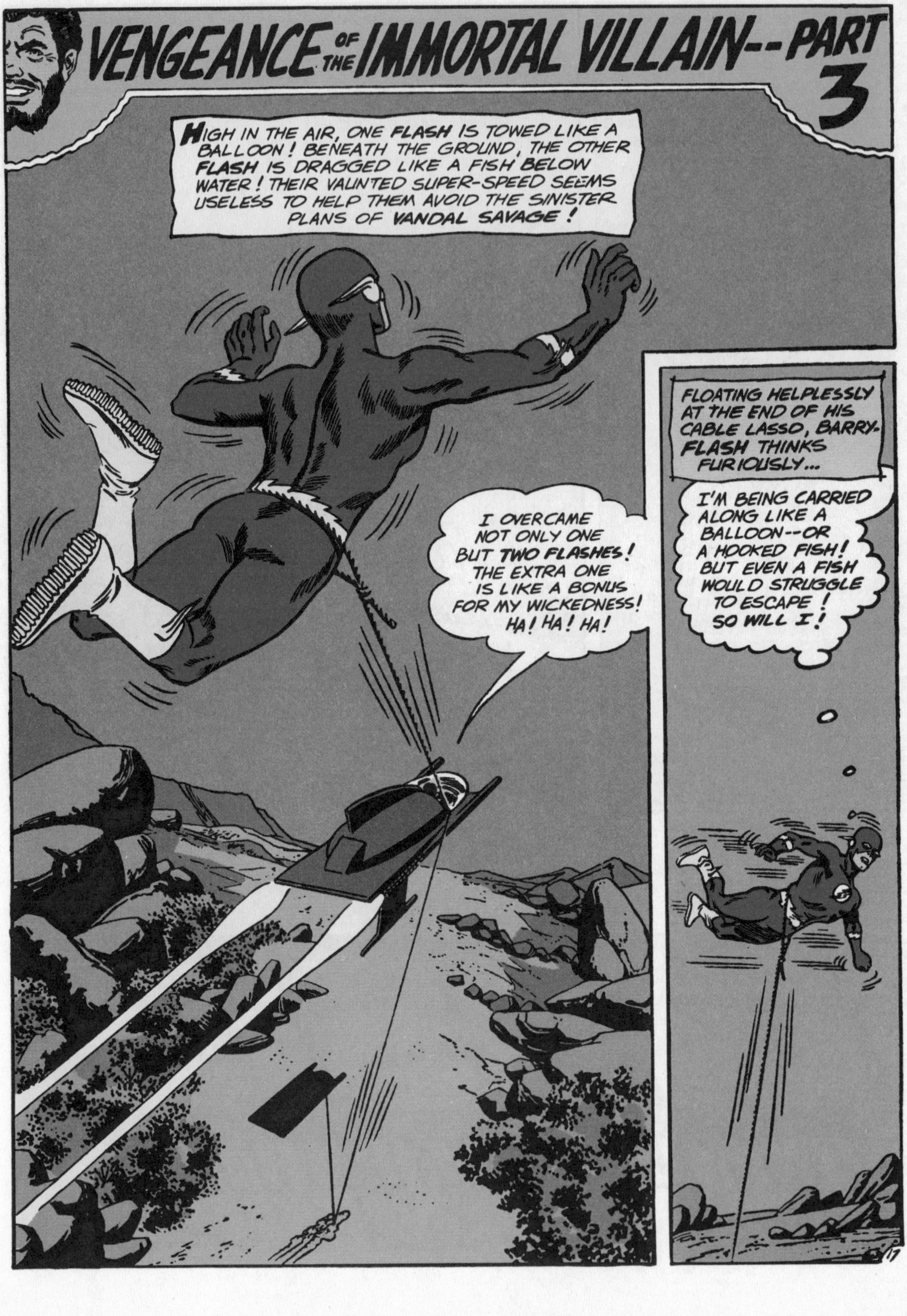
VENGEANCE OF THE IMMORTAL VILLAIN--PART 3
HIGH IN THE AIR, ONE FLASH IS TOWED LIKE A BALLOON! BENEATH THE GROUND, THE OTHER FLASH IS DRAGGED LIKE A FISH BELOW WATER! THEIR VAUNTED SUPER-SPEED SEEMS USELESS TO HELP THEM AVOID THE SINISTER PLANS OF VANDAL SAVAGE!
I OVERCAME NOT ONLY ONE BUT TWO FLASHES! THE EXTRA ONE IS LIKE A BONUS FOR MY WICKEDNESS! HA! HA! HA!
FLOATING HELPLESSLY AT THE END OF HIS CABLE LASSO, BARRY-FLASH THINKS FURIOUSLY...
I'M BEING CARRIED ALONG LIKE A BALLOON--OR A HOOKED FISH! BUT EVEN A FISH WOULD STRUGGLE TO ESCAPE! SO WILL I!
17

GRASPING THE CABLE LASSO, HE BEGINS TO VIBRATE IT WITH TERRIFIC SWIFTNESS...

THIS OUGHT TO SHAKE THAT VILLAIN UP A BIT!

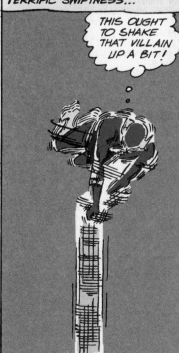

FAR BELOW HIM, JAY-FLASH HAS THOUGHT OF THE SAME TRICKY MANEUVER AND...

BY SHAKING THE LASSO AT SUPER-SWIFT SPEED-- I OUGHT TO BE ABLE TO MAKE THE PLANE VIBRATE UNCONTROLLABLY!

WITHIN MOMENTS THE DOUBLE-POWERED VIBRATIONS OF THE LASSOS SET UP A COMPENSATORY VIBRATION WITHIN THE PLANE ITSELF...

MY PLANE'S GOING OUT OF CONTROL! EVERYTHING'S SHAKING SO MUCH-- I CAN'T HOLD IT ON COURSE!

ITS STEERING MECHANISM WRECKED BY THE INCESSANT VIBRATIONS, THE LAB PLANE PLUNGES GROUNDWARD...

THROWN CLEAR OF THE WRECKAGE, VANDAL SAVAGE SEES THE TWO FLASHES DRAG THEMSELVES TOWARD HIS FLYING LABORATORY...

THEY CAN TURN MY OWN WEAPONS AGAINST ME! I'M NOT PREPARED TO FIGHT TWO FLASHES ARMED WITH MY WEAPONS! I'VE GOT TO GET AWAY!

18

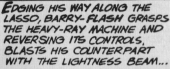

EDGING HIS WAY ALONG THE LASSO, BARRY-FLASH GRASPS THE HEAVY-RAY MACHINE AND REVERSING ITS CONTROLS, BLASTS HIS COUNTERPART WITH THE LIGHTNESS BEAM...

A LITTLE LESS LIGHTNESS, BARRY! I'M STARTING TO FLOAT, NOW!

THANKS, PAL! I'M BACK TO NORMAL! NOW LET ME RETURN THE COMPLIMENT!

OKAY! I WAS NEVER CUT OUT TO BE A BALLOON!

AFTER BEING RESTORED TO PROPER WEIGHT, THE MONARCHS OF MOTION BEGIN THEIR HUNT FOR VANDAL SAVAGE...

NO TRACE OF HIM! WE COULD SPEND HOURS-- DAYS-- SEARCHING FOR HIS HIDE-OUT...

SECONDS, BARRY! NOW THAT I KNOW VANDAL SAVAGE IS BEHIND THIS--I KNOW--FROM THE JUSTICE SOCIETY'S PREVIOUS ENCOUNTER WITH HIM--WHERE HE MAKES HIS HIDE-OUT!

OUTSIDE THE MAMMOTH CAVES IN KENTUCKY, AT THAT MOMENT...

I'VE BORROWED IDEAS FROM MY FELLOW MEMBERS OF THE INJUSTICE SOCIETY--BUT I ALSO INVENTED A FEW OF MY OWN! THIS UNIFORM, FOR INSTANCE, WHICH IS GIMMICKED TO FLY ME THROUGH THE AIR, ENABLED ME TO ESCAPE THE FLASHES!

I USED THE LAB PLANE TO MEET THEM INSTEAD OF FLYING UNDER MY OWN POWER BECAUSE I WANTED TO HAVE WEAPONS WITH WHICH TO OVERCOME THEM! NOW THAT FLASH KNOWS WHO IS BEHIND THE SKYLIGHTS MENACE, HE'LL ALSO REMEMBER I HAVE A HIDE-OUT UNDER MAMMOTH CAVES!

INTO THE CAVES HE RUNS AND TO HIS HIDE-OUT, WHERE...

MY OTHER WEAPONS FAILED-- BUT THIS INVENTION OF DEGATON'S WON'T! MY OLD INJUSTICE SOCIETY FELLOW MEMBER DIDN'T GO FAR ENOUGH WITH IT, HOWEVER! HE USED IT MERELY TO PARALYZE THE WILL! I'VE IMPROVED HIS BEAM--SO I CAN CONTROL THE WILL!

19

BY PREVENTING THE *FLASHES* FROM TEAMING UP AGAINST ME--BY USING THE *WILL-CONTROLLER* TO MAKE THEM BATTLE EACH OTHER INSTEAD OF ME--IT'LL ENABLE ME TO CAPTURE THEM BOTH!

WHEN THE BEAM FROM THIS *WILL-CONTROLLER* HITS THEM, IT WILL DIRECT THEM TO FIGHT ONE ANOTHER--FOR THE PRIVILEGE OF CAPTURING ME! WHEN THEY'RE SO WEAK THEY CAN'T FIGHT ANY MORE--I'LL ENCASE THEM IN MY CUBES!

UNAWARE OF THE GRIM TRAP INTO WHICH THEY ARE HEADING, THE *FLASH* PAIR RACES INTO MAMMOTH CAVES...

I'VE HIT THEM WITH THE INVISIBLE BEAMS OF THE *WILL-PARALYZER.* NOW THEY'LL BE TOO BUSY FIGHTING EACH OTHER TO BOTHER ABOUT ME!

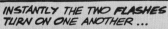

INSTANTLY THE TWO *FLASHES* TURN ON ONE ANOTHER ...

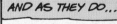

AND AS THEY DO...

WHILE THE TWO *FLASHES* FIGHT IT OUT FOR THE PRIVILEGE OF CAPTURING ME, I'LL MAKE MY GETAWAY... TO SET A TRAP AND CAPTURE THE WINNER--IF THERE IS ONE!

BEHIND HIM, BARRY- *FLASH* DRUMS HIS FEET ON THE ROCKY GROUND OF THE VAST CAVERNS...

I MUST OVER-COME JAY--SO I AND I ALONE CAN CAPTURE THIS VANDAL SAVAGE!

As HIS FEET SET UP TREMENDOUS VIBRATIONS, JAGGED STALACTITES SNAP OFF AND DROP IN A DEADLY SHOWER TOWARD JAY-FLASH...

IF BARRY THINKS HE'S GOING TO CAPTURE MY OLD ENEMY--HE'S GOT ANOTHER THINK COMING!

DARTING BETWEEN THE FALLING STONE SPEARS, JAY-FLASH ROTATES HIS ARM AT FURIOUS SPEED...

I CAN MOVE JUST AS FAST AS HE CAN! LET'S SEE HOW HE LIKES BEING A TARGET FOR THOSE STALACTITES!

--COMING STRAIGHT AT ME!

BUT BARRY-FLASH-- DODGING AND DARTING THOSE DEADLY MISSILES--CIRCLES FASTER AND FASTER ABOUT HIS FELLOW SCARLET SPEEDSTER...

THIS VORTEX OF SUPER-HURRICANE PROPORTIONS IS MAKING ME SPIN LIKE A TOP! THERE'S ONLY ONE THING TO DO!

DESPERATELY JAY-FLASH REACHES OUT--GRASPS HIS COUNTERPART BY AN ARM ...

TWO CAN PLAY AT THIS SORT OF GAME!

21

NOW IT IS THE TURN OF BARRY-FLASH TO CIRCLE AROUND AND AROUND...

WHEN I LET GO--HE'LL BE HURLED WITH SUPER-SPEED AND CENTRIFUGAL FORCE AGAINST THE ROCKY CAVERN WALL!

ONE SCARLET SPEEDSTER RELEASES HIS HOLD--AND THE OTHER SAILS LIKE A BULLET TOWARD THE JAGGED ROCKS...

IN MID-FLIGHT, BARRY-FLASH'S PALMS PUSH BACK AGAINST THE AIR IN A SWIMMING MOTION SO SWIFTLY THAT THEY BRAKE HIS PROGRESS...

INCHES FROM THE DEADLY WALL, HE DROPS LIGHTLY TO THE GROUND AND...

JAY IS OLDER THAN I AM-- AND CAN'T KEEP UP THIS SPEED DUEL AS LONG AS I! I'LL TRY OUT A SUPER-WIND ON HIM AND SEE WHAT HAPPENS!

JAY-FLASH IS WILLING--BUT HIS BODY, SO LONG OUT OF RETIREMENT--IS CLOSE TO EXHAUSTION. HE IS HURLED BACKWARD BY THE GALE...

THAT TAKES CARE OF HIM! NOW TO GO AFTER VANDAL SAVAGE AND CAPTURE HIM!

AS BARRY-FLASH SPEEDS OFF, VANDAL SAVAGE SLIPS OUT FROM BEHIND A STALAGMITE...

NOW I CAN PUT MY OLD ENEMY IN A CUBE FROM WHICH THIS TIME THERE'LL BE NO ESCAPE! AH--THERE GOES THE OTHER FLASH--VIBRATING HIMSELF INTO INVISIBILITY!

BUT IF HE THINKS TO OVERCOME ME THAT WAY, HE'S WRONG--DEAD WRONG! EVEN INVISIBILITY CAN'T SAVE HIM FROM THE CLEVER TRAP I ARRANGED! I ANTICIPATED HIS POSSIBLE USE OF INVISIBILITY-- AND GUARDED AGAINST IT!

MEANWHILE, BARRY-FLASH IS RACING FROM THE CAVES INTO THE SCIENTIFIC HIDE-OUT BELOW THEM...

THERE'S VANDAL SAVAGE NOW--WAITING TO DROP ME AS SOON AS HE SEES ME! BUT HE'LL NEVER GET THE CHANCE TO SEE ME ...

UNAWARE THAT THIS VANDAL SAVAGE IS ONLY A CREATED IMAGE OF THE REAL VILLAIN, THE FASTEST MAN ALIVE LEAPS FORWARD...

ONE SOLID BLOW WILL KNOCK HIM COLD !

THEN IN MID-AIR HE HALTS HIS PUNCH...

WAIT! THERE'S SOMETHING WRONG HERE!

FROM A SAFE DISTANCE HE TOSSES A STONE AT THE FIGURE OF VANDAL SAVAGE AND...

I WAS RIGHT! IF I'D MADE CONTACT WITH THAT IMAGE OF VANDAL SAVAGE-- HIS INESCAPABLE CUBE WOULD HAVE INSTANTLY FORMED AND TRAPPED ME INSIDE!

VROOM!

23

MOMENTS LATER, HAVING HEARD THE EXPLODING IMAGE OF HIS DUPLICATE, VANDAL SAVAGE RACES INTO HIS HIDE-OUT...

THE TRAP'S BEEN SPRUNG! I CAUGHT HIM! SINCE HE WAS INVISIBLE WHEN THE CUBE FORMED ABOUT HIM, HE'LL REMAIN INVISIBLE FOR ALL ETERNITY! NOW ALL THE JUSTICE SOCIETY MEMBERS WHO IMPRISONED ME--ARE MY PRISONERS!

THAT'S WHAT YOU THINK, VANDAL SAVAGE!

HUH? YOU-- YOU'RE ALL FREE! BUT I CREATED THE PERFECT DUPLICATE! WHAT COULD HAVE GIVEN IT AWAY?

WHEN YOU CREATED IT, THE IMAGE--MAKING MACHINE MUST HAVE USED SO MUCH POWER, THE LIGHTS DIMMED! IN THAT DIM LIGHT THE IRISES OF YOUR EYES EXPANDED! YOUR IDENTICAL IMAGE SHOWED THOSE SAME EXPANDED IRISES-- WHEN WITH BRIGHT LIGHTS SHINING, THEY SHOULD HAVE BEEN CONTRACTED!

WARNED THAT YOUR IMAGE WASN'T REAL, I TOSSED A STONE AT IT--THEN WENT AND FREED MY FRIEND, THE FLASH!

WHEREUPON WE RACED BACK AND FREED MY FELLOW JUSTICE SOCIETY MEMBERS-- WHILE YOU WERE RUNNING INTO THIS HIDE-OUT FROM THE CAVES OUTSIDE!

THE JUSTICE SOCIETY MEMBERS CONVERSE AMONG THEM-SELVES AS THE TWO FLASHES TAKE VANDAL SAVAGE BACK TO PRISON...

WE'LL SHUT OFF THIS MASTER CONTROL OF THE CUBE-MAKING MACHINES NEAR THE SKY-LIGHTS ENGINES-- SO WE CAN DISMANTLE THEM WITHOUT DANGER!

YOU KNOW, BOYS-- I'VE BEEN THINKING--

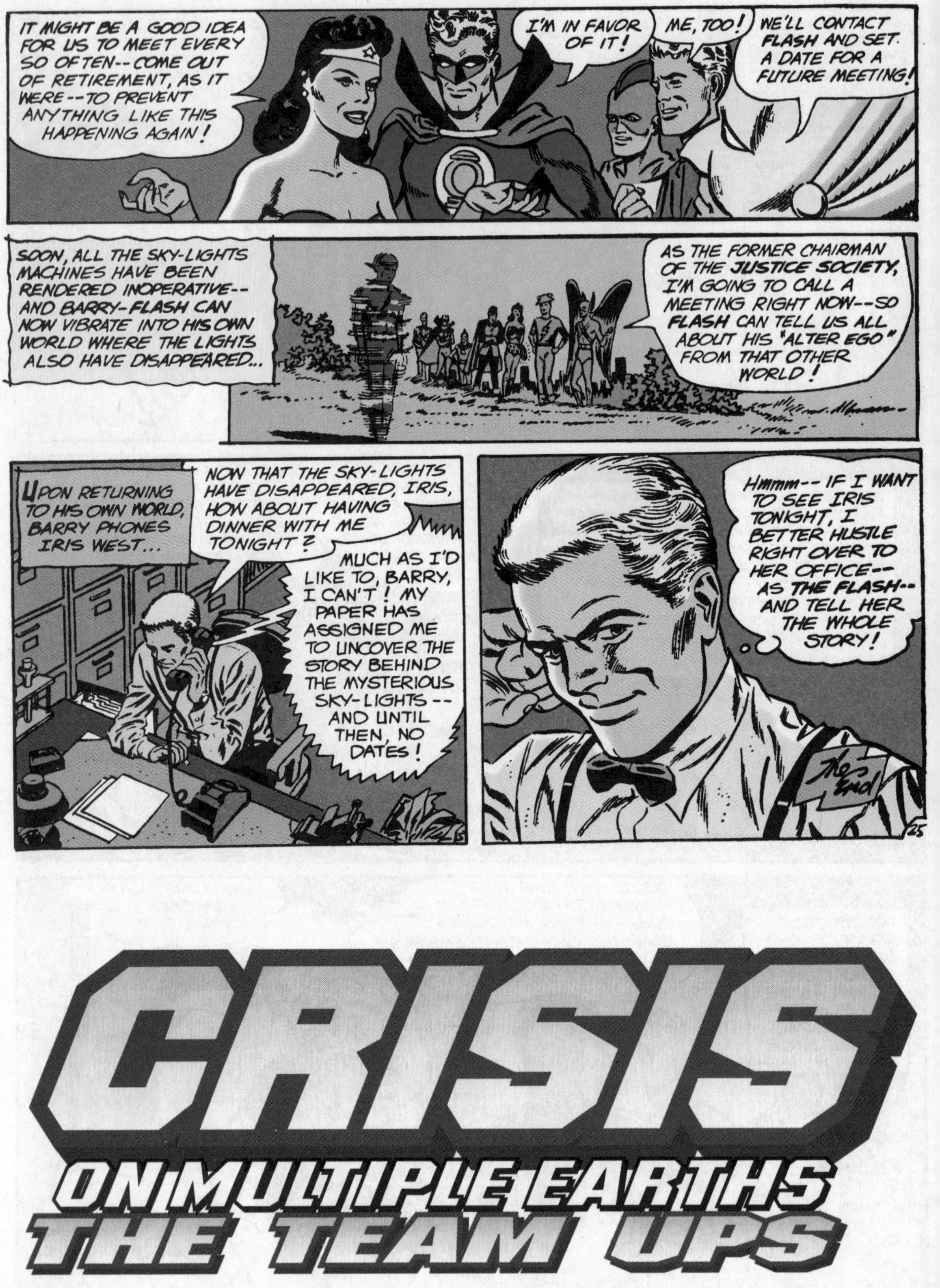
IT MIGHT BE A GOOD IDEA FOR US TO MEET EVERY SO OFTEN--COME OUT OF RETIREMENT, AS IT WERE--TO PREVENT ANYTHING LIKE THIS HAPPENING AGAIN!
I'M IN FAVOR OF IT!
ME, TOO!
WE'LL CONTACT FLASH AND SET A DATE FOR A FUTURE MEETING!
SOON, ALL THE SKY-LIGHTS MACHINES HAVE BEEN RENDERED INOPERATIVE--AND BARRY-FLASH CAN NOW VIBRATE INTO HIS OWN WORLD WHERE THE LIGHTS ALSO HAVE DISAPPEARED...
AS THE FORMER CHAIRMAN OF THE JUSTICE SOCIETY, I'M GOING TO CALL A MEETING RIGHT NOW--SO FLASH CAN TELL US ALL ABOUT HIS "ALTER EGO" FROM THAT OTHER WORLD!
UPON RETURNING TO HIS OWN WORLD, BARRY PHONES IRIS WEST...
NOW THAT THE SKY-LIGHTS HAVE DISAPPEARED, IRIS, HOW ABOUT HAVING DINNER WITH ME TONIGHT?
MUCH AS I'D LIKE TO, BARRY, I CAN'T! MY PAPER HAS ASSIGNED ME TO UNCOVER THE STORY BEHIND THE MYSTERIOUS SKY-LIGHTS--AND UNTIL THEN, NO DATES!
Hmmm--IF I WANT TO SEE IRIS TONIGHT, I BETTER HUSTLE RIGHT OVER TO HER OFFICE--AS THE FLASH--AND TELL HER THE WHOLE STORY!
The End
25

CRISIS ON MULTIPLE EARTHS THE TEAM UPS

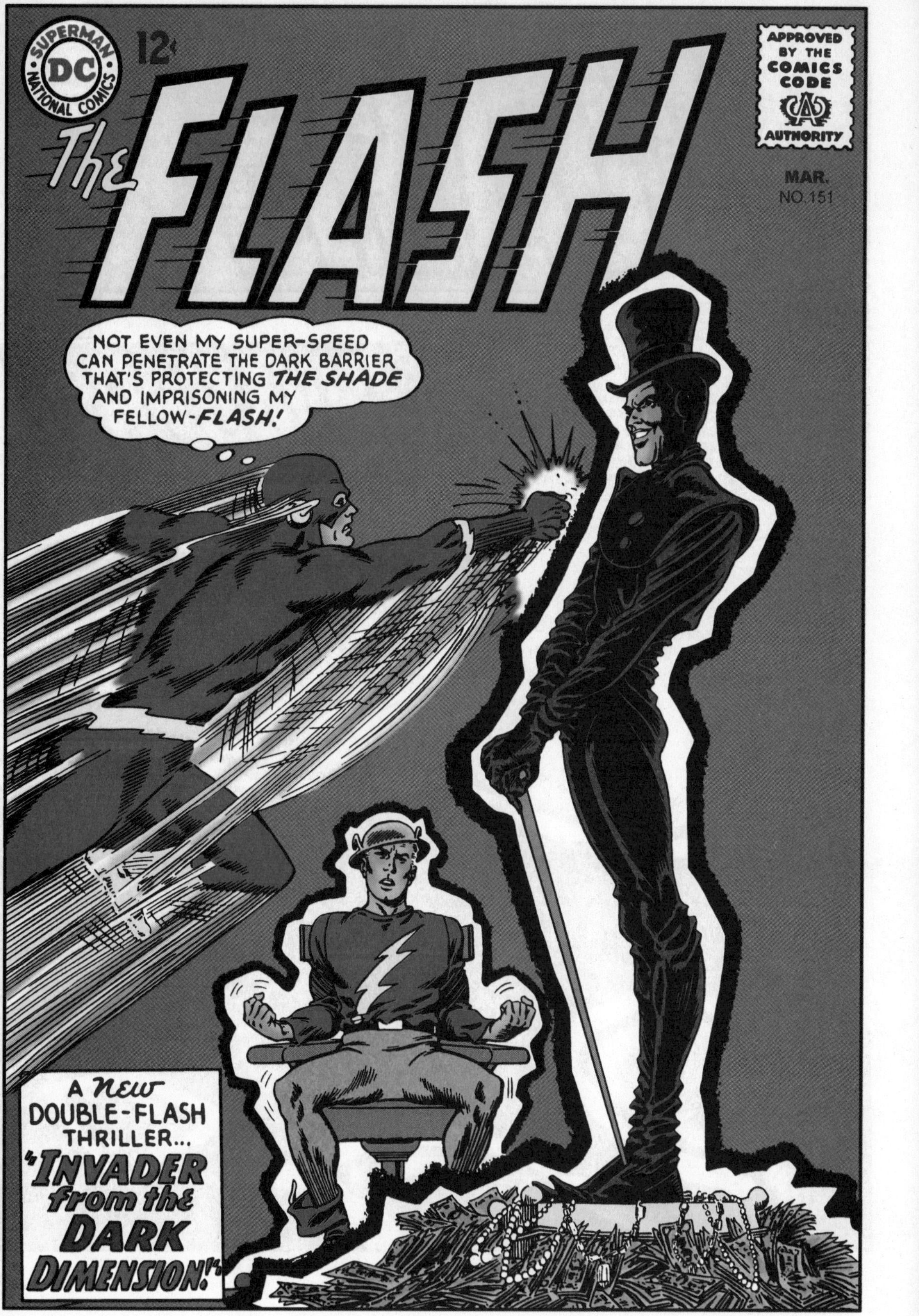
SUPERMAN DC NATIONAL COMICS
12¢
The FLASH
APPROVED BY THE COMICS CODE AUTHORITY
MAR. NO.151
NOT EVEN MY SUPER-SPEED CAN PENETRATE THE DARK BARRIER THAT'S PROTECTING THE SHADE AND IMPRISONING MY FELLOW-FLASH!
A NEW DOUBLE-FLASH THRILLER... "INVADER from the DARK DIMENSION!"

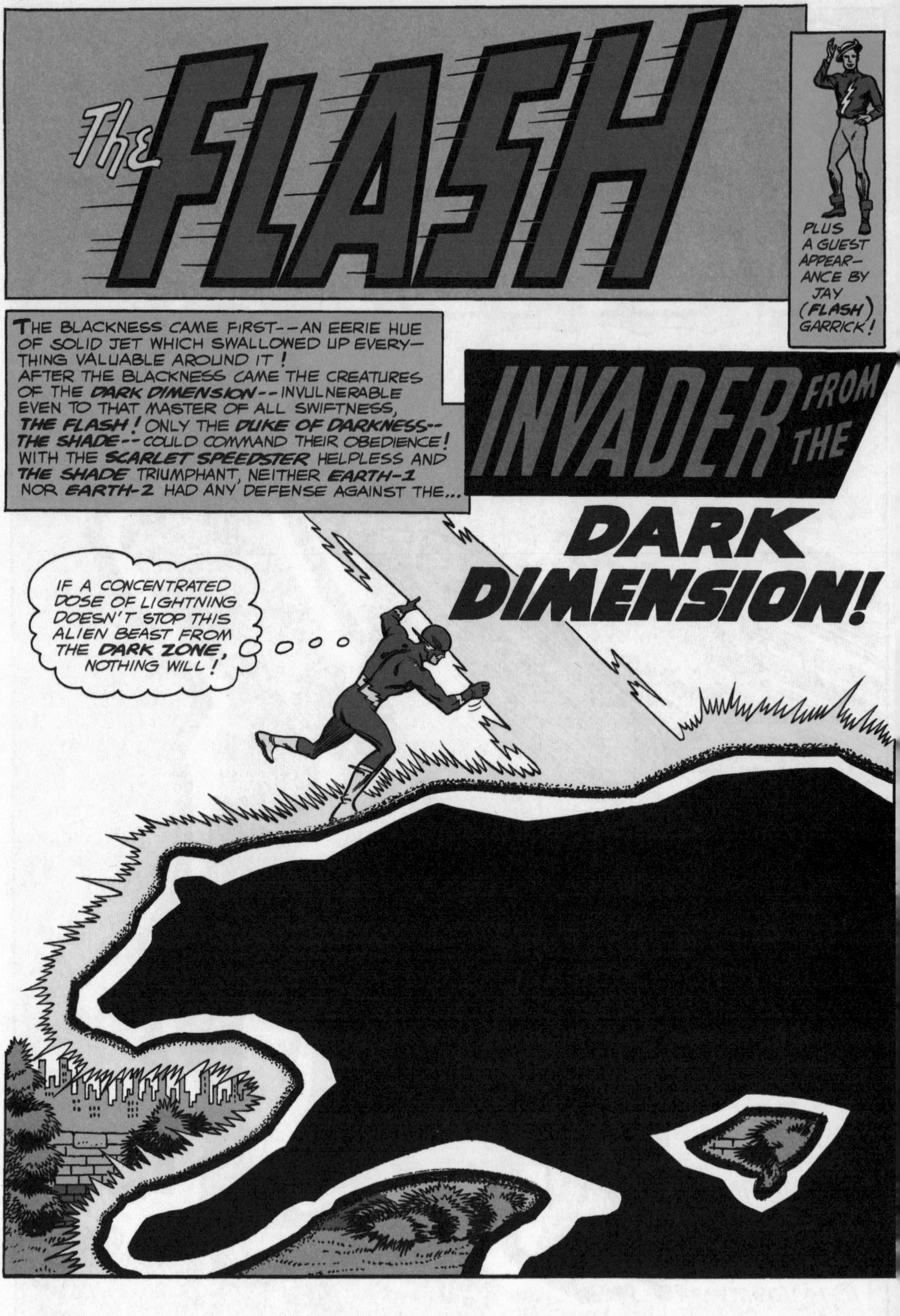
THE FLASH
PLUS A GUEST APPEAR-ANCE BY JAY (FLASH) GARRICK!
THE BLACKNESS CAME FIRST--AN EERIE HUE OF SOLID JET WHICH SWALLOWED UP EVERY-THING VALUABLE AROUND IT! AFTER THE BLACKNESS CAME THE CREATURES OF THE DARK DIMENSION--INVULNERABLE EVEN TO THAT MASTER OF ALL SWIFTNESS, THE FLASH! ONLY THE DUKE OF DARKNESS--THE SHADE--COULD COMMAND THEIR OBEDIENCE! WITH THE SCARLET SPEEDSTER HELPLESS AND THE SHADE TRIUMPHANT, NEITHER EARTH-1 NOR EARTH-2 HAD ANY DEFENSE AGAINST THE...
INVADER FROM THE DARK DIMENSION!
IF A CONCENTRATED DOSE OF LIGHTNING DOESN'T STOP THIS ALIEN BEAST FROM THE DARK ZONE, NOTHING WILL!

THE STREET KNOWN AS THE *DIAMOND MART* IN *CENTRAL CITY* IS THE JEWEL BOX OF THE MIDWEST. ALONG ITS THOROUGHFARE ONE DAY A WOMAN'S VOICE RINGS OUT TRIUMPHANTLY!...

BARRY, THERE IT IS! I FINALLY FOUND IT-- AFTER TWO YEARS OF HUNTING ALL OVER!

WHA-WHAT DID YOU FIND, IRIS?

THERE! THE ONE RING IN THE WORLD I WANT FOR MY ENGAGEMENT RING! ALL ALONG-- EVEN WHILE YOU PLEADED WITH ME TO LET YOU GIVE ME A RING TO SEAL OUR ENGAGEMENT-- I COULD NEVER FIND THE RING I HAD MY HEART SET ON!

BUBBLING OVER WITH HAPPINESS (BECAUSE TWO YEARS IS A LONG TIME TO BE LOOKING FOR AN ENGAGEMENT RING WITHOUT FINDING IT), IRIS WEST DRAGS A BEAMING BARRY *(FLASH)* ALLEN INTO THE JEWEL SALON ...

IT'S BEEN WORTH THE WAIT, DARLING!

MOMENTS LATER, BEAMING EYES EXAMINE THE UNUSUAL JEWEL IN ITS UNUSUAL SETTING ...

I MUST TRY IT ON! OH, BARRY-- I'M SO THRILLED!

ME, TOO! I WAS BEGINNING TO THINK YOU'D NEVER OWN AN ENGAGEMENT RING, HONEY! LET'S SEE HOW IT LOOKS!

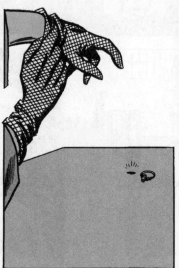

AS IRIS PUTS DOWN THE RING TO PULL OFF HER GLOVE, SHE DOES NOT NOTICE A *BLACK SPOT* MATERIALIZE ON THE DISPLAY COUNTER...

THE SPOT GROWS AND GROWS-- SWIFTLY AND SILENTLY-- ENCOMPASSING THE RING, SO THAT WHEN IRIS REACHES FOR IT....

OHHH! BARRY, IT'S CAUGHT! SOMETHING HAS HOLD OF IT!

WITH A SCREAM OF MINGLED FEAR AND ANGER, THE GIRL SEES THE DARK BLOTCH ENLARGE UNTIL...

OH, MY GOODNESS! IT'S SWALLOWED UP MY RING! BARRY-- GET IT OUT!

I'M TRYING TO-- BUT THIS BLACK STUFF IS AS HARD AS STEEL!

LARGER GROWS THE INCREDIBLE DARKNESS UNTIL...

THIS IS THE MOST FANTASTIC THING I'VE EVER SEEN! I BETTER GET HELP!

I'LL GO WITH THE CLERK, BARRY! YOU STAY PUT-- KEEP TABS ON IT!

AS IRIS AND THE CLERK RUN TO SOUND THE ALARM, BARRY USES THE SUPER-SPEED OF HIS HANDS TO TRY AND CRACK THE STRANGE SUBSTANCE...

NOBODY CAN SEE WHAT I'M DOING, SO IT'S SAFE TO-- UHH! I CAN'T EVEN DENT IT!

LARGER GROWS THE EERIE BARRIER UNTIL IT FILLS HALF THE STORE...

BARRY! WHAT A STORY FOR THE PICTURE NEWS!

HUH? HOW ABOUT THAT! AFTER HUNTING TWO YEARS FOR A RING-- AFTER FINDING IT--THEN LOSING IT-- HER MAIN CONCERN IS FOR THE SCOOP SHE'S GETTING FOR HER NEWSPAPER! I GUESS I'LL NEVER UNDERSTAND WOMEN!

POLICE SIRENS WAIL AS PROWL CARS PULL UP TO THE SITE OF THE OCCURRENCE! IRIS COMMANDEERS A STREET CORNER PHONE BOOTH! PEOPLE SURROUND THE STORE FRONT! AND ALONE, OFF TO ONE SIDE ...

HERE'S MY CHANCE TO SWITCH TO THE FLASH! WITH ALL THIS COMMOTION, NOBODY'LL NOTICE ME!

FROM HIS POCKET, BARRY SLIPS ON A SPECIAL RING AND PRESSES A SECRET SPRING-- CAUSING A TINY RED COSTUME TO ERUPT FROM IT AND EXPAND WHEN IT HITS THE AIR...

BEFORE A SECOND CAN TICK BY, THE *SCARLET SPEEDSTER* FLASHES TOWARD THE DARK BARRIER LOOMING IN THE STORE DOORWAY...

EVERY-BODY BACK!

I SHOULD HAVE THE ENDING FOR THE STORY IN A MINUTE! *THE FLASH* JUST SHOWED UP--!

VIBRATING SO SWIFTLY THAT HIS BODY IS A BLUR, THE *FASTEST MAN ON EARTH* SLAMS INTO THE BLACKNESS...

ONCE I VIBRATE INSIDE THAT THING, I'LL FIND OUT WHAT THIS IS ALL ABOUT!

NEXT INSTANT, HE BOUNCES BACK OFF THE WEIRD EBON SUBSTANCE...

INCREDIBLE!

AT MY SPEED I CAN VIBRATE THROUGH THE DENSEST MATERIAL! WHAT CAN THIS STUFF BE MADE OF?

HE TRIES THE FRICTION OF HANDS RUBBED WITH SUPER-SWIFTNESS OVER THE SMOOTH BLACK SURFACE...

THIS DOESN'T WORK--!

...AND THE AWE-SOME TENSION OF FEET DRUMMED WITH THE FORCE OF A THOUSAND TRIPHAMMERS AGAINST THE EBONY MATERIAL...

--NOR THIS!

HE GOES UNDER THE DARK BLOB-- ONLY TO LEARN IT IS AS SOLID ON THE BOTTOM AS IT IS ON TOP...

CAN'T EVEN SCRATCH IT!

HE VIBRATES THROUGH THE STEEL AND GLASS OF THE BUILDING TO STAND ON TOP OF THE BLOB-- WITH THE SAME NEGATIVE RESULTS...

I'VE EXHAUSTED MY REPERTOIRE OF SPEED TRICKS! WHAT DO I DO NOW?

THEN--AS FLASH DASHES OUTSIDE AGAIN, DESPERATELY HOPING TO COME UP WITH ANOTHER COURSE OF ACTION...

NICE WORK, FLASH! IT'S SHRINKING! SOON AS IT DISAPPEARS, I'LL GET MY RING-- AND YOUR EXCLUSIVE STORY! WHAT A DAY THIS HAS BEEN!

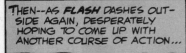

JEWELRY

IN THE DOORWAY OF THE STORE, A SOB OF DESPAIR RISES FROM HER THROAT AS IRIS SEES...

OHHH! THE BLACK BLOB HAS GONE-- BUT SO ARE ALL THE JEWELS IN THE STORE-- INCLUDING MY ENGAGEMENT RING!

NOTHING MORE THE FLASH CAN DO HERE! AND SINCE IRIS WILL BE EXPECTING TO SEE BARRY RIGHT ABOUT NOW, I'D BETTER CHANGE BACK TO MY OTHER SELF!

OUT OF SIGHT OF CURIOUS EYES, FLASH DOFFS HIS UNIFORM AND PRESSES ANOTHER PART OF HIS RING-- WHICH DRAWS THE RAPIDLY SHRINKING UNIFORM BACK INSIDE IT WITH A SMALL BUT POWERFUL SUCTION DEVICE...

MOMENTS LATER...

OH, THERE YOU ARE, BARRY! WELL, THE RING'S GONE! EVEN *THE FLASH* COULDN'T GET IT BACK!

SO I HEARD! er--HOW ABOUT A DRIVE AROUND TOWN-- MIGHT GET YOUR MIND OFF ALL THIS...

AS IRIS PULLS OUT INTO TRAFFIC, HER CAR RADIO COMES ALIVE...

--TO BRING YOU THE FOLLOWING NEWS BULLETIN! STRANGE CREATURES SURROUNDED BY A BLACK BARRIER HAVE BEEN SIGHTED IN THE NORTH END OF *CENTRAL CITY!*

BARRY-- LISTEN TO *THAT!*

THESE DARK BEINGS ARE FLYING-- LEAPING-- CRAWLING ALONG THE GROUND-- STEALING EVERYTHING VALUABLE IN THEIR PATH!

MY REPORTER'S INSTINCT TELLS ME THERE'S SOME SORT OF TIE-UP BETWEEN THOSE CREATURES AND THE BLACK ODDBALLS WHO STOLE MY RING!

LIPS TIGHT WITH DE-TERMINATION, THE GIRL REPORTER SPEEDS SKILLFULLY THROUGH THE CITY TRAFFIC...

SOON AS *THE FLASH* HEARS ABOUT THOSE THIEVING ALIEN CREATURES--HE'LL BE AROUND TO STOP THEM! BARRY, I'M GOING THERE TOO!

OKAY, HON-- BUT LET ME OFF FIRST!

BARRY, YOU'RE A *POLICEMAN!* IT SEEMS TO ME YOU'D WANT TO *HELP!*

I *DO* WANT TO HELP! BUT I'M A *LABORATORY ANALYST,* NOT A *FIELD INVESTIGATOR!* MY JOB IS TO ANALYZE INFORMATION OTHER POLICEMEN BRING ME! I'LL GO DIRECTLY TO THE LAB -- AND HELP FROM THERE!

6

SCARCELY DOES IRIS DROP HER FIANCÉ AT A NEARBY SIDEWALK THAN...

I CHANGED INTO MY *FLASH* OUTFIT EVEN BEFORE IRIS PULLED AWAY FROM THE CURB! NOW WHEN SHE ARRIVES IN THE NORTH END OF TOWN--SHE'LL FIND *FLASH* ALREADY AT WORK--TRYING TO SUCCEED WHERE HE FAILED BEFORE!

SOME DISTANCE AHEAD OF THE *SCARLET SPEEDSTER*, A MASSIVE *SOMETHING* IS TRUDGING INTO THE *NORTHSIDE BANK*...

WHAT *IS* IT?

WHERE'D IT *COME* FROM?

BANK OF WOR

WHERE IT PASSES-- ALL MONEY DISAPPEARS! POLICE BULLETS BOUNCE OFF THE BLACK SHELL AROUND IT...

OKAY, *FLASH*! TAKE OVER--

WE'RE GETTING NOWHERE AGAINST THAT NIGHTMARE!

THE *MONARCH OF MOTION* SPINS LIKE A SUPER DERVISH-- HURLING A TORRENT OF VIBRATIONS AT THE UNCANNY PRESENCE...

I'VE SET UP SHOCK-WAVES EQUAL TO THOSE CREATED BY A SMALL ATOM-- BOMB--ONLY THEY DON'T SEEM TO BOTHER IT!

7

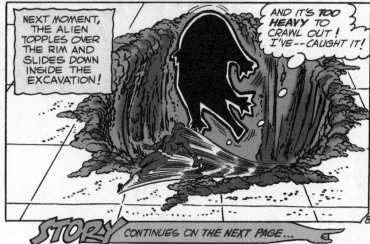

STORY CONTINUES ON THE NEXT PAGE...

CRISIS
ON MULTIPLE EARTHS
THE TEAM UPS

INVADER FROM THE DARK DIMENSION!

PART 2

THE BEATING OF DARK WINGS OVERHEAD ALERTS THE *SCARLET SPEEDSTER* TO THE FACT THAT HIS WORK HAS ONLY BEGUN! SWOOPING LOW ABOVE THE CITY STREETS-- HEADING TOWARD A DISPLAY OF ART OBJECTS IN A PUBLIC PARK--COMES ANOTHER MONSTROSITY OUT OF NIGHTMARE! BUT WHAT CAN THE *FASTEST MAN ON EARTH* DO AGAINST A FOE THAT IS SEEMINGLY OUT OF HIS REACH?

GOT TO TRACK THIS ONE DOWN-- FIND ANOTHER WAY OF CAPTURING IT!

AS THE WINGED CREATURE SKIMS THE ART DISPLAY--ABSORBING RARE TREASURES AS IT DOES SO--THE *CRIMSON COMET* SPURTS FORWARD,...

WHILE I CAN'T MAKE DIRECT CONTACT WITH IT, I *CAN* BATTLE IT WITH A CYCLONIC-- LIKE WIND!

TO ONE SIDE, AN OVERJOYED IRIS WEST HOPS UP AND DOWN TO ENCOURAGE THE MAN SHE IS COUNTING ON TO GET HER ENGAGEMENT RING BACK,...

GO TO IT, *FLASH!* POLISH THEM OFF-- *FLASH-STYLE!*

AROUND AND AROUND GOES THE *FASTEST MAN ON EARTH,* SETTING UP A TITANIC WHIRL-- WIND THAT GRIPS THE ALIEN CREATURE AND SPINS IT....

THINGS ARE GOING MY WAY AT LAST! IT WON'T BE STEALING ANY MORE STATUES WHILE IT STAYS "PUT"!

THERE IS NO TIME FOR FURTHER SELF-CONGRATULATION-- FOR AT THIS MOMENT *THE FLASH* SEES ANOTHER THREAT LOOMING UP...

OHH! THIS ONE LOOKS TOUGHER THAN THE OTHER TWO COMBINED!

whew I HAVE MY WORK CUT OUT FOR ME WITH THAT MONSTROUS THING!

NEITHER SUPER-SWIFT VIBRATIONS NOR AWESOME PIT NOR CYCLONIC WIND HAS ANY EFFECT ON THE MIGHTY COLOSSUS!...

I'VE FOUGHT SOME FORMIDABLE OPPONENTS IN MY TIME--

--BUT THIS ONE COPS THE PRIZE--

-- FOR SHEER INVULNERABILITY!

SUDDENLY, THE *SCARLET SPEEDSTER* CUTS OFF HIS SUPER-SPEED STUNTS AND...

FLASH, WHAT ARE YOU GAPING AT? THERE'S NOTHING UP THERE TO HELP YOU--

I WONDER--THAT DARK CLOUD ON THE HORIZON AND THAT BOLT OF LIGHTNING--MAY BE THE "WEAPON" I NEED TO STOP THAT COLOSSUS!

SPEEDING PAST THE OUTSKIRTS OF TOWN, HE WINDMILLS HIS ARMS TO BLOW THE DARK CLOUD BEFORE HIM...

ACTUALLY "LIGHTNING" IS INVISIBLE! WHAT THE EYE SEES IS THE PATH OF BURNING AIR THROUGH WHICH THE BOLT OF ELECTRICITY HAS JUST PASSED!

AS THE CLOUD MOVES ABOVE THE DARK MONSTER, JAGGED YELLOW BOLTS STAB DOWNWARD--TOUCHING AND HAMMERING ITS COLOSSAL BULK!...

THEY AREN'T EVEN TICKLING IT! YET LIGHTNING CONTAINS UP TO 340,000 AMPERES--AND ONLY 2400 ARE NEEDED TO KILL A MAN! I'VE GOT TO DO SOMETHING MORE AND-- I THINK I KNOW WHAT IT IS!

MOVING EVEN MORE SWIFTLY THAN THE LIGHTNING BOLTS THEMSELVES, THE *SCARLET SPEEDSTER* PUSHES AGAINST THEM--PROTECTED BY THE AURA OF HIS SUPER-SWIFT BODY--JOINING THEM INTO A SINGLE MASSIVE BOLT!...

ZZZTT!

THEN AS *FLASH* AND IRIS WATCH, THE ALIEN CREATURE FADES AWAY...

FLASH--YOU DID IT! YOU MADE ALL THESE ALIEN CREATURES GO BACK WHERE THEY CAME FROM! NOW HOW ABOUT GOING AFTER THEM AND GET BACK MY RING?

I--I CAN'T, IRIS! THERE'S NO WAY FOR ME TO PENETRATE THE MYSTERIOUS BLACK BARRIER THAT PROTECTS THEM!

DESPAIR SLUMPS THE GIRL REPORTER'S SHOULDERS...

I--I WAS COUNTING ON YOU SO MUCH! I--I GUESS I'LL NEVER WEAR AN ENGAGEMENT RING NOW-- BECAUSE THERE'S NO OTHER ONE LIKE IT ON EARTH!

HEY--WAIT! ON EARTH-1, MAYBE! BUT HOW ABOUT ON-- EARTH-2?

EARTH-2 IS ANOTHER EARTH, SEPARATED FROM OURS BY A VIBRATIONAL BARRIER! I'VE HAD ADVENTURES IN IT--AND JAY GARRICK, WHO IS *THE FLASH* ON THAT OTHER EARTH, CAME TO *EARTH-1* TO GET A DUPLICATE METEOR HE NEEDED TO SAVE HIS EARTH*!

*Editor's Note: SEE *FLASH* #129: "DOUBLE DANGER ON EARTH!"

THERE ARE DOUBLES OF PRACTICALLY EVERYTHING ON THOSE TWO EARTHS! SO THERE'S A GOOD CHANCE THERE'S A DUPLICATE OF IRIS' LOST RING ON *EARTH-2!* BUT I CAN'T GO THERE AT THIS CRITICAL MOMENT-- WHEN I'M IN THE MIDDLE OF A CASE TRACKING DOWN THOSE EBONY ALIENS!

12

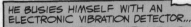

As Barry Allen, he returns to his police laboratory where...

I noticed that whenever I came close to those alien creatures, my body started vibrating in an odd manner! By analyzing those vibrations, I may come up with some clue as to their origin!

He busies himself with an electronic vibration detector...

Just as fingerprints leave their telltale marks, so do vibrations! I'll record those still lingering in my body on a punched card...

Armed with a pattern of the vibrations, he feeds the data into a computer, and soon after...

Good gosh! These vibrations match those I obtained from the cane of THE SHADE -- when I last tangled with him! *

* Editor's Note: See THE FLASH #123: "Flash of Two Worlds!"

THE SHADE lives on EARTH-2! But I doubt that those alien creatures came from there -- so how is THE SHADE involved in this mystery? My starting point for clearing up this mystery is to vibrate myself into EARTH-2!

As he has done a number of times in the past, THE FLASH races into the old theater which is a gateway between the two Earths, where...

Soon as I get there, I'll contact THE FLASH of EARTH-2 -- JAY GARRICK! Perhaps he knows something about THE SHADE that will explain matters!

Soon after, in answer to the SCARLET SPEEDSTER'S knock on the door of the Garrick home...

Good gosh! There's the same ring Iris wanted for an engagement ring!

THEN THE DOOR SWINGS WIDE AND HE FINDS HIMSELF STARING AT MRS. JAY GARRICK--THE FORMER JOAN WILLIAMS...

FLASH! IT'S GOOD TO SEE YOU--Hmmm! YOU'RE STARING AT MY RING-- AND NO WONDER! IT WAS MY ENGAGEMENT RING-- THE ONLY ONE LIKE IT ON EARTH!

THEN THERE IS A DOUBLE OF IRIS' RING HERE! BUT-- I COULDN'T POSSIBLY ASK JOAN TO PART WITH IT!

AS JOAN LEADS HIM INTO THE LIVING ROOM...

HI, BARRY! WHAT BRINGS YOU TO EARTH-2?

THE SHADE! LET ME TELL YOU OF THE INCREDIBLE HAPPENINGS OF THE PAST HALF DOZEN HOURS ON EARTH-1!

WHEN HIS STORY IS CONCLUDED, THE EARTH-2 FLASH DRAWS A DEEP BREATH, THEN PLUNGES INTO HIS OWN RECITAL...

ODDLY ENOUGH, THE CASE I WAS JUST ABOUT TO GO OUT ON ALSO CONCERNS THE SHADE! LATELY, HE'S BEEN SPENDING MONEY AS IF IT WERE GOING OUT OF STYLE!

"THE SHADE WAS RELEASED FROM PRISON FOR GOOD CONDUCT AFTER WE LAST PUT HIM THERE. SOON AFTER, HE BEGAN 'LIVING IT UP'..."

I'M TREATING EVERYONE IN THE PLACE TO DINNER!

"SINCE THE SHADE NEVER EARNED AN HONEST DOLLAR IN HIS LIFE, ALL HIS MONEY MUST HAVE COME FROM ROBBERIES--ONLY THERE HAVE BEEN NO REPORTS OF ANY SUCH ROBBERIES! SO I DECIDED TO TRAIL HIM ..."

I'LL KEEP HIM IN VIEW UNTIL I LEARN WHERE HE GETS THE FORTUNE HE'S BEEN SQUANDERING! I'LL VIBRATE SO SWIFTLY HE WON'T KNOW HE'S BEING FOLLOWED!

"SURE ENOUGH, I CAUGHT HIM VISITING AN ART DEALER-- A FENCE WHO TURNS STOLEN GOODS INTO CASH-- WITH A RARE *CELLINI VASE...*"

HOLD IT! THAT'S THE *CELLINI CUP!* THERE'S ONLY ONE LIKE IT--AND IT BELONGS TO A FOREIGN MUSEUM!

ON THE CONTRARY, *FLASH--* IT BELONGS TO *ME!*

"A QUICK CHECK BROUGHT THE *ASTONISHING* NEWS THAT *TWO* SUCH MASTERPIECES MUST EXIST, FOR..."

THE MUSEUM STILL HAS ITS *CUP!* YET THAT ONE IS A PERFECT DUPLICATE OF IT! I DON'T UNDER- STAND IT...

LET'S JUST SAY I'M TOO CLEVER FOR YOU, *FLASH!*

NOW, OF COURSE, I UNDER- STAND EVERYTHING! *THE SHADE* HAS BEEN ROBBING ON *EARTH-1!*

AND HE MUST HAVE BEEN ROBBING FOR QUITE A WHILE, PERHAPS SECRETLY AT FIRST! NOW HE'S COME RIGHT OUT INTO THE OPEN! I'M CON- VINCED HE'S BE- HIND THE MYSTERIOUS DARK CREATURES THAT HAVE APPEARED ON MY EARTH!

WITHIN MOMENTS, THE FLASHES OF TWO WORLDS RACE OUT OF *KEYSTONE CITY...*

WE'LL PAY *THE SHADE* A VISIT AND CON- FRONT HIM WITH THE TRUTH!

BUT SINCE *THE SHADE* IS SO TRICKY-- I'M GOING TO REMAIN *IN- VISIBLE!* THAT WAY, I'LL HAVE A COUNTERMOVE FOR ANY TRICK HE TRIES TO SPRING ON YOU!

SOON AFTERWARD, *JAY-FLASH* RACES INTO THE HOUSE OF THE *DUKE OF DARKNESS...*

THE FLASH! SO GOOD OF YOU TO VISIT ME! COME IN, COME IN, BY ALL MEANS!

YOU WON'T SWEET-TALK YOUR WAY OUT OF THIS, *SHADE--* YOU'VE BEEN ROBBING ON *EARTH-1!*

BY EREBUS! I'M SURPRISED YOU DIDN'T TUMBLE TO IT SOONER, *FLASH!* YES, YOU'RE PERFECTLY RIGHT! I MADE A FORTUNE -- A DOZEN FORTUNES! -- ON *EARTH-1,* THANKS-- TO YOU!

THANKS-- TO *ME??*

HAVE A CHAIR, *FLASH--* AND I'LL TELL YOU ALL ABOUT IT!

"YES, *FLASH*-- IT WAS *YOU* WHO SHOWED ME HOW TO VIBRATE FROM *EARTH-2* INTO *EARTH-1* ! YOU SEE, I'D HAD MY EYE ON YOU FOR SOME TIME AND WAS WATCHING WHEN YOU CARVED A PATHWAY BETWEEN WORLDS !"...

HE'S VIBRATING IN AN ODD MANNER. WHAT'S HE UP TO ?

"I CAUGHT THOSE VIBRATIONS WITH MY CANE-- BUT WHEN I DUPLICATED THEM BY PRESSING DOWN THE PLUNGER THAT ACTIVATES MY WALKING STICK ... "

I'M IN A STRANGE ZONE OF UTTER DARKNESS ! FORTUNATELY, HOW- EVER, THE SPECIAL CONTACT LENSES I WEAR ENABLE ME TO SEE PERFECTLY !

"FROM THAT DARK DIMENSION I COULD LOOK INTO BOTH *EARTH-1* AND *EARTH-2* ... "

TWO EARTHS ! SIMPLY FAN- TASTIC ! WHY, I COULD ROB IN ONE-- AND ENJOY MY ILL-GOTTEN GAINS IN THE OTHER-- AND NO ONE WOULD BE THE WISER !

"WITH THE POWERS OVER THE DARK ZONE AND ITS ALIEN INHABITANTS WHICH MY CANE GAVE ME, I WAS SOON ROBBING ON *EARTH-1* WHERE AND WHEN I WILLED !... "

I CAN EXTEND THE IMPENETRABLE BLACKNESS OF THE DARK ZONE SO IT WILL ADMIT ONLY OBJECTS OF VALUE THROUGH IT AND TO ME-- THANKS TO MY MARVELOUS CANE !

AS *THE SHADE* CONCLUDES HIS NARRATIVE...

NOW THAT YOU'VE ADMITTED YOUR GUILT-- I'LL TAKE YOU INTO *EARTH-1* FOR PUNISHMENT !

OH, COME NOW, *FLASH* ! YOU UNDERESTIMATE ME ! DO YOU REALLY THINK I'D HAVE TOLD YOU ALL THAT-- IF THERE WAS THE SLIGHTEST CHANCE OF YOUR STOPPING ME ?

TO HIS HORROR, THE *EARTH-2 FLASH* DISCOVERS THAT HE CANNOT RISE FROM THE CHAIR...

WH-WHAT HAVE YOU DONE TO ME ?

ALL THE WHILE I'VE BEEN TALKING TO YOU, *INVISIBLE BLACK LIGHT* HAS BEEN BEAMING DOWN ON YOU-- THE CUMULATIVE EFFECT OF WHICH IS TO BAR YOU FROM EVER LEAVING IT ! WHAT A TRIUMPH OVER MY ARCH-FOE ! *HA, HA !*

At THE SHADE'S mocking laughter, the EARTH-1 FLASH leaps forward...

AM I EVER GLAD I HAD THE FORESIGHT TO REMAIN IN- VISIBLE! NOW TO TURN THE SHADE'S TRIUMPH INTO DEFEAT-- AND FREE MY FELLOW-FLASH!

BUT--EVEN AS HIS FIST SLAMS AGAINST THE SHADE...

OHHH! I'VE BECOME VISIBLE!

eh? BY EREBUS-- IT'S MY OTHER VAUNTED FOE, THE EARTH-1 FLASH! YOU SEE, I REMEMBER YOU! AND--I'M 'WAY AHEAD OF YOU, I MIGHT ADD!

I SURROUNDED MYSELF WITH AN UNSEEN BLACK AURA IN CASE THE FLASH OF MY WORLD TRIED ANY INVISIBILITY TRICKS ON ME! IT MADE YOU APPEAR AS SOON AS YOU TOUCHED "ME"! I NEVER FIGURED I'D CATCH YOU THIS WAY, THOUGH! HOWEVER-- NOW THAT YOU'RE HERE--

GO AHEAD! TRY TO CAPTURE ME! DON'T LET ME JUST STAND HERE--!

NO, WAIT! I HAVE A BETTER IDEA!

I'LL STAND ON TOP OF MY ACCUMULATED WEALTH TO MAKE IT MORE INVITING FOR YOU! ALL YOU HAVE TO DO IS OVERCOME ME AND RE- COVER THE LOOT OF MY MANY EARTH-1 ROBBERIES! WELL, COME ON! GIVE IT THAT OLD SUPER- SPEED TRY!

I KNOW HE'S TEMPT- ING ME-- BUT ONE THING'S SURE! I WON'T CAP- TURE HIM JUST BY STARING AT HIM! SO HERE GOES--

BARRELING IN LIKE A HUMAN BULLET, THE SCARLET SPEEDSTER HURLS HIMSELF AT HIS MOCKING ENEMY...
JUST AS I ANTICIPATED, I CAN'T PENETRATE THE DARK BARRIER THAT PROTECTS HIM! BUT THERE MUST BE A WAY--
NOTHING CAN HARM ME IN THE ZONE OF DARKNESS, FLASH--ABSOLUTELY NOTHING!
THEN BEFORE HIS EYES, THE DUKE OF DARKNESS BEGINS TO DISAPPEAR...
HAD I KNOWN YOU WERE COMING HERE, I'D HAVE ARRANGED TO CAPTURE YOU TOO, BUT--SINCE YOU CAN NEVER CAPTURE ME IN THE ZONE OF DARKNESS, IT REALLY MAKES NO DIFFERENCE!
ONLY A TAUNTING VOICE REVEALS WHERE THE SHADE ONCE STOOD...
JUST AS IT WAS IMPOSSIBLE FOR YOU TO HARM ME, SO IT IS IMPOSSIBLE FOR YOU TO ENTER MY DARK DIMENSION--OR CAPTURE ME! I AM NOW FREE TO GO ON ROBBING IN EARTH-1 AS I HAVE BEEN DOING! FAREWELL!
DESPITE ALL HIS BOASTS, I'LL FIND A WAY TO BEAT HIM AND FREE MY FELLOW-FLASH!
STORY CONTINUES ON FOLLOWING PAGE
18

CRISIS ON MULTIPLE EARTHS THE TEAM UPS

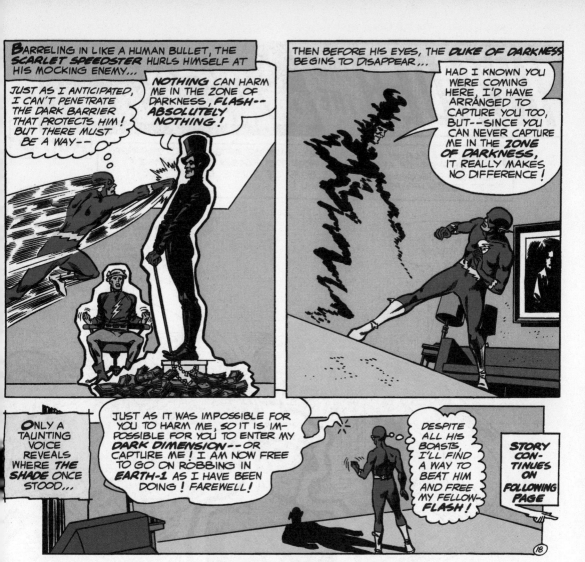

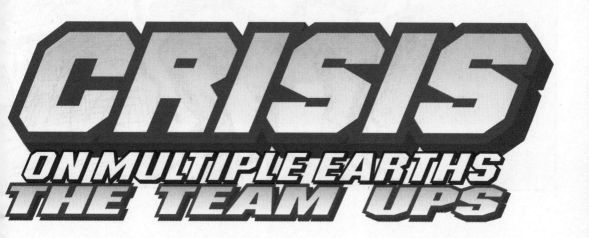

INVADER FROM THE DARK DIMENSION!

PART 3

THE *EARTH-1 FLASH* BREAKS SPEED BARRIER AFTER SPEED BARRIER IN A DESPERATE ATTEMPT TO FREE *THE FLASH* OF *EARTH-2!* ALWAYS HE IS BALKED BY THE BAND OF INVISIBLE BLACK LIGHT THAT HOLDS HIS FRIEND IN THRALL!

I'LL FIND A WAY YET TO FREE YOU, JAY!

YOUR BEST BET IS TO RETURN TO *EARTH-1* AND SOMEHOW-- IN SOME WAY--CAPTURE *THE SHADE* AND TAKE HIS CANE AWAY FROM HIM! IT'S THE CANE WHICH CONTROLS THIS BLACK LIGHT THAT HOLDS ME PRISONER!

YOU'RE RIGHT! I HATE TO RUN OUT ON YOU LIKE THIS--BUT THE SOONER I GET AFTER *THE SHADE* THE SOONER YOU'LL BE FREE!

GOOD HUNTING-- AND GOOD LUCK, BARRY!

EVEN AS THE *SCARLET SPEEDSTER* VIBRATES INTO HIS OWN WORLD--FOUR TERRIBLE MENACES ARE STIRRING TO LIFE ON *EARTH-1* UNDER THE COMMAND OF *THE SHADE* AND HIS EBON CANE..

WHERE THE GROUND SHUDDERS AND SPLITS APART UNDER A BATTERING FROM THE DARK DIMENSION--AN EERIE "MAN" OF ANTHRACITE COAL RISES OUT OF A FISSURE IN THE GROUND...

MILES AWAY IN THE *CENTRAL CITY MUSEUM,* AN EMPTY SUIT OF BLACK ARMOR BEGINS TO MOVE WITH METALLIC STIFFNESS,...

IT'S--ALIVE!

LET'S GET OUT OF HERE--!

A QUEER FIGURE FORMED OF *BLACK 8-BALLS* CLICKS ALONG A SUPER-- HIGHWAY...

WHILE A MASSIVE BLOB OF ANIMATED *INDIA INK* FLOWS ACROSS THE FENCES AND DITCHES OF A COUNTRYSIDE...

As the coal "man" passes through a factory—absorbing its payroll cash within its vast bulk—*the flash* appears...

This is *the shade's* handiwork—and it's up to me to undo it!

So swiftly does *flash* travel that he causes air on all sides of the coal-man to ignite—but...

The coal must be protected from the fire by the same blackness which protected *the shade!*

He leaves one awesome menace and races to where the *"black knight"* is raiding an art gallery...

I ought to be able to kayo at least *one* of these thieving menaces!

From a fire hydrant, *flash* frees a stream of water—and directs it with pulse-stunning force at the black armor as it emerges from the art gallery...

Incredible! That water would knock over a dozen men—but the empty suit of armor keeps on moving!

Again he abandons one foe to seek another...

It's just robbed that bank! Perhaps I can blow those 8-balls apart!

THE AWESOME WIND THAT SWEEPS THE *CENTRAL CITY* STREET AND BATTERS AGAINST THE 8-BALL GIANT IS STRONGER THAN A HURRICANE, YET...

FAILED AGAIN! I HAVE ONE LAST HOPE-- TO STOP THAT FLOW OF INDIA INK!

BUT EVEN AS HE SLIDES TO A HALT BEFORE THE ADVANCING TORRENT OF BLACK INK, THE *SCARLET SPEEDSTER* SLAPS HIS FOREHEAD IN DISGUST!...

OHHHH-- WHAT AN *IDIOT* I'VE BEEN!

THE SOLUTION TO MY PROBLEM HAS BEEN IN FRONT OF ME RIGHT ALONG! I'VE SEEN IT HALF A DOZEN TIMES-- YET IT MADE NO IMPRESSION ON ME UNTIL THIS MOMENT! IT'S SO *SIMPLE*! NOW I KNOW HOW TO GO INTO THE "IM-PENETRABLE" DARK DIMENSION AFTER *THE SHADE*!

WHAT CAN *THE FLASH* HAVE IN MIND AS HE TURNS AND SPEEDS AWAY FROM THE ADVANCING INK BLOTCH EVEN AS IT MOVES IN TO LOOT THE CITY MUSEUM?...

22

RACING HUNDREDS OF MILES AWAY IN THE WINK OF AN EYELID, THE *FASTEST MAN ON EARTH* ARRIVES AT A BRANCH OF THE *UNITED STATES MINT*...

I'LL FIND WHAT I NEED IN HERE! I'LL HAVE TO BORROW WHAT I WANT--AND RETURN IT AS SOON AS POSSIBLE!

MOVING WITH THAT SAME INCREDIBLE SWIFTNESS, HE SNATCHES UP MICRO-THIN SHEETS OF 22-KARAT GOLD LEAF AND PLASTERS THEM OVER HIS BODY...

I MUST MAKE MYSELF LOOK LIKE A STATUE OF SOLID GOLD!

THEN HE RACES BACK TO THE MUSEUM--AND STANDS RIGIDLY NEXT TO OTHER GOLDEN OBJECTS AS THE INDIA INK FLOWS TOWARD THEM...

THE ONLY WAY I HAVE OF GETTING INTO THE DARK DIMENSION WHERE *THE SHADES* HIDE-OUT IS-- TO BE *TAKEN THERE* BY ONE OF *THE SHADE'S* ANIMATED "CROOKS"!

SLOWLY-- QUESTINGLY-- THE INDIA INK TOUCHES THE *GOLDEN FLASH*-- FLOWS ABOUT HIM-- AND ABSORBS HIM...

THE SHADE HAS OBVIOUSLY INSTRUCTED THE INK TO TAKE ONLY VALUABLE OBJECTS--SO I'VE FOOLED IT INTO THINKING I'M A PRIZE PIECE OF LOOT!

MOMENTS LATER, INSIDE THE DARK DIMENSION...

THERE HE IS! THINKING HIMSELF COMPLETELY SAFE IN THIS PLACE, *THE SHADE* WON'T HAVE ANY OF HIS PROTECTION ABOUT HIM!

23

INSTANTLY THE **SULTAN OF SPEED** VIBRATES SO SWIFTLY HE SENDS A RAIN OF GOLD LEAVES OVER HIS **EARTH-2** FOE...

OH, NO! THE FLASH! HOW DID YOU-- GLUBBB!

NOW TO GRAB HIS CANE AWAY FROM HIM!

AS **FLASH'S** FIST SLAMS INTO THE GOLDEN CHEEK OF **THE DUKE OF DARKNESS**, HIS OTHER HAND SNATCHES AWAY THE CANE...

THERE! NOW I HAVE THE CANE AND CAN VIBRATE US BOTH OUT OF THIS PLACE WITH ALL HIS STOLEN LOOT!

BUT--AS THE **SCARLET SPEEDSTER** IS ABOUT TO PRESS THE PLUNGER AND ACTIVATE THE WONDROUS WALKING-- STICK...

FLASH--NO! DON'T DO IT! IF YOU PRESS DOWN THE PLUNGER-- NEITHER OF US WILL EVER BE ABLE TO LEAVE THIS PLACE!

THERE IS THE RING OF TRUTH IN **THE SHADE'S** ALMOST HYSTERICAL VOICE...

HERE, GIVE IT BACK TO ME AND I'LL SET YOU FREE! YOU JUST DON'T REALIZE WHAT TERRIBLE FORCES OF DARKNESS YOU'RE TAM- PERING WITH!

IF **THE SHADE** CAN WORK THE CANE-- WHY CAN'T I? SURELY THE CANE DOESN'T KNOW WHO'S USING IT! WHAT GIVES **THE SHADE** HIS POWER OVER IT?

FOR A LONG MOMENT, THE **SCARLET SPEEDSTER** STANDS IMMOBILE. THEN WITH A GRIN HE BENDS FORWARD AND WITH HIS HANDS BLURRING IN SUPER- SPEED, HE STRIPS OFF **THE SHADE'S** GLOVES!...

OF COURSE! IT HAS TO BE YOUR GLOVES! THEY MUST BE TREATED IN SOME MANNER THAT PROTECTS YOU FROM THE AWESOME POWERS CONTAINED IN YOUR WALKING STICK!

NEXT MOMENT, **FLASH** PRESSES THE CANE PLUNGER--AND FREES **THE SHADE** AND HIMSELF-- TOGETHER WITH **THE SHADE'S** LOOT--FROM THE DARK DIMENSION...

YOUR NEXT STOP, **SHADE**-- IS POLICE HEADQUARTERS!

SIMULTANEOUSLY, THE LIFE-FORCE THAT WAS IN THE COAL-MAN, THE BLACK ARMOR, THE 8-BALLS, AND THE INK DIES OUT...

AFTER LEAVING HIS PRISONER WITH THE POLICE OF *EARTH-1*, *FLASH* RACES INTO *EARTH-2* WHERE...

I'M GOING TO LEAVE HIS CANE WITH YOU, JAY! WITH *THE SHADE* IN AN *EARTH-1* JAIL AND HIS CANE IN *EARTH-2*, WE'LL BE SAFE FOR SOME TIME TO COME!

I NEVER DOUBTED FOR A MOMENT YOU'D SUCCEED, *FLASH!*

ONE THING REMAINS TO BE DONE! *FLASH* RETURNS IRIS' "STOLEN" ENGAGEMENT RING TO HER SO THAT LATER, WHEN HE VISITS HER AS *BARRY ALLEN*...

WHEN WE'RE MARRIED, BARRY-- YOU JUST *HAVE* TO ASK *THE FLASH* TO BE YOUR BEST MAN AFTER ALL HE'S DONE FOR US!

YES, DEAR!

I'LL FACE *THAT* PROBLEM WHEN I COME TO IT!

The End

25

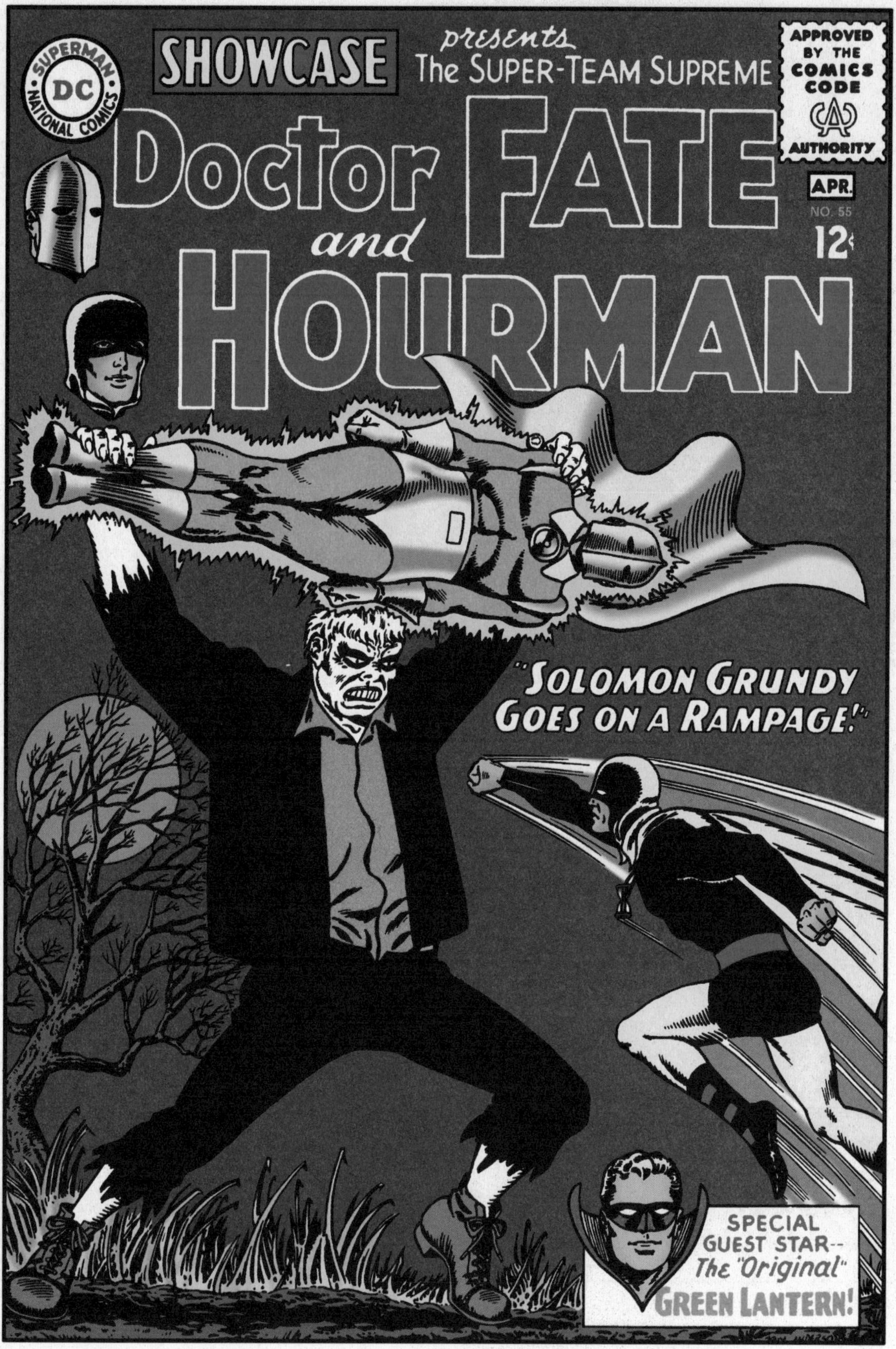

SUPERMAN DC NATIONAL COMICS
SHOWCASE
presents
The SUPER-TEAM SUPREME
APPROVED BY THE COMICS CODE AUTHORITY
Doctor FATE
and
HOURMAN
APR.
NO. 55
12¢
"SOLOMON GRUNDY GOES ON A RAMPAGE!"
SPECIAL GUEST STAR-- The "Original" GREEN LANTERN!

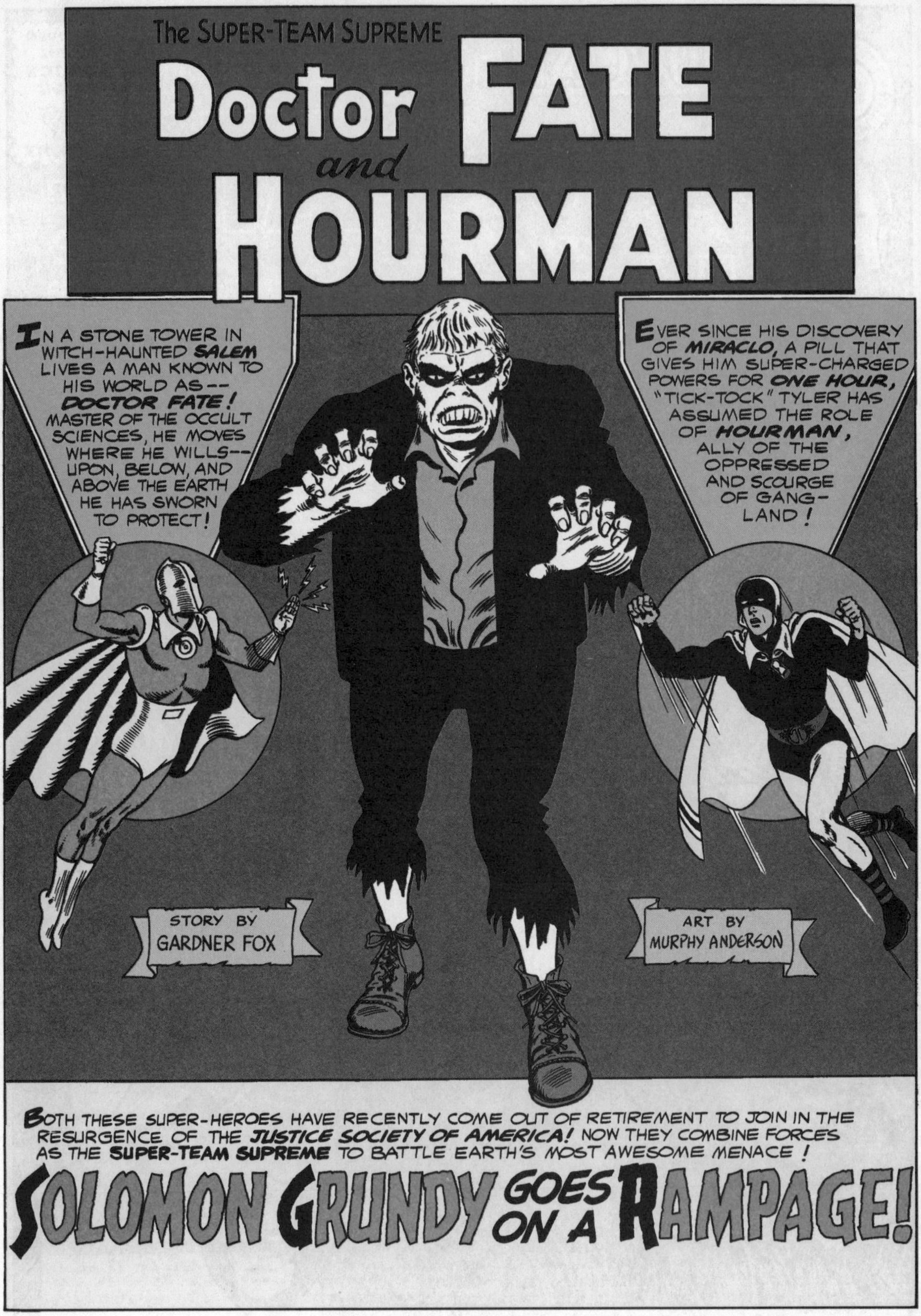
The SUPER-TEAM SUPREME
Doctor FATE and HOURMAN
IN A STONE TOWER IN WITCH-HAUNTED SALEM LIVES A MAN KNOWN TO HIS WORLD AS-- DOCTOR FATE! MASTER OF THE OCCULT SCIENCES, HE MOVES WHERE HE WILLS-- UPON, BELOW, AND ABOVE THE EARTH HE HAS SWORN TO PROTECT!
EVER SINCE HIS DISCOVERY OF MIRACLO, A PILL THAT GIVES HIM SUPER-CHARGED POWERS FOR ONE HOUR, "TICK-TOCK" TYLER HAS ASSUMED THE ROLE OF HOURMAN, ALLY OF THE OPPRESSED AND SCOURGE OF GANG-LAND!
STORY BY GARDNER FOX
ART BY MURPHY ANDERSON
BOTH THESE SUPER-HEROES HAVE RECENTLY COME OUT OF RETIREMENT TO JOIN IN THE RESURGENCE OF THE JUSTICE SOCIETY OF AMERICA! NOW THEY COMBINE FORCES AS THE SUPER-TEAM SUPREME TO BATTLE EARTH'S MOST AWESOME MENACE!
SOLOMON GRUNDY GOES ON A RAMPAGE!

SOLOMON GRUNDY GOES ON A RAMPAGE-- PROLOGUE *

NOT REAL LIFE--ONLY A WEIRD DISTORTION OF IT--SOLOMON GRUNDY IS SAID TO HAVE BEEN CREATED BY THE STRANGE CHEMICAL REACTION OF SIZZLING SUNLIGHT BEATING DOWN ON THE DECAYED VEGETATION OF SOGGY SWAMPLAND...

"IMPOSSIBLE," SAID SCIENTISTS ! WELL, MAYBE IT WAS ! BUT, BEFORE LONG, A CRIMINAL BAND FOLLOWED A NEW CHIEF-- SOLOMON GRUNDY !

SOON--TOO SOON-- AN ENTIRE NATION WAS TREMBLING BEFORE THE OMINOUS ONSLAUGHTS OF A RAGING COLOSSUS OF CRIME WHO COULDN'T BE STOPPED BY BULLETS.

FINALLY TRAILED TO THE PETRIFIED FOREST BY INDOMITABLE GREEN LANTERN, A TRULY TITANIC BATTLE ENSUED...

YOU--HURT--ME --

THAT CHASE ACROSS THE CONTINENT DIDN'T HELP HIM ANY ! MY RAY IS WEAKENING HIM--

BULLETS COULDN'T KILL HIM-- JAILS COULDN'T HOLD HIM-- ONLY THE EMERALD ENERGY OF GREEN LANTERN HAD ANY EFFECT ON SOLOMON GRUNDY...

CAN'T--MOVE-- I'M CAUGHT !

AND, TODAY, HERE IS THAT VISION OF TERROR--STILL IMPRISONED IN A BUBBLE OF EMERALD ENERGY !

SOME DAY--GET OUT-- DESTROY ENEMY-- GREEN LANTERN-- SOME DAY--

CANNOT KILL ME--LIVE FOREVER--MUST COME TIME WHEN AM FREE ! THEN--KILL-- GREEN LANTERN !

*EDITOR'S NOTE: THIS IS A RE-CREATION OF A PAGE THAT ORIGINALLY APPEARED IN "THE REVENGE OF SOLOMON GRUNDY!", PUBLISHED IN ALL STAR COMICS #33 (FEBRUARY-MARCH, 1947).

SOLOMON GRUNDY GOES ON A RAMPAGE! *chapter 1*

OUT OF THE SKY IT COMES, STREAKING EARTHWARD IN A FURIOUS BLAST OF FLAME AND THUNDER--TO CRASH AND HURL SKYWARD A SPRAY OF DIRT AND BURNING VEGETATION! ...

THERE IS AN EERIE SILENCE. IS THIS MYSTERIOUS EXPLODING OBJECT A METEOR? A FALLEN SATELLITE? A STRAY ASTEROID? OR SOME OTHER VISITOR FROM OUTER SPACE?

FOR THINGS FROM OUTER SPACE *DO* FALL ON EARTH--YET THIS IS TOTALLY UNLIKE ANYTHING ELSE THAT HAS EVER LANDED ON OUR PLANET!

FOR FROM THE WISPING REMNANTS OF THE SHATTERED GLOBE RISES A CREATURE WITH A HATE-TWISTED FACE...

EXILED INTO OUTER SPACE BY *GREEN LANTERN*, *SOLOMON GRUNDY* HAS RETURNED TO THE EARTH THAT SPAWNED HIM!

THE FIGURE STUMBLES AWAY FROM THE IMPACT POINT, THROUGH THE WOODS...

I FIND HIM! WHEN I FIND HIM--I KILL!

IT STRIDES INTO A LAKE, PROCEEDING FORWARD EVEN AS THE WATERS CLOSE ABOUT ITS HEAD, NOT BREATHING, NOT NEEDING TO BREATHE...

UNTIL IT COMES TO A HIGH STONE WALL SURROUNDING WHAT USED TO BE--LONG AGO-- THE WATERY MARSH-LANDS KNOWN AS *SLAUGHTER SWAMP*...

WALL NO STOP ME! I GO BACK TO BIRTH WATERS!

CRAACK

③

THE WALL GOES DOWN BEFORE THE GIANT STRENGTH OF THE EERIE HUMANOID-- REVEALING A GLOWING MARSHLAND INTO WHICH **SOLOMON GRUNDY** HURLS HIMSELF HEADLONG ...

FAR AWAY IN THE WITCH-HAUNTED HILLS OF **OLD SALEM** STANDS A STONE TOWER, WHICH EMITS A PULSING GLOW INTO THE NIGHT AS...

KENT--LOOK! THE TOWER IS GIVING OFF SOME SORT OF STRANGE RADIANCE!

NOT THE TOWER--BUT THE CRYSTAL BALL INSIDE IT, HONEY! THIS HASN'T HAPPENED IN A LONG TIME!

ARCHEOLOGIST **KENT NELSON** AND HIS LOVELY WIFE, THE FORMER **INZA CRAMER**, HURRY INTO THE STONE TOWER--WHICH HAS NO DOOR!...

THE CRYSTAL BALL GLOWS OF ITS OWN ACCORD-- ONLY WHEN SOME TERRIBLE EVIL WALKS THE EARTH! HURRY-- I MUST LOOK INTO ITS DEPTHS!

TO THE TOPMOST ROOM HURRIES THE MARRIED COUPLE-- BUT ONLY KENT NELSON DARES STARE INTO THAT BRILLIANT GLOBE...

ODD-- I SEE THE RADIOACTIVE MARSHLANDS ATTACHED TO THE **TYLER CHEMICAL COMPANY** PLANT! HOW CAN *THAT* BE EVIL?

I'LL GET YOUR COSTUME, DEAR! I KNOW TROUBLE WHEN I SEE IT!

NEXT MOMENT, THE MASTER OF MAGIC-- **DOCTOR FATE**-- STANDS ARRAYED IN THE UNIFORM GIVEN HIM BY **NABU THE WISE** *...

I'LL DIRECT THE CRYSTAL BALL TO SHOW ME WHERE THE EVIL COMES FROM, TO RETRACE ITS STEPS!

* *Editor's Note:*

FOR AN EXPLANATION OF THE ORIGIN AND POWERS OF *DOCTOR FATE*, SEE THE TEXT PAGE AT THE END OF THIS STORY.

4

HURLING HIMSELF UPWARD FROM THE TOWER AND MERGING HIS ATOMIC STRUCTURE WITH THE VERY WIND, *DOCTOR FATE* QUICKLY ARRIVES AT THE IMPACT POINT WHERE THE CELESTIAL GLOBE STRUCK THE EARTH...

WHATEVER IT WAS THAT FELL HERE IS...GONE! BY REASSEMBLING ITS ATOMS, I CAN RECONSTRUCT ITS ORIGINAL FORM!

WITH THE ANCIENT WISDOM OF THE *CHALDEANS*, HE GATHERS THE ATOMS OF THE DISSIPATED BUBBLE OF FORCE AND RESHAPES THEM...

BY ISHTAR! THIS WAS ONCE A BUBBLE OF FORCE--CREATED BY MY FELLOW *JUSTICE SOCIETY OF AMERICA* MEMBER-- *GREEN LANTERN*! HMMM-- ALL THE MORE REASON TO HURRY TO THE RADIOACTIVE MARSHLAND POOL!

SOME MILES AWAY IN THE *TYLER CHEMICAL COMPANY* PLANT OFFICE, THE PRESIDENT OF THE COMPANY-- *REX TYLER*-- IS ENTERING A VAULT KNOWN ONLY TO HIMSELF...

GOOD THING I WAS WORKING LATE TONIGHT SO I COULD BE HERE WHEN THE ALARM SOUNDED! SOME MAN OR ANIMAL HAS BLUNDERED INTO THE MARSH WHERE WE EMPTY THE RADIOACTIVE WASTE FROM OUR CYCLOTRON!

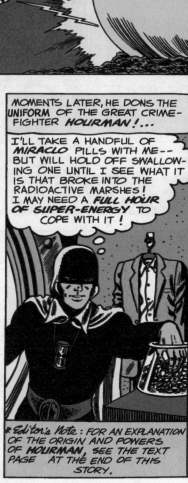

MOMENTS LATER, HE DONS THE UNIFORM OF THE GREAT CRIME- FIGHTER *HOURMAN*!...

I'LL TAKE A HANDFUL OF *MIRACLO* PILLS WITH ME-- BUT WILL HOLD OFF SWALLOW- ING ONE UNTIL I SEE WHAT IT IS THAT BROKE INTO THE RADIOACTIVE MARSHES! I MAY NEED A *FULL HOUR OF SUPER-ENERGY* TO COPE WITH IT!

* *Editor's Note*: FOR AN EXPLANATION OF THE ORIGIN AND POWERS OF *HOURMAN*, SEE THE TEXT PAGE AT THE END OF THIS STORY.

SOON AFTER, THE *MAN OF THE HOUR* STANDS BEFORE THE GLOWING WASTES OF *SLAUGHTER SWAMP*-- AND LIFTS OUT A *MIRACLO* PILL AT SIGHT OF...

SOLOMON GRUNDY! I'VE HEARD *GREEN LANTERN* SPEAK OF THAT MOST BITTER OF ALL FOES--AND HOW HE PUT HIM AWAY ON A DISTANT PLANET-- PRESUMABLY "FOR ETERNITY"!

SWALLOWING A *MIRACLO PILL*, *HOURMAN* VAULTS INTO THE AIR AT THE MACABRE MAN-THING...

I MUST STOP HIM, THEN TELL *GREEN LANTERN*--

NO TELL *GREEN LANTERN!* I TELL HIM! I *HATE GREEN LANTERN!!*

10:15 P.M.

BUT INSTEAD OF ATTACKING WITH HIS UPRAISED ARM, *SOLOMON GRUNDY* SWINGS HIS LEFT ARM UPWARD...

OOOOOF!

I MUST BE RUSTY--TO LET HIM BOOBY-TRAP ME WITH THAT RIGHT HAND--

THUMMMMP!

10:15¼ P.M.

EVEN AS *HOURMAN* SLAMS INTO THE BOLE OF A THICK TREE-- FROM THE SKY ABOVE SWOOPS THE *WONDER WIZARD*, BOLTS OF LIGHTNING RUNNING FROM HIS FINGERTIPS...

SOLOMON GRUNDY! I NEVER FOUGHT AGAINST HIM--BUT I'VE HEARD THE *JUSTICE SOCIETY* MEMBERS TELL OF THEIR HOMERIC BATTLE WITH HIM!

DOCTOR FATE INFECTS THE SWAMPLAND TREES WITH A *PSEUDO-LIFE-FORCE* AND DIRECTS IT TO ATTACK THE BELLOWING MAN-THING...

AAARRGHHH!

6

MAD WITH RAGE-- LIVID WITH THE URGE TO REND AND TEAR-- *SOLOMON GRUNDY* REACHES OUT AND RIPS ANOTHER TREE FROM ITS EARTH-BED...

WHAT ENORMOUS STRENGTH HE HAS--TO FIGHT OFF MY MAGIC-RIDDLED TREES AND RIP UP ANOTHER ONE!

WITH THAT FLAIL IN HIS HANDS, THE *MARSHLAND MONSTER* SWEEPS THE AIR ABOVE HIM, SEEKING TO "BAT DOWN" HIS FOE...

I KILL! NO STOP ME! I KILL!

QUICKLY, *DOCTOR FATE* DIVERTS SOME OF HIS MAGIC TO SHRED THE TREE-CLUB INTO POWDER...

IT IS EVIDENT THAT *SOLOMON GRUNDY*--BEING ONLY A PSEUDO-LIFE-FORM-- IS NOT AS BADLY AFFECTED BY MY MAGIC AS A TRUE HUMAN WOULD BE!

WITH A HUGE ROAR OF DEFIANCE, THE MAN-THING RIPS THE TREES FROM HIS BODY-- EVEN AS THE *WONDER WIZARD* FREEZES THE VERY AIR ABOUT HIM!...

7

MAGICALLY FORM THE FROST CRYSTALS! SWIFTLY THEY BUILD AND CLING TO ONE ANOTHER--UNTIL AN IMMENSE ICE-BLOCK STANDS ON THE RIM OF *SLAUGHTER SWAMP!*...

I'VE IMPRISONED HIM! NOW I'LL SEE TO *HOURMAN!*

BUT THE *MARSHLAND MAN-THING* IS NO ORDINARY FOE! THE HATE THAT SURGES THROUGH HIS BODY POWERS MUSCLES THAT HAVE NO HUMAN EQUAL!...

CRAAAACK!

INCREDIBLE! I NEVER THOUGHT ANYTHING COULD BURST THE ICE I FORMED AROUND HIM! HIS INCREDIBLE STRENGTH CALLS FOR-- NEW WAYS TO USE MY MAGIC!

AS THE RENDING BURST OF CRACKING ICE FILLS THE NIGHT, A GROGGY *HOURMAN* LIFTS HIS HEAD,...

I'LL DELIBERATELY LET *GRUNDY* GRAB HOLD OF ME--AND WHEN HE SWINGS ME UP TO HURL ME DOWN AT THE GROUND--

DOCTOR FATE-- IN DANGER!

10:28 P.M.

AS *DOCTOR FATE* HAS ANTICIPATED, *SOLOMON GRUNDY* GRIPS AND LIFTS THE *MAGIC MASTER*, SWINGING HIM HIGH INTO THE AIR,...

NOW THAT I'M IN *CONTACT* WITH HIM-- I'LL FILL HIS BODY WITH *ELECTRICAL MAGIC!*

HIGH UP, THE *MAN-THING* SWINGS HIS FOE-- WHILE FROM *DOCTOR FATE* A FLOOD OF CRACKLING ELECTRICAL MAGIC FREEZES THE *MARSHLAND MONSTER* MOTIONLESS!...

DOCTOR FATE NEEDS A HELPING HAND! I'VE GOT TO KNOCK *GRUNDY* OUT WITH ONE WELL-TIMED BLOW!

10:29 P.M.

8

117

EVEN AS SOLOMON GRUNDY STANDS HELPLESS-- ELECTROCUTED BY MAGIC!--HOURMAN ROCKETS TO THE DEFENSE OF HIS FRIEND--UNAWARE THAT BY SO DOING-- HE WILL BRING ABOUT THEIR OWN DEFEAT!...
10:29 :02 p.m.
FOR AS HE JETS INTO ACTION--THE DEADLY MAGIC SUDDENLY SEEPS OUT OF SOLOMON GRUNDY AND BACK INTO THE BODY OF THE WONDER WIZARD! THUS, AS HOURMAN SLAMS HOME HIS ENERGY-PACKED FIST--HE FREES THE MAN-THING FROM HIS SPELL! ...
I KILL!
WHA--WHAT'S HAPPENING TO ME? MY MIRACLO POWERS--FADING AWAY! BUT--THE HOUR ISN'T UP! WHAT'S WRONG?
STORY CONTINUES ON THE FOLLOWING PAGE!
10:29 :03 p.m.
9

CRISIS ON MULTIPLE EARTHS THE TEAM UPS

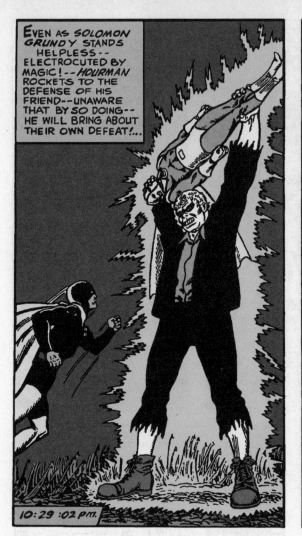

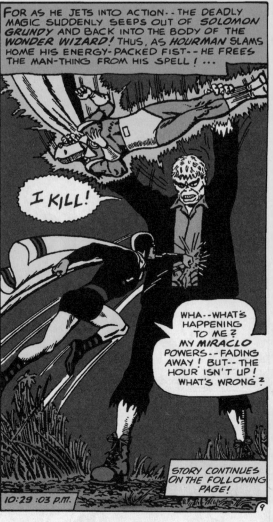

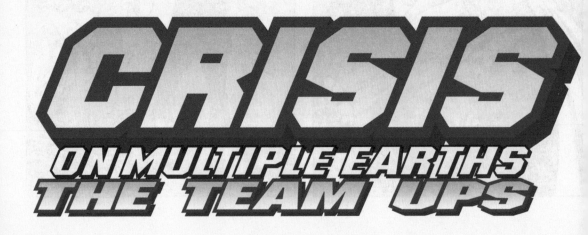

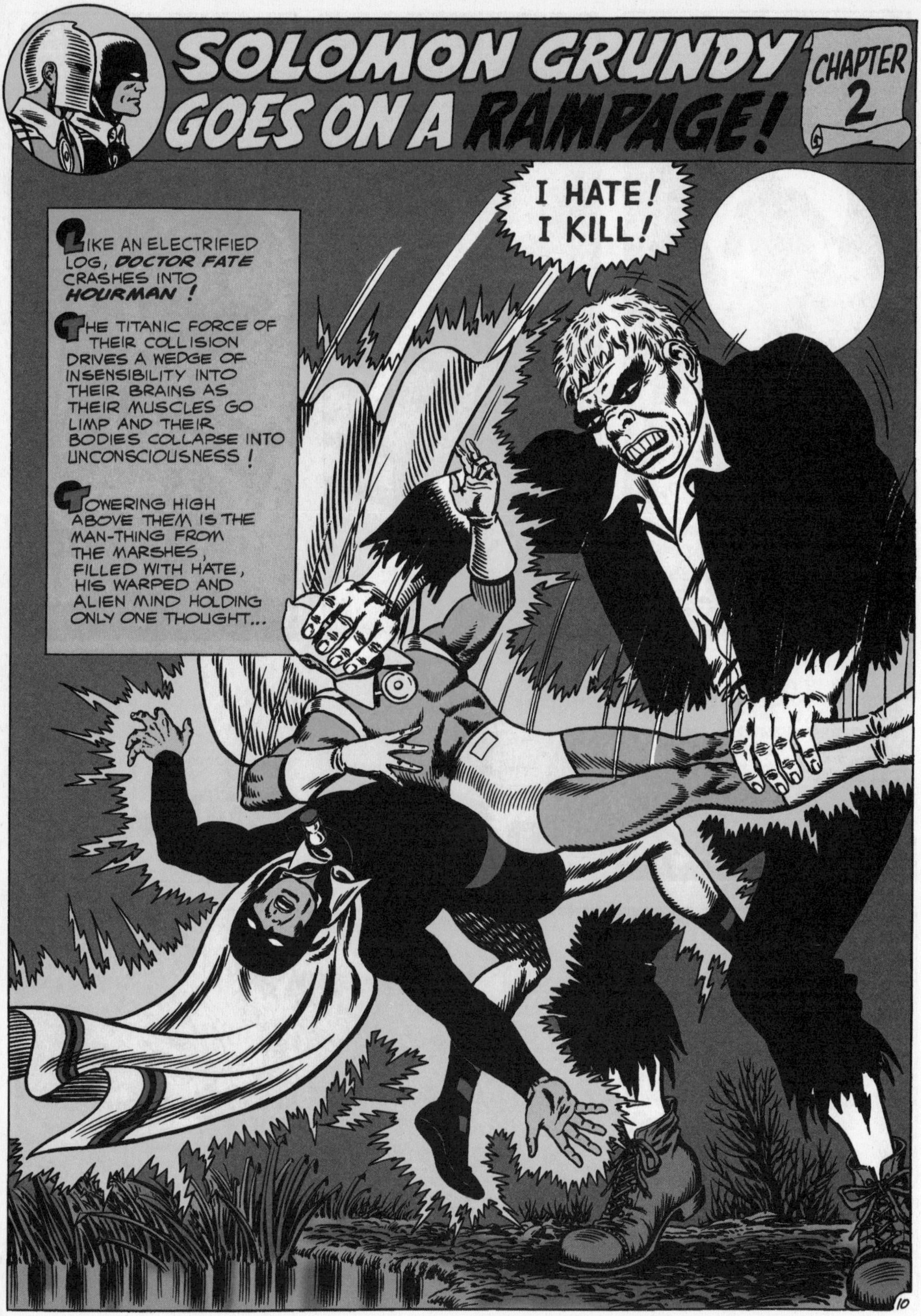
SOLOMON GRUNDY GOES ON A RAMPAGE!
CHAPTER 2
LIKE AN ELECTRIFIED LOG, DOCTOR FATE CRASHES INTO HOURMAN!
THE TITANIC FORCE OF THEIR COLLISION DRIVES A WEDGE OF INSENSIBILITY INTO THEIR BRAINS AS THEIR MUSCLES GO LIMP AND THEIR BODIES COLLAPSE INTO UNCONSCIOUSNESS!
TOWERING HIGH ABOVE THEM IS THE MAN-THING FROM THE MARSHES, FILLED WITH HATE, HIS WARPED AND ALIEN MIND HOLDING ONLY ONE THOUGHT...
I HATE! I KILL!
10

FOR A MOMENT *SOLOMON GRUNDY* STARES DOWN AT THE CRUMPLED, INERT FORMS OF HIS FOES--THEN TURNS AND PLODS OFF THROUGH THE NIGHT...

WHILE HE SHUFFLES ALONG THE ROAD LEADING TOWARD *GOTHAM CITY*, HIS BODY GLOWS WITH WEIRD BRILLIANCE, WHICH SPREADS TO NEARBY OBJECTS MADE OF *WOOD*...

QUIVERING WITH HALF-LIFE, A GLOWING FENCE YANKS FREE OF THE GROUND THAT HOLDS IT AND JOINS A GLOWING BARREL IN AN EERIE FLIGHT THROUGH THE NIGHT AIR AFTER THE DEMONIAC MAN-THING...

IN AN EERIE *DANSE MACABRE*, DOZENS OF WOODEN OBJECTS--ALL AFFLICTED WITH A RADIOACTIVE PART-LIFE GIVEN THEM BY *SOLOMON GRUNDY*--TRAIL HIM INTO *GOTHAM CITY*!...

POCKETING AN AXE-HANDLE, HE GRIPS THE DOORS OF A LOCAL BANK AND...

I FIND! I MAKE HIM COME TO ME! I ROB! HE NO LIKE ANYONE TO ROB!

RRRRIIIPPPPP!

INSIDE THE BANK HIS FINGERS FASTEN ON THE HEAVY VAULT DOOR AND...

I BRING HIM SOON, NOW! I TAKE MONEY! HE COME STOP ME! THEN I-- KILL!

SCREEEEE

MOMENTS LATER, THE POCKETS OF HIS RAGGED, ROTTING GARMENTS STUFFED WITH GREENBACKS, THE MAN-THING LURCHES FROM THE BANK WHERE HIS WOODEN SLAVES HAVE BEEN HOVERING..

WHERE IS HE? HE BE HERE SOON, I THINK!

AS HE HOWLS HIS FURY TO THE STARS...

COME GET ME! WHERE YOU HIDE? I WAIT! I WAIT! WHERE YOU? WHERE YOU?

THERE HE IS! HE COME AT LAST!

IT HARDLY SEEMS POSSIBLE! I LEFT SOLOMON GRUNDY TRAPPED ON A COLD, LIFELESS PLANET! HOW COULD HE HAVE ESCAPED MY GLOBE OF EMERALD ENERGY?

FROM THE POWER RING SHOOTS A VERDANT BEAM OF ENERGY-- AND AS IT HITS THE MACABRE MAN-THING AND SPREADS-- IT FORMS ANOTHER BUBBLE OF FORCE WITH WHICH TO CONTAIN HIM...

THERE-- THAT DOES IT! LET'S SEE GRUNDY ESCAPE FROM THAT!

FOR THOSE READERS WHO MAY BE PUZZLED AT THE UNFAMILIAR COSTUME OF GREEN LANTERN, BE ADVISED THAT THIS IS THE GREEN LANTERN OF EARTH-TWO!

IN THIS OTHER EARTH-- AS CONTRASTED TO EARTH-ONE, WHERE GREEN LANTERN IS REALLY TEST PILOT HAL JORDAN-- THE EMERALD CRUSADER'S CIVILIAN IDENTITY IS THAT OF ALAN SCOTT, EX - RADIO ANNOUNCER AND NOW PRESIDENT OF THE GOTHAM CITY BROADCASTING COMPANY!

12

FROM HIS PERSON, **SOLOMON GRUNDY** LIFTS A RADIO-ACTIVE AXE-HANDLE AND SLASHES OUT WITH IT -- DENTING AND CRACKING HIS **POWER RING** PRISON !...

NO! I NOT GO TO FARAWAY PLANET AGAIN! I STAY HERE-- AND SMASH **GREEN LANTERN!**

WHEW! HE SURE SHOWED **ME!**

THE QUEER, HALF-ALIVE WOOD SMASHES THE POWER GLOBE-- AS THE MARSHLAND MONSTER HOWLS HIS TRIUMPH...

IN THE LONG YEARS WHEN HE WAS IMPRISONED ON THAT PLANET WITH PLENTY OF TIME TO THINK, HE MUST HAVE REMEMBERED OUR BATTLES AND REALIZED-- THAT **WOOD** IS MY **WEAKNESS** AND **NEMESIS!**

AAAARRGHHH!

NEXT MOMENT, THE **MAN-THING** WAVES HIS "WOODEN SOLDIERS" TO THE ATTACK...

HIT! HIT! KNOCK HIM DOWN TO ME-- SO I GRAB HIM!

QUICKLY, THE **EMERALD CRUSADER** DEFLECTS THE PATH OF A DISTANT CYCLONE TO BLOW AWAY THOSE DEADLY OBJECTS...

SOME OF THOSE WOODEN OBJECTS ARE GETTING THROUGH TO ME-- BATTERING ME...

WITH HIS **POWER RING** HE FASHIONS TONGUES OF FLAMES TO LEAP UP AT THOSE WOODEN WEAPONS...

I'LL PUT OUT THAT FIRE AND RESTORE THINGS TO NORMAL-- AFTER I OVERCOME THAT WOODEN BARRAGE!

13

BUT ALWAYS THAT ARMY OF WOOD INCREASES SO THAT THE UNENDING BLOWS FELL THE *GREEN GLADIATOR*...

I WIN! I WIN!

AT THIS CRITICAL MOMENT, FROM SOUTH OF *GOTHAM CITY* STREAKS *DOCTOR FATE*, FULLY RECOVERED FROM HIS KNOCKOUT BLOW...

GRUNDY'S GRABBING *GREEN LANTERN!* FORTUNATELY I WAS ABLE TO TRACK HIM HERE BY HIS RADIO-ACTIVE FOOTPRINTS!

SPOTTING THE *WONDER WIZARD,* THE MACABRE *MAN-THING* POINTS--AND INSTANTLY HIS WOODEN ARMY RE-GROUPS ITSELF AND...

KILL! KILL!

WOOD IS NO NEMESIS OF THE *MASTER OF MAGIC,* HOWEVER! HIS BODY POURS OUT OCCULT POWERS AND UNDER THEIR EERIE SPELL...

I'LL RESHAPE THEIR ATOMS TO FORM A MIGHTY WEAPON TO USE AGAINST THAT PSEUDO-LIFE-FORM!

MEANWHILE, *HOURMAN* HAS ALSO BEEN TRAILING *SOLOMON GRUNDY* AS SWIFTLY AS HE CAN...

ALMOST TWO HOURS HAVE PASSED SINCE I TOOK THE *MIRACLO* PILL! IN ANOTHER FEW SECONDS--AN HOUR HAVING INTERVENED AFTER MY HOUR OF ENERGY-CHARGED POWERS--I CAN TAKE ANOTHER!

CRASH!

12:14 A.M.

EVEN AS HE SWALLOWS A *MIRACLO* PILL, HE SEES THE *SWAMPLAND SCARECROW* LIFT *DOCTOR FATE'S* WOODEN MALLET AND SWING IT...

I HOPE THAT *THIS* "HELPING HAND" I GIVE *DOCTOR FATE* WILL TURN OUT BETTER THAN THE LAST ONE!

12:15 A.M.

BUT--AS *DOCTOR FATE* SWERVES ASIDE FROM THE MALLET, "TICK-TOCK" TYLER SEES HIS FELLOW SUPER-HERO COME STRAIGHT FOR *HIM!*...

ALL OF A SUDDEN-- I HAVE A GREAT COMPULSION TO DESTROY *HOURMAN!*

I MUST BATTLE AND OVERCOME *DOCTOR FATE*-- AT ALL COSTS!

12:15½ A.M.

15

CRISIS
ON MULTIPLE EARTHS
THE TEAM UPS

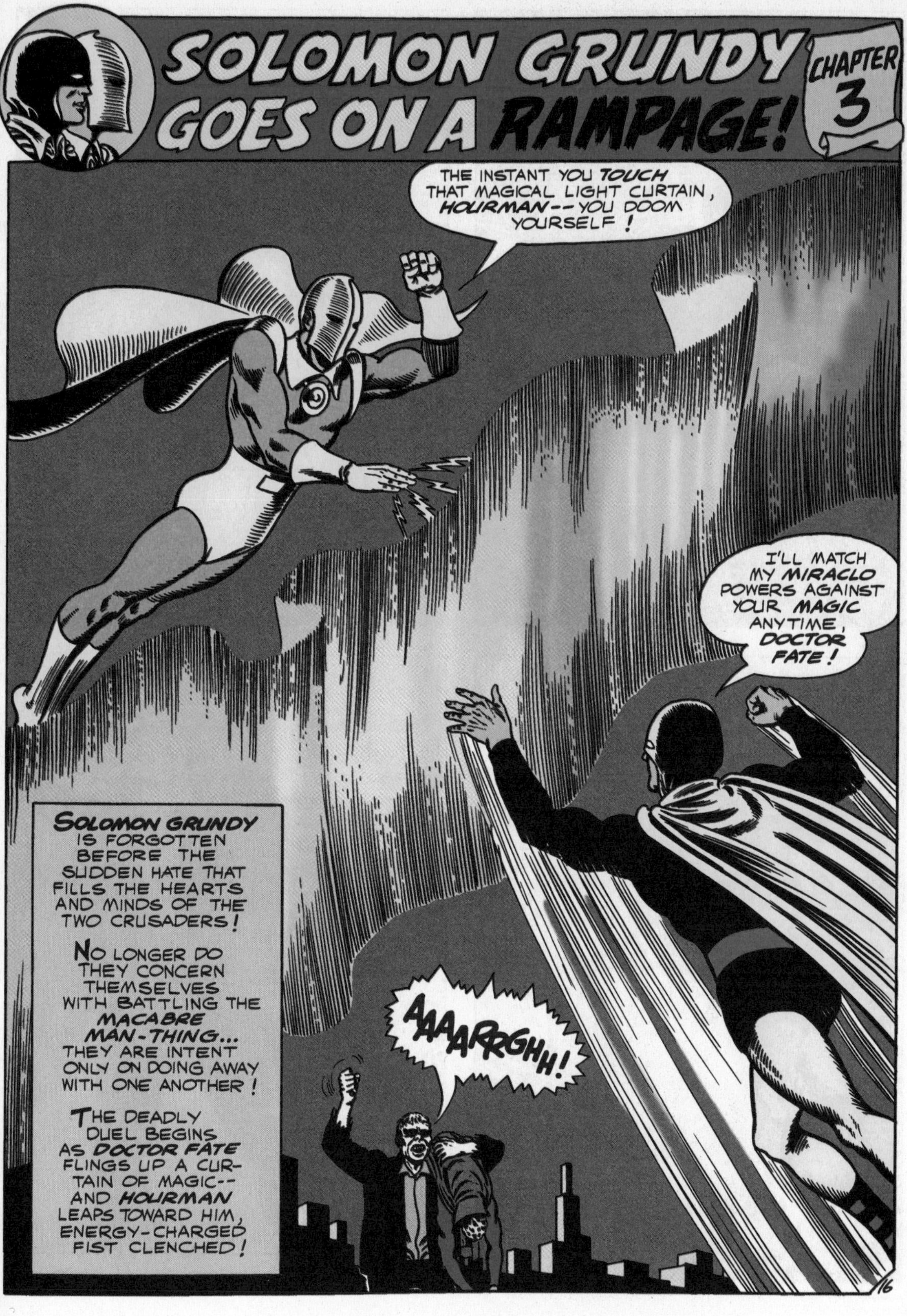
SOLOMON GRUNDY GOES ON A RAMPAGE!
CHAPTER 3
THE INSTANT YOU TOUCH THAT MAGICAL LIGHT CURTAIN, HOURMAN-- YOU DOOM YOURSELF!
I'LL MATCH MY MIRACLO POWERS AGAINST YOUR MAGIC ANYTIME, DOCTOR FATE!
SOLOMON GRUNDY IS FORGOTTEN BEFORE THE SUDDEN HATE THAT FILLS THE HEARTS AND MINDS OF THE TWO CRUSADERS!
NO LONGER DO THEY CONCERN THEMSELVES WITH BATTLING THE MACABRE MAN-THING... THEY ARE INTENT ONLY ON DOING AWAY WITH ONE ANOTHER!
THE DEADLY DUEL BEGINS AS DOCTOR FATE FLINGS UP A CURTAIN OF MAGIC-- AND HOURMAN LEAPS TOWARD HIM, ENERGY-CHARGED FIST CLENCHED!
AAAARRGHH!
16

CONFIDENTLY, THE *MAN OF THE HOUR* SPRINGS INTO THE SHIMMERING DRAPE OF AWESOME ENCHANTMENT ! ...

HA! HIS BODY IS STIFFENING -- HIS MIND REELING...

BUT EVEN THOUGH *HOURMAN* SINKS INTO UNCONSCIOUSNESS...

HE HAD SO MUCH MOMENTUM BEHIND HIM, IT CARRIED HIM CLEAR THROUGH MY MAGICAL CURTAIN -- : UNNGH :

SOK

HEAD OVER HEELS, THE INERT SUPER-HEROES TUMBLE TOWARD THE GROUND...

THE INSTANT THEY THUD TO EARTH, THE *MARSHLAND MONSTER* TRUDGES OFF INTO THE NIGHT,...

17

AS HE SHUFFLES ALONG THE ROAD TOWARD *SLAUGHTER SWAMP, SOLOMON GRUNDY* IS SUDDENLY FRAMED IN A PAIR OF BRILLIANT HEADLIGHTS...

FOR PETE'S SAKE! LOOK THERE! IT'S OUR OLD PAL -- *SOLOMON GRUNDY!*

WHERE YA BEEN ALL THESE YEARS?

THE MAN-THING PAUSES, RECOGNIZING HIS GANG OF YEARS BEFORE...

AND HE'S GOT HIS ARCH-ENEMY-- *GREEN LANTERN!* HOW ABOUT THAT!

GREEN LANTERN PUT ME ON DEAD PLANET--LONG TIME AGO! VERY COLD, VERY DARK THERE! ME NOT LIKE!

"THEN LONG TIME LATER, BIG THING LIKE SHOOTING STAR PASS HIGH UP...PULL EVERYTHING OFF PLANET NOT HELD DOWN. I GO TOO..."

NOW ME FIND *GREEN LANTERN!* ME GET REVENGE!

"I RIDE THROUGH SPACE. NOT NEED TO BREATHE. FEEL COLD, BUT NOT FREEZE..."

MOVE GREEN BALL BY HOLDING SIDES! MAKE IT GO WHERE ME WANT!

"TOOK LONG TIME--BUT AT LAST I STEER IT 'HOME'..."

18

URGED ON BY HIS EAGER FRIENDS, *SOLOMON GRUNDY* AGREES TO HELP THEM PULL OFF ANOTHER JOB -- FOR OLD TIMES' SAKE...

ATTABOY, *SOLOMON!* WE'LL TAKE OVER NOW!

MAN, WHAT A HAUL!

WHILE THE *SWAMPLAND SCARECROW* CONTINUES ON HIS WAY -- *DOCTOR FATE* AND *HOURMAN* SLOWLY STIR -- RISE TO THEIR FEET...

:WHEW: WHAT CAME OVER US? FOR A WHILE THERE, I FELT YOU WERE MY ENEMY!

SAME HERE! BUT I BELIEVE I'M BEGINNING TO UNDERSTAND. MY HATE FOR YOU BEGAN WHEN -- YOU SWALLOWED THAT *MIRACLO* PILL!

12:30 A.M.

SOMETHING ABOUT YOUR *MIRACLO* AFFECTS MY MAGIC, JUST AS MY MAGIC HAS AN ADVERSE INFLUENCE ON YOU WHEN YOU GO INTO ACTION NEAR ME!

FIRST IT WEAKENED US SO *SOLOMON GRUNDY* COULD THROW OFF YOUR MAGIC ELECTRICITY AND HURL YOU AT ME! THEN IT MADE US FIGHT ONE ANOTHER! PERHAPS THE RADIOACTIVITY OF *SOLOMON GRUNDY'S* BODY HAD SOMETHING TO DO WITH IT!

MERGING HIS BODY-ATOMS WITH THE WIND HE CREATES WITH HIS MAGIC, THE *WONDER WIZARD* ROCKETS INTO THE AIR AS THE *MAN OF THE HOUR* IS DRAWN UP AFTER HIM...

I'LL CREATE A NON-GRAVITIC PATHWAY IN THE AIR BEHIND ME -- SO YOU CAN RIDE ALONG, DRAWN AFTER ME BY THE SPEED OF MY FLYING!

SINCE WE HAVE TO BE REASONABLY CLOSE TO HAVE MY *MIRACLO* AFFECT YOUR MAGIC, I'LL MAKE SURE TO KEEP MY DISTANCE!

12:31 A.M.

WITH THE *MASTER MAGE* LEADING THE WAY, "TICK-TOCK" TYLER SPEEDS ALONG BEHIND HIM WITH THE EASE OF AN "AIR-SKIER" -- UNTIL...

DOCTOR FATE -- LOOK BELOW YOU!

12:33 A.M.

19

NEXT MOMENT, *HOURMAN* BREAKS OUT OF THAT ANTI-GRAVITIC PATHWAY AS...

CROOKS--ROBBING THAT JEWELRY STORE! I'M GOING DOWN TO STOP THEM-- WHILE YOU GO ON AHEAD AFTER SOLOMON GRUNDY! I'LL JOIN YOU LATER!

REGAL JEWELERS

12:33 1/2 A.M.

THE *MAN OF THE HOUR* DROPS LIKE AN AVENGING COMET FROM THE SKY...

THUD!

12:33 3/4 A.M.

LIKE A CAT, HE DROPS TO HIS FEET-- THEN LASHES OUT WITH A SUPER- CHARGED FIST...

ZOK

12:33 7/8 A.M.

A GUN BLASTS IN THE NIGHT-- BUT BEFORE THE BULLET CAN REACH HIM, *HOURMAN* LEAPS ABOVE IT...

BLAMM!

12:34 A.M.

HE COMES DOWN HARD-- LIKE A LIVING BOMB!...

KLONK!

WRAPPED THAT UP IN LESS THAN A MINUTE! I'LL TURN THEM OVER TO THE POLICE-- THEN REJOIN DOCTOR FATE!

12:34 1/4 A.M.

FAR AHEAD OF HIM, THE *MASTER OF MAGIC* IS SWOOPING LOW OVER *SLAUGHTER SWAMP*, KEEN EYES SCANNING ITS RADIO-ACTIVE WATERS...

NO SIGN OF *SOLOMON GRUNDY*-- YET HIS RADIOACTIVE FOOT-PRINTS SHOW HE CAME HERE!

SUDDENLY THE WATERS PART AS THE *MACABRE MAN-THING* RISES UPWARD TO COME TO GRIPS WITH HIS TORMENTOR...

AH, THERE YOU ARE! YOU NOT ONLY HAVE ME TO DEAL WITH *GRUNDY*-- BUT ALSO--*GREEN LANTERN!*

AAAARRGH!

THE STUNNED EYES OF THE *SWAMPLAND SCARECROW* TURN TOWARD THE EDGE OF THE MARSHLAND, WHERE...

GREEN LANTERN? NO! YOU IN SWAMP! ME PUT YOU THERE-- MAKE YOU JUST LIKE ME--HELP ME FIGHT ENEMIES! THAT--NOT YOU!

I FIGURED THAT *MAGICAL GREEN LANTERN* I CREATED WOULD MAKE HIM BLURT OUT THE WHERE-ABOUTS OF THE REAL *GREEN LANTERN!*

DESPITE HIS CLAIM TO HAVE IMPRISONED THE *EMERALD GLADIATOR*, THE SIGHT OF HIS LONG-TIME FOE MADDENS *SOLOMON GRUNDY...*

I TAKE YOU BACK INTO WATER! I MAKE YOU MAN-THING--LIKE ME!

THE *MARSHLAND MONSTER* DISCOVERS THAT THE "*MAGICAL GREEN LANTERN*" HAS AN EERIE STRENGTH ALL HIS OWN!...

YOU HIT HARD--BUT I KNOCK YOU OUT! YOU WAIT! YOU SEE!

21

TO ONE SIDE, *DOCTOR FATE* HAS CAST AN ANCIENT SPELL, LIFTING THE GLOWING WATERS OF *SLAUGHTER SWAMP* UPWARD INTO THE AIR--REVEALING...

A MONSTROUS *GREEN LANTERN!* SOLOMON GRUNDY BROUGHT HIM HERE TO MAKE THESE RADIOACTIVE WATERS TURN HIM INTO A PSEUDO-LIFE-FORM LIKE HIMSELF!

SHAMBLING FORWARD, THE TRANSFORMED *GREEN LANTERN* HURLS HIMSELF STRAIGHT AT THE *WONDER WIZARD*...

HE DOESN'T KNOW WHO *HE* IS OR WHO *I* AM! HE IS COMPLETELY UNDER THE SPELL OF THE RADIOACTIVE SWAMPLANDS!

A BEAM FROM THE *POWER RING* FORMS A GREAT GREEN MACE THAT PLUMMETS DOWNWARD AT THE *MYSTICAL MAGE*...

I KILL!

WITH HIS LEFT HAND *DOCTOR FATE* CATCHES AND HOLDS THE MACE AS HIS RIGHT HAND HURLS TINY SUNS AT HIS FELLOW *JUSTICE SOCIETY* MEMBER...

YOU HAVE GREAT POWERS, *GREEN LANTERN*--BUT SO HAVE I! AND MY BRAIN IS KEEN AND ALERT, WHILE YOURS IS POSSESSED ONLY WITH THE DESIRE TO DESTROY!

22

THE MINIATURE SUNS BEAT DOWN UPON *GREEN LANTERN* WITH THEIR MYSTIC POWERS! HE WRITHES, HE TWISTS TO ESCAPE THE MAGICAL RAYS THAT BATHE HIS BODY!...

SUDDENLY, A STARTLING CHANGE COMES OVER THE *EMERALD CRUSADER!* HIS MONSTROUS FEATURES DISAPPEAR, HIS TORN AND RIDDLED CLOTHES FIRM BACK TO NORMAL-- UNTIL IN EXHAUSTION AT HIS ORDEAL, HE DROPS TO HIS KNEES...

WITH A BELLOW OF RAGE, *SOLOMON GRUNDY* TURNS FROM THE *MAGICAL GREEN LANTERN* TOWARD THE REAL ONE--AND SEES *DOCTOR FATE* STANDING IN HIS PATH...

YOU DO THIS! YOU TRICK ME! I--GET YOU!

NOW THE *WONDER WIZARD* IS IN CONTROL, HOWEVER! HIS MAGIC IS NEVER STRONGER AS HE HURLS A SORCEROUS BATTERING RAM AT HIS EERIE FOE...

HYEEAH!

THEN OUT OF THE NIGHT RACES *HOURMAN*-- EAGER TO BE IN AT THE FINISH!...

ATTABOY, *DOCTOR FATE!* YOU KNOCKED HIM WITHIN RANGE OF MY FISTS! HOLD OFF ON YOUR MAGIC WHILE I GIVE HIM A DOSE OF MY *SUPER-ENERGY!*

23

IT'S -- YOUR TURN NOW!

12:47 P.M.

As THE MACABRE MAN-THING HURTLES BACK TOWARD HIM, THE WONDER-WIZARD WHIPS HIM AROUND AND AROUND UNTIL...

COMING RIGHT BACK AT YOU, HOURMAN!

THIS IS LIKE A WRESTLING TAG-TEAM MATCH! AS LONG AS WE WORK IN TURNS, WE CAN EACH USE OUR SUPER-POWERS!

12:47 1/2 P.M.

UPWARD INTO THE AIR JETS HOURMAN HIGH ABOVE THE SWAMP-LAND SCARE-CROW...

12:47 3/4 P.M.

REVERSING DIRECTION IN MID-AIR, HE POWERS A PULVERIZING BLOW DOWN ON SOLOMON GRUNDY...

12:47 7/8 P.M.

24

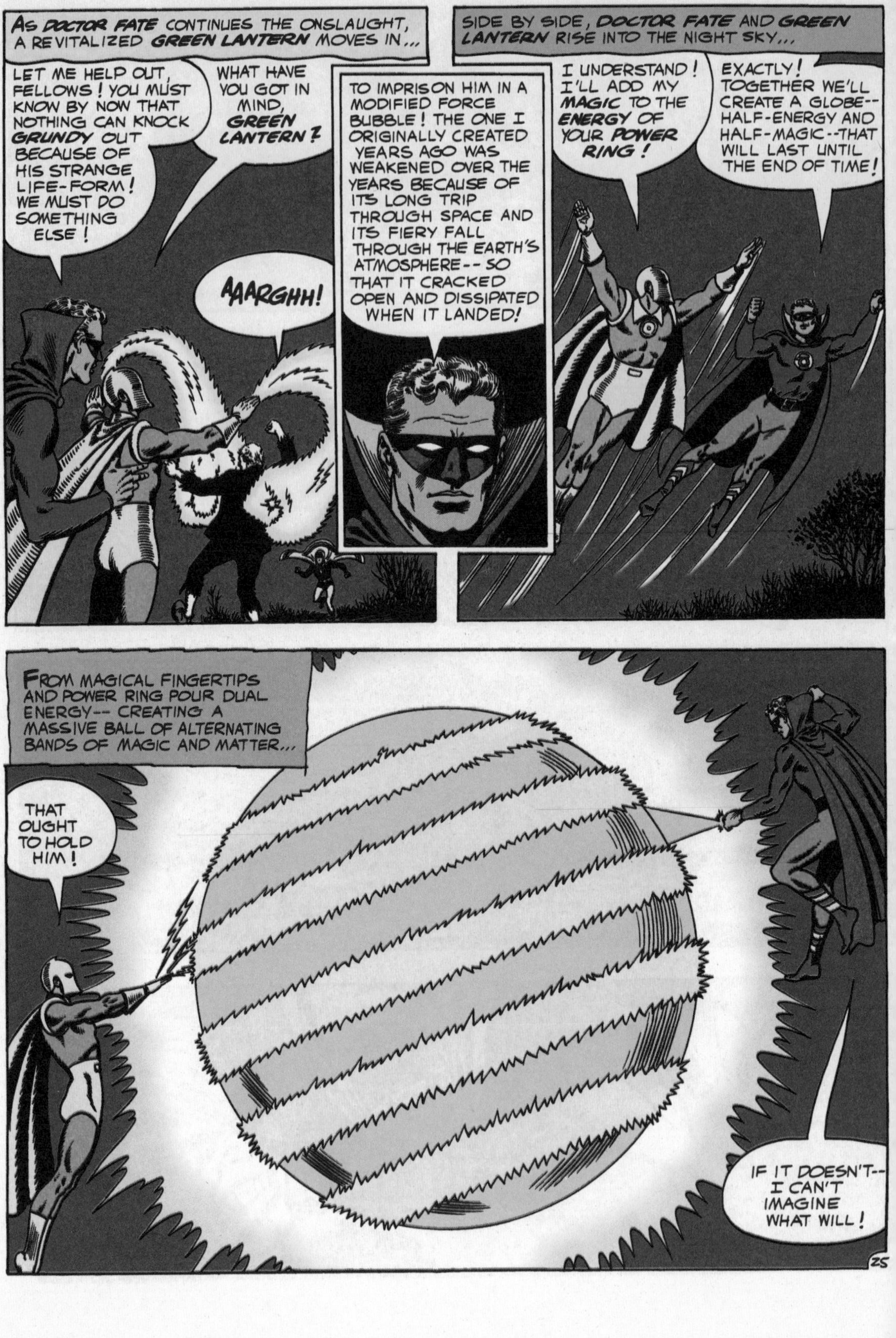
AS DOCTOR FATE CONTINUES THE ONSLAUGHT, A REVITALIZED GREEN LANTERN MOVES IN...
LET ME HELP OUT, FELLOWS! YOU MUST KNOW BY NOW THAT NOTHING CAN KNOCK GRUNDY OUT BECAUSE OF HIS STRANGE LIFE-FORM! WE MUST DO SOMETHING ELSE!
WHAT HAVE YOU GOT IN MIND, GREEN LANTERN?
AAARGHH!
TO IMPRISON HIM IN A MODIFIED FORCE BUBBLE! THE ONE I ORIGINALLY CREATED YEARS AGO WAS WEAKENED OVER THE YEARS BECAUSE OF ITS LONG TRIP THROUGH SPACE AND ITS FIERY FALL THROUGH THE EARTH'S ATMOSPHERE-- SO THAT IT CRACKED OPEN AND DISSIPATED WHEN IT LANDED!
SIDE BY SIDE, DOCTOR FATE AND GREEN LANTERN RISE INTO THE NIGHT SKY...
I UNDERSTAND! I'LL ADD MY MAGIC TO THE ENERGY OF YOUR POWER RING!
EXACTLY! TOGETHER WE'LL CREATE A GLOBE-- HALF-ENERGY AND HALF-MAGIC--THAT WILL LAST UNTIL THE END OF TIME!
FROM MAGICAL FINGERTIPS AND POWER RING POUR DUAL ENERGY-- CREATING A MASSIVE BALL OF ALTERNATING BANDS OF MAGIC AND MATTER...
THAT OUGHT TO HOLD HIM!
IF IT DOESN'T-- I CAN'T IMAGINE WHAT WILL!
25

THEN FROM BELOW, *HOURMAN* LIFTS HIS FIST IN A MAGNIFICENT UPPERCUT-- DRIVING THE *MACABRE MAN-THING* UPWARD TOWARD THE MAGICAL PRISON PREPARED FOR HIM...

SO AWESOME IS THAT BLOW THAT WITHIN MOMENTS...

NOW WHAT DO WE DO WITH *SOLOMON GRUNDY*?

WITH OUR COMBINED POWERS, WE'LL PUT HIM IN ETERNAL ORBIT AROUND THE EARTH! THAT WAY, WE CAN MAINTAIN A 24-HOUR VIGILANCE ON HIM!

UPWARD AND OUTWARD INTO AN ORBIT ABOUT THE PLANET GOES THE *MACABRE MAN-THING*, ENDLESSLY CIRCLING THE WORLD THAT SPAWNED HIM...

MY *CRYSTAL BALL* AND YOUR *POWER RING* WILL GLOW IN A UNIQUE WAY IF *SOLOMON GRUNDY* EVER ESCAPES FROM THAT PRISON!

PERSONALLY, I DON'T THINK HE'LL EVER BOTHER US AGAIN!

I-- WONDER!

The End 26

THE ORIGIN OF

DR. FATE   HOURMAN

Doctor Fate is a student of those ancient mysteries the secrets of which were lost when Julius Caesar burned the library in Alexandria. He delves into the sciences of the occult and the weird, being both an alchemist and a mage. He has learned the ultimate secret of the universe, the true conversion of energy into matter and matter into energy.

He lives in a doorless stone tower in witch-haunted Salem. In his civilian identity of Kent Nelson, archeologist, he is married to Inza Cramer, who shared his many adventures as originally reported in *More Fun Comics*, from his initial appearance in the May, 1940 issue, number 55, through issue number 98. *Doctor Fate* also appeared in many *All-Star* adventures, as a member of the famed super-hero organization, the *Justice Society of America*.

The son of an archeologist, young Kent Nelson accompanied his father Sven to the Valley of Ur, in his quest to solve the riddle of the building of the pyramids. There Kent discovered the living but inert body of *Nabu the Wise* in a casket. By pushing a lever, Kent sent a flood of gas into *Nabu's* casket, releasing him from the state of hibernation in which he had lain for centuries.

When Kent found his father dead, *Nabu* remained with him, teaching him the secrets of the universe, the lost mystical arts of Chaldea and Egypt, Babylon and Sumer. *Nabu* was from *Cilia*, a planet that orbits close to Earth once every several thousand years. When he was about to return home, he gave Kent Nelson the blue-and-gold uniform which he was to wear in his adventurous career as *Doctor Fate*.

Recently, *Doctor Fate* reappeared with the revived *Justice Society* to help its counterpart on another Earth, the *Justice League*, combat the *Crime Champions* and the *Crime Syndicate of America*.

For one hour, thanks to the *Miraclo* pills, he became endowed with super-charged energy! At the end of that hour, he once again was a normal human being! His name was Rex Tyler, and he made his first appearance in *Adventure Comics* in the March, 1940 issue, as—*Hourman*.

The inventor of *Miraclo*, "Tick-Tock" Tyler soon discovered that this powerful chemical transformed him from a meek, mild chemist to *Hourman*—a fleet-footed man with the strength of a giant, the leaping ability of a super-athlete and a body insensible to harm. Since his great powers lasted precisely one hour, he hung an *hourglass* about his neck to keep track of the time.

When he first began his adventures, his superior at the chemical plant assured him he would never amount to anything because of his meekness, but today he owns that chemical plant and runs it with business skill and acumen!

Hourman, too, was a charter member of the *Justice Society of America* but was granted a leave of absence and replaced by *Starman* in *All-Star* number 8. Subsequently, in issue 83, *Hourman* was given another leave of absence, this time from *Adventure Comics*. Until his recent appearance in *Justice League of America*, he has remained in quiet retirement. Until, that is, he was summoned out of that retirement, as was *Doctor Fate*, by the *Crises on Earth-One and Earth-Two!* Battling side by side with such former friends as *Flash, Green Lantern, Atom, Hawkman* and the *Black Canary, Hourman* found a new love of life!

Today he keeps his *Miraclo* pills and his *Hourman* costume in a secret vault in the Tyler Chemical Company plant, ready for any sudden emergency such as the one he is presented with in this issue—the reappearance of the marshland monster, *Solomon Grundy!*

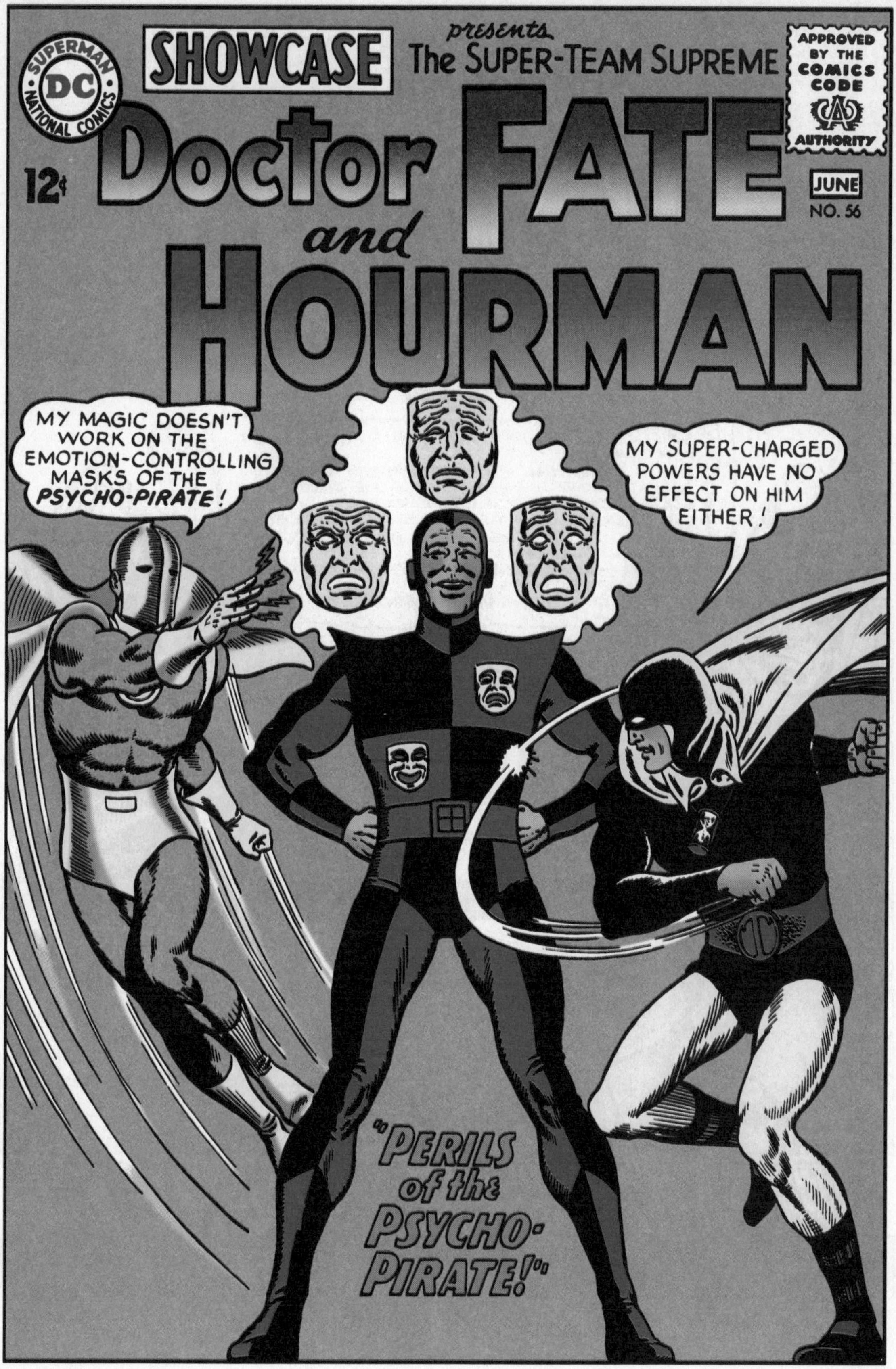
SHOWCASE
presents
The SUPER-TEAM SUPREME
SUPERMAN DC NATIONAL COMICS
APPROVED BY THE COMICS CODE AUTHORITY
12¢
Doctor FATE and HOURMAN
JUNE
NO. 56
MY MAGIC DOESN'T WORK ON THE EMOTION-CONTROLLING MASKS OF THE PSYCHO-PIRATE!
MY SUPER-CHARGED POWERS HAVE NO EFFECT ON HIM EITHER!
"PERILS of the PSYCHO-PIRATE!"

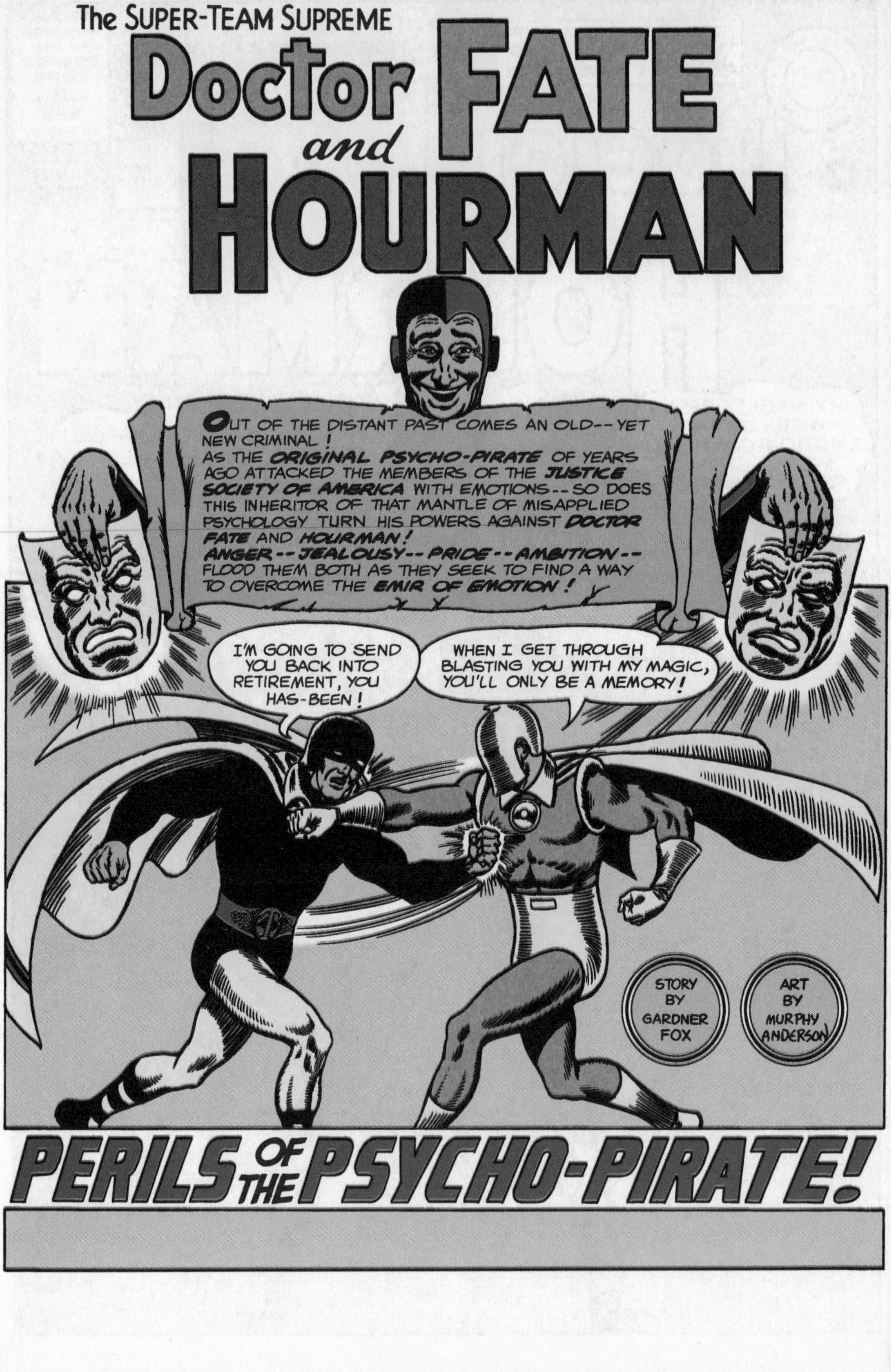
The SUPER-TEAM SUPREME
Doctor FATE and HOURMAN
OUT OF THE DISTANT PAST COMES AN OLD--YET NEW CRIMINAL! AS THE ORIGINAL PSYCHO-PIRATE OF YEARS AGO ATTACKED THE MEMBERS OF THE JUSTICE SOCIETY OF AMERICA WITH EMOTIONS--SO DOES THIS INHERITOR OF THAT MANTLE OF MISAPPLIED PSYCHOLOGY TURN HIS POWERS AGAINST DOCTOR FATE AND HOURMAN! ANGER--JEALOUSY--PRIDE--AMBITION--FLOOD THEM BOTH AS THEY SEEK TO FIND A WAY TO OVERCOME THE EMIR OF EMOTION!
I'M GOING TO SEND YOU BACK INTO RETIREMENT, YOU HAS-BEEN!
WHEN I GET THROUGH BLASTING YOU WITH MY MAGIC, YOU'LL ONLY BE A MEMORY!
STORY BY GARDNER FOX
ART BY MURPHY ANDERSON
PERILS OF THE PSYCHO-PIRATE!

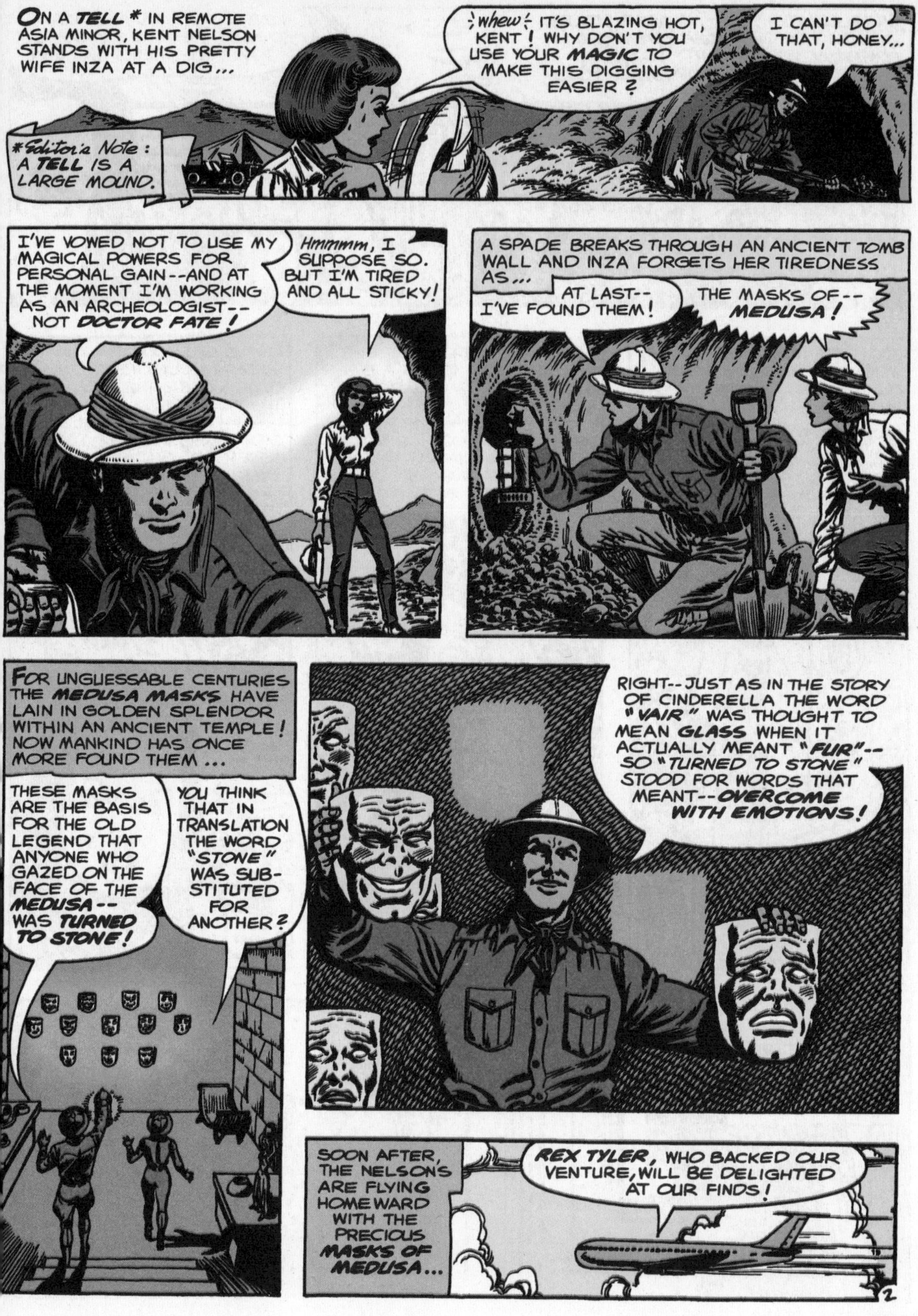
ON A TELL * IN REMOTE ASIA MINOR, KENT NELSON STANDS WITH HIS PRETTY WIFE INZA AT A DIG...
*Editor's Note: A TELL IS A LARGE MOUND.
-whew- IT'S BLAZING HOT, KENT! WHY DON'T YOU USE YOUR MAGIC TO MAKE THIS DIGGING EASIER?
I CAN'T DO THAT, HONEY...
I'VE VOWED NOT TO USE MY MAGICAL POWERS FOR PERSONAL GAIN--AND AT THE MOMENT I'M WORKING AS AN ARCHEOLOGIST--NOT DOCTOR FATE!
Hmmmm, I SUPPOSE SO. BUT I'M TIRED AND ALL STICKY!
A SPADE BREAKS THROUGH AN ANCIENT TOMB WALL AND INZA FORGETS HER TIREDNESS AS...
AT LAST--I'VE FOUND THEM!
THE MASKS OF--MEDUSA!
FOR UNGUESSABLE CENTURIES THE MEDUSA MASKS HAVE LAIN IN GOLDEN SPLENDOR WITHIN AN ANCIENT TEMPLE! NOW MANKIND HAS ONCE MORE FOUND THEM...
THESE MASKS ARE THE BASIS FOR THE OLD LEGEND THAT ANYONE WHO GAZED ON THE FACE OF THE MEDUSA--WAS TURNED TO STONE!
YOU THINK THAT IN TRANSLATION THE WORD "STONE" WAS SUBSTITUTED FOR ANOTHER?
RIGHT--JUST AS IN THE STORY OF CINDERELLA THE WORD "VAIR" WAS THOUGHT TO MEAN GLASS WHEN IT ACTUALLY MEANT "FUR"--SO "TURNED TO STONE" STOOD FOR WORDS THAT MEANT--OVERCOME WITH EMOTIONS!
SOON AFTER, THE NELSONS ARE FLYING HOMEWARD WITH THE PRECIOUS MASKS OF MEDUSA...
REX TYLER, WHO BACKED OUR VENTURE, WILL BE DELIGHTED AT OUR FINDS!
2

IN CELEBRATION, REX (*HOURMAN*) TYLER, PRESIDENT OF THE *TYLER CHEMICAL COMPANY*, HOSTS A PARTY TO DISPLAY THE GOLDEN TREASURES...

KENT, I WANT YOU AND INZA TO MEET THE GIRL I'M GOING TO MARRY -- WENDI HARRIS!

SOON, WITH WIDE EYES, ACTRESS WENDI HARRIS STUDIES THE *MEDUSA MASKS*, AWED AND ENCHANTED...

THEY'RE BREATH-TAKING!

SO ENRAPTURED IS SHE THAT SHE DOES NOT NOTICE A BYSTANDER LIFT A CIGARETTE-LIGHTER AND...

THE MASK WILL DO ITS WORK AS SOON AS THE IRRADIATED GAS IN MY LIGHTER MAKES CONTACT WITH IT!

AS THE GAS TOUCHES THE MASK-- A CURIOUS CHANGE COMES OVER THE FACE OF THE ACTRESS...

I MUST OWN THOSE MASKS! I'VE NEVER HAD SUCH AN *AVID DESIRE* FOR ANYTHING IN ALL MY LIFE!

GREED PICTURES ITSELF ON HER LOVELY FEATURES AS SHE YANKS THE MASKS OFF THE WALL...

WENDI, HONEY-- WHAT IN THE WORLD ARE YOU DOING?

NOTHING MUST STOP ME! NOTHING!

3

THE MYSTERIOUS CIGARETTE-LIGHTER FLARES AGAIN...

AND A RIPPLE OF LAUGHTER RUNS THROUGH THE ASSEMBLED GUESTS...

HA! HA! WENDI IS SURE PUTTING ON A SHOW!

WHAT A SUPERB ACTRESS! HA! HA!

APPLAUSE RINGS OUT AS WENDI HARRIS MAKES HER EXIT, CLINGING TO THE GOLDEN MASKS AS IF UNABLE TO LET THEM GO...

BRAVO! BRAVO!

HOW ABOUT AN ENCORE?

CLAP

CLAP

CLAP

IN A LITTLE WHILE THE LAUGHTER STOPS, AS MEN AND WOMEN STARE AT ONE ANOTHER IN DISMAY...

WHAT MADE US THINK THAT ACT OF WENDI'S WAS SO FUNNY?

I--I CAN'T IMAGINE! IT WAS AS IF I WERE COMPELLED TO LAUGH FOR SOME REASON!

AS ONE, THEY RUN OUT INTO THE STREET, WHERE...

WENDI, WHAT HAPPENED? WHERE ARE THE MASKS?

I--I DON'T KNOW!

SHAME AND EMBARRASSMENT FLOOD THE ACTRESS AS...

I COULD JUST DIE! I DON'T KNOW WHAT POSSESSED ME TO STEAL THOSE MASKS! I WAS SO -- SO *GREEDY!* AND THEN WHEN I RAN OUT OF THE BUILDING...

"I SAW A BEGGAR AND FELT SUCH *PITY* FOR HIM I PRACTICALLY SHOVED THE MASKS INTO HIS HANDS..."

HERE, MAYBE THESE WILL HELP YOU GET A NEW START IN LIFE!

KENT NELSON DRAWS REX TYLER TO ONE SIDE...

I'VE A FEEL-ING WE HAVEN'T HEARD THE LAST OF THOSE MASKS!

WE'LL GO AFTER THEM -- AS *DOCTOR FATE* AND *HOURMAN* JUST AS SOON AS I TAKE WENDI HOME!

SOON, IN A STONE TOWER NEAR WITCH-HAUNTED SALEM, KENT NELSON DONS THE BLUE-AND-GOLD GARB OF *DOCTOR FATE*...

STRANGE! MY CRYSTAL BALL IS UNABLE TO PICK UP ANYTHING ABOUT THE MASKS! THEY MUST HAVE A MAGICAL POWER OF THEIR OWN WHICH PROTECTS THEM!

AT THIS MOMENT, THE *MASKS OF MEDUSA* ARE IN THE SEACOAST MANSION THAT IS THE HIDE-OUT OF ROGER HAYDEN -- WHO ALSO CALLS HIMSELF THE *PSYCHO-PIRATE*...

MY PLAN WORKED PERFECTLY -- INGENIOUSLY! I STOLE AN INVITATION TO THE TYLER PARTY -- THEN USED HIS OWN FIANCÉE TO STEAL THE MASKS FOR ME! THEN I GRABBED THEM FROM THE BEGGAR!

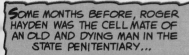

SOME MONTHS BEFORE, ROGER HAYDEN WAS THE CELL MATE OF AN OLD AND DYING MAN IN THE STATE PENITENTIARY...

I'VE TOLD YOU ALL MY *PSYCHO-PIRATE* * SECRETS, ROGER -- TAUGHT YOU ALL I KNOW OF HUMAN EMOTIONS, THEIR CAUSES AND RESULTS!

NOW YOU SHALL BE THE "*NEW*" *PSYCHO-PIRATE*, FOR I CANNOT LAST MUCH LONGER! IN YOU, MY SKILLS SHALL LIVE ON -- AND THROUGH YOU, I SHALL GAIN MY REVENGE ON THE FORCES OF LAW AND ORDER WHO IMPRISONED ME!

SOON AFTER ROGER HAYDEN WAS RELEASED FROM PRISON, HE READ ABOUT THE ARCHEOLOGICAL FIND OF THE *MASKS OF MEDUSA* ...

THIS IS MY CHANCE TO TAKE ADVANTAGE OF WHAT THE "*ORIGINAL*" *PSYCHO-PIRATE* TOLD ME! HE KNEW THE MEDUSA MASKS EXISTED. HE DID RESEARCH ON THEM -- AND DISCOVERED THE SECRET OF HOW TO ACTIVATE THEM!

* Editor's Note; THE PSYCHO-PIRATE FIRST APPEARED IN ALL-STAR COMICS # 23 (WINTER ISSUE, 1944)

IN HIS SEACOAST MANSION, THE PRESENT *EMIR OF EMOTION* HANGS THE MASKS BETWEEN A NUMBER OF TORCHES THAT FLOOD THEM WITH A SPECIAL TYPE OF IRRADIATING GASES...

NOW FOR THE GREAT EXPERIMENT!

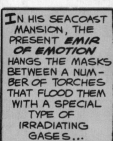

AS HE STARES UP AT THOSE AUREATE DOMINOES, THE FACE OF THE *PSYCHO-PIRATE* UNDERGOES A NUMBER OF WEIRD CHANGES. ONE BY ONE -- ENVY, HATE, FEAR, GREED, PRIDE, DESPAIR, CONCEIT AND OTHER EMOTIONS STAMP THEMSELVES INDELIBLY ON HIS FEATURES...

NOW I SHALL BE ABLE TO...

...CAUSE OTHERS TO FEEL THESE SAME EMOTIONS...

...BY A SIMPLE GESTURE OF MY HAND OVER MY FACE!

SUSPICION

DISDAIN

FURY

LATE THE FOLLOWING AFTERNOON, JUST BEFORE CLOSING TIME, ROGER HAYDEN ENTERS A *GOTHAM CITY* BANK AND...

I COULDN'T WEAR THE COSTUME I DESIGNED FOR MY USE AS THE *PSYCHO-PIRATE* BECAUSE I'D ATTRACT TOO MUCH ATTENTION... JUST AS THIS NEWSPAPER IS GOING TO DO!

HIS HAND MOVES BEFORE HIS FACE AND AS IT DROPS...

AS I RELEASE THE *CURIOSITY MASK--* I INFECT EVERYONE IN HERE WITH OVER-WHELMING CURIOSITY ABOUT THAT DISCARDED NEWSPAPER!

A WAVE OF THAT INTENSE CURIOSITY SWEEPS ACROSS THE BANK, AS TELLERS AND OFFICIALS JOIN CUSTOMERS ABOUT THE NEWS-PAPER...

WHAT DO THE HEADLINES SAY?

I MUST FIND OUT!

I'LL GO OUT OF MY MIND UNLESS I KNOW--!

HIS MOBSTERS DASH PAST THE GRINNING ROGER HAYDEN AS HE STATIONS HIMSELF AT THE BANK DOOR...

GO AHEAD--DO YOUR STUFF! NOBODY WILL BOTHER YOU! THEY'RE ALL TOO BUSY TO PAY ANY ATTENTION! I'LL MAKE ANYONE ELSE GOING INTO THE BANK JUST AS *CURIOUS!*

ONLY ONE MAN IN ALL THE WORLD SEES WHAT IS HAPPENING IN THE BANK...

ODD! I CANNOT LOCATE THE MASKS--YET MY CRYSTAL BALL PICKS UP THAT MAN IN A BANK! *Hmmm!* PERHAPS I'D BETTER INVESTIGATE, JUST ON THE ODD CHANCE THAT *HE* HAS SOMETHING TO DO WITH THEM!

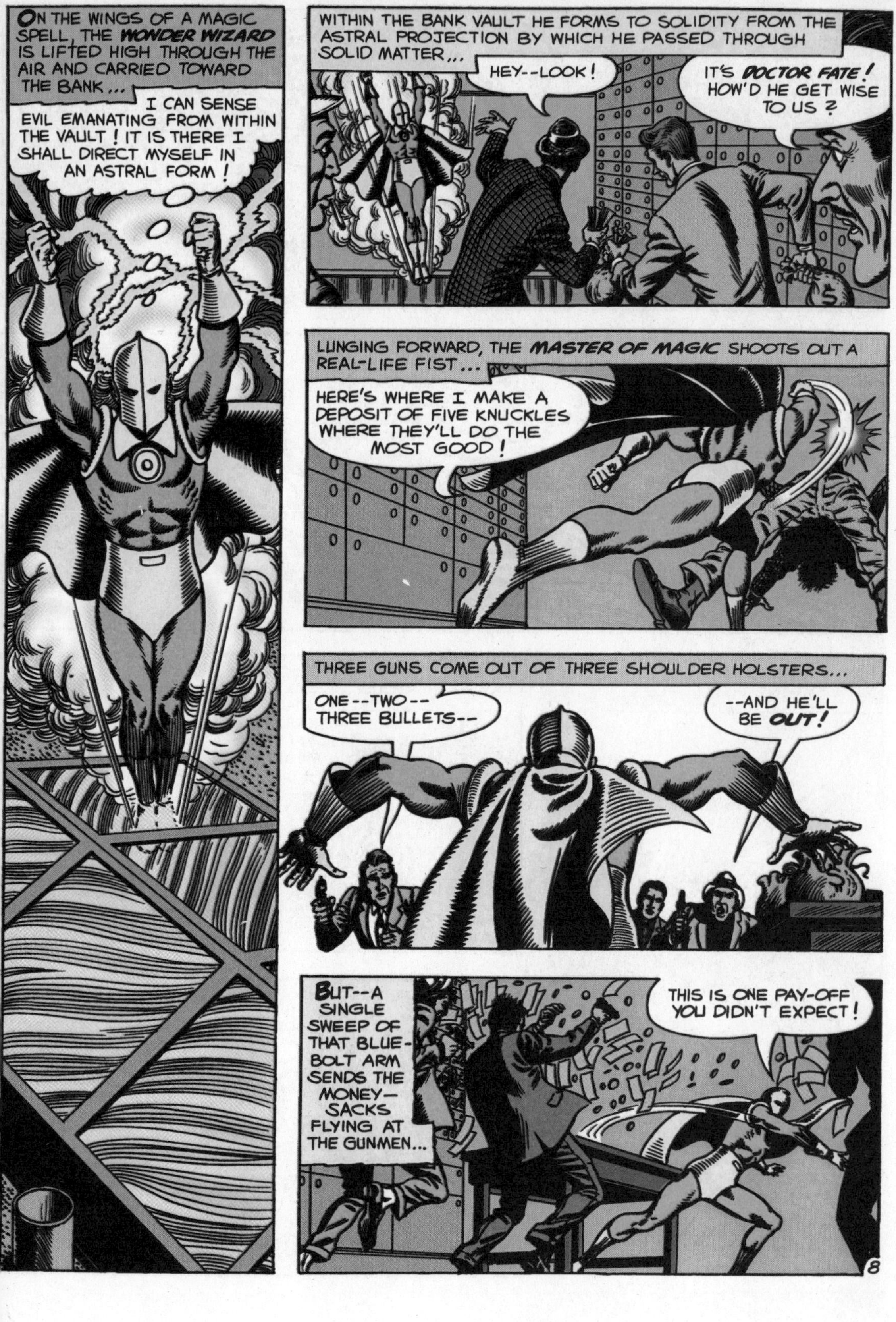
ON THE WINGS OF A MAGIC SPELL, THE WONDER WIZARD IS LIFTED HIGH THROUGH THE AIR AND CARRIED TOWARD THE BANK...
I CAN SENSE EVIL EMANATING FROM WITHIN THE VAULT! IT IS THERE I SHALL DIRECT MYSELF IN AN ASTRAL FORM!
WITHIN THE BANK VAULT HE FORMS TO SOLIDITY FROM THE ASTRAL PROJECTION BY WHICH HE PASSED THROUGH SOLID MATTER...
HEY--LOOK!
IT'S DOCTOR FATE! HOW'D HE GET WISE TO US?
LUNGING FORWARD, THE MASTER OF MAGIC SHOOTS OUT A REAL-LIFE FIST...
HERE'S WHERE I MAKE A DEPOSIT OF FIVE KNUCKLES WHERE THEY'LL DO THE MOST GOOD!
THREE GUNS COME OUT OF THREE SHOULDER HOLSTERS...
ONE--TWO--THREE BULLETS--
--AND HE'LL BE OUT!
BUT--A SINGLE SWEEP OF THAT BLUE-BOLT ARM SENDS THE MONEY-SACKS FLYING AT THE GUNMEN...
THIS IS ONE PAY-OFF YOU DIDN'T EXPECT!
8

HE FOLLOWS THAT FLYING MONEY WITH A FLYING FIST THAT DOES DOUBLE DUTY...

A PILE-DRIVER SHOULDER TAKES THE LEGS OUT FROM UNDER A THIRD MOBSTER...

HE PIVOTS AND BRINGS AN UPPERCUT UP FROM THE FLOOR TILES...

OUTSIDE THE BANK, THE LONG DELAY MAKES ROGER HAYDEN NERVOUS...

WHAT'S KEEPING THEM? THEY SHOULD BE OUT WITH THE LOOT BY NOW! THE SPELL OF THE CURIOSITY MASK LASTS ONLY FOR A SHORT TIME!

HOURS
MON.-THURS. 9:
FRIDAY 9:00-

HE ENTERS THE VAULT AND AS HE SEES THE STELLAR SORCERER, HIS HAND LIFTS TO HIS FACE...

DOCTOR FATE! I MUST DO SOMETHING FAST! I'LL BOMBARD HIM WITH PRIDE!

IMMEDIATELY, A CHANGE OF EXPRESSION COMES OVER THE FACE OF THE *PSYCHO-PIRATE*...

IN A MOMENT, *DOCTOR FATE*, YOUR PRIDE IN YOUR GREAT PROWESS AS A CRIME-FIGHTER WILL CAUSE YOU TO REMEMBER SOME OF THE AWESOME VILLAINS YOU HAVE OVERCOME IN THE PAST!

AND THEN HIS FEATURES ALTER AGAIN...

--BUT *FRUSTRATION* WILL SO GRIP YOU, YOU WILL BE UNABLE TO DEFEAT THEM AS ONCE YOU DID!

AS THE FACE OF THE *PSYCHO-PIRATE* MIRRORS *PRIDE*-- AND THEN *FRUSTRATION*-- SO ALSO DOES THE HELMET OF THE *WONDER WIZARD*!..

MY FORMER ENEMIES -- COMING BACK TO FIGHT ME -- TOGETHER!

FROM ONE OF THOSE IMAGINARY BUBBLES INDUCED BY THE MEMORY CENTERS OF *DOCTOR FATE'S* BRAIN LEAPS A VISIONARY VILLAIN...

WOTAN!

YES--I HAVE COME BACK WHENCE YOU CAST ME TO WORK MY EVIL ON YOU!

AS *DOCTOR FATE* LEAPS BACKWARD TO AVOID THAT LUNGE, HE HURLS MAGICAL BOLTS AT HIS FOE...

I'LL PARALYZE YOU WITH A--

FOOLISH *DOCTOR FATE!* YOU CANNOT DESTROY ME! YOU KNOW IN YOUR HEART--THAT'S RIGHT!

10

AND THEN FROM OUT OF THE SUN-LIGHT BRILLIANCE ABOUT *WOTAN'S* HEAD EMERGES...

THE MAGE OF THE YUCATAN JUNGLES-- *MAYOOR!*

WITH A HIDEOUS LAUGH, THE TERRIBLE *MAYOOR* TURNS THE FLOOR TO WET OOZE...

THIS TIME IT IS *I* WHO SHALL BE VICTORIOUS!

THE VERY ATOMS OF THE FLOOR ARE GRIPPING ME, SEEKING TO DRAG ME DOWN AS IF THEY WERE QUICKSAND!

BUT THE WISDOM OF THE ANCIENT *CHALDEANS* DOES NOT DESERT THE *WONDER WIZARD*...

MY MAGIC SEEMS TO HAVE NO EFFECT ON THEM! ALL I CAN DO IS SAVE MYSELF--BY USING MAGIC LIGHTNING TO BLAST MYSELF UPWARD--LIKE A ROCKET!

AND THEN--SO ABRUPTLY THAT HE GASPS WITH SURPRISE, THE *STELLAR SORCERER* FINDS HIM-SELF ALONE...

WHAT..? WHY--OF COURSE! I ONLY *IMAGINED* THOSE OLD ENEMIES OF MINE! SOMEONE USED MY MOMENTARY LAPSE TO HELP THE BANK ROBBERS GET AWAY!

STORY CONTINUES ON NEXT PAGE!

CRISIS
ON MULTIPLE EARTHS
THE TEAM UPS

PERILS OF THE PSYCHO-PIRATE! PART 2

IN A LOCKED ROOM DEEP IN THE SUBTERRANEAN QUARTERS OF THE *TYLER CHEMICAL COMPANY* HANGS THE DARK, GRIM UNIFORM OF *HOURMAN*, WITH A SMALL HOURGLASS ON A CHAIN, TO KEEP TRACK OF HIS HOUR OF SUPER-CHARGED POWER...

FOR WHEN REX TYLER DONS THAT COSTUME AND HANGS THE HOUR-GLASS ABOUT HIS NECK, HE CHANGES FROM PRESIDENT OF HIS COMPANY TO HEROIC CRIME-FIGHTER.

MIRACLO, THE AMAZING CHEMICAL TAKEN IN THE FORM OF A PILL, GIVES HIM SUPER-POWERS-- BUT ONLY FOR ONE HOUR!

TO RE-ACQUIRE THESE GREAT ABILITIES, HE MUST WAIT ANOTHER SIXTY MINUTES...

I MUST DISCOVER WHY WENDI HARRIS STOLE THOSE MASKS! BECAUSE SHE UNACCOUNTABLY DID-- SHE NOW SAYS SHE CANNOT MARRY ME! SOMEHOW, I KNOW IT WASN'T HER FAULT--AND I INTEND TO PROVE IT!

HEARING OF THE ROBBERY AT THE *GOTHAM CITY* BANK, *HOURMAN* RACES TO THE FINANCIAL ESTABLISHMENT ONLY TO LEARN THAT...

DOCTOR FATE WAS HERE AT THE TIME OF THE ROBBERY, *HOURMAN!* HE--er--TOUCHED THIS NEWSPAPER, THEN SET OFF IN PURSUIT OF THE ROBBERS!

I'LL BORROW THAT PAPER, IF I MAY!

WITH THE NEWSPAPER AND A DESCRIPTION OF THE MAN WHO OWNED IT, THE SIXTY-MINUTE *SUPER-HERO* VISITS A CORNER NEWSSTAND...

SURE, I REMEMBER THE GUY THAT BOUGHT IT--BECAUSE HE CAME IN A RED FOREIGN CAR--A *MERCEDES-BENTLY!*

SWALLOWING THE *MIRACLO PILL, HOURMAN* HURTLES INTO THE AIR...

I'LL LEAP HIGH ABOVE THE CITY--AND SCAN ALL THE STREETS IN THE VICINITY FOR THAT *MERCEDES-BENTLY!*

3:10 P.M.

UPWARD HE SOARS AS HIS KEEN EYES DRINK IN CAR AFTER CAR--BUT THERE IS NO SIGN OF THE *PSYCHO-PIRATE'S* VEHICLE...

GOT TO MAKE ANOTHER JUMP--AND KEEP ON UNTIL I SPOT HIM!

3:18 P.M.

THEN--OUTSIDE AN OPEN AIR ART MUSEUM DISPLAY...

EVERYONE HERE EXCEPT US--THANKS TO THE *COUNTER-EMOTIONAL* CAPSULE WE ALL TOOK--IS OVERCOME BY THE EMOTION--*DESPAIR!* IT LEAVES US A CLEAR FIELD TO CLEAR OUT THIS PLACE!

THERE THEY ARE!

3:39 P.M.

13

DROPPING LIKE A BOMB, HE RAMS BOTH FEET INTO AN IRON ART ABSTRACTION AND...

3:39:01

ROGER HAYDEN QUICKLY RECOVERS HIS BALANCE AND LIFTS A HAND TO HIS FACE...

I'LL PUT A STOP TO *HOURMAN*-- WITH AN EMOTIONAL DISTURBANCE!

3:39:04

BUT BEFORE HE CAN CAUSE A FACIAL CHANGEOVER...

3:39:05

HE DIVES THROUGH A MARBLE FREE-ART FORM...

HE WON'T BE SO ACROBATIC WHEN I BOUNCE THIS STATUE OFF HIS NOGGIN!

3:39:10

BUT THE MIGHTY MUSCLES OF THE *TICK-TOCK TORNADO* REACT INSTANTLY AS...

IT WOULD BE A SHAME TO BREAK THAT PRICELESS PIECE OF STATUARY-- SO I'LL CATCH IT IN FLIGHT!

3:39:11

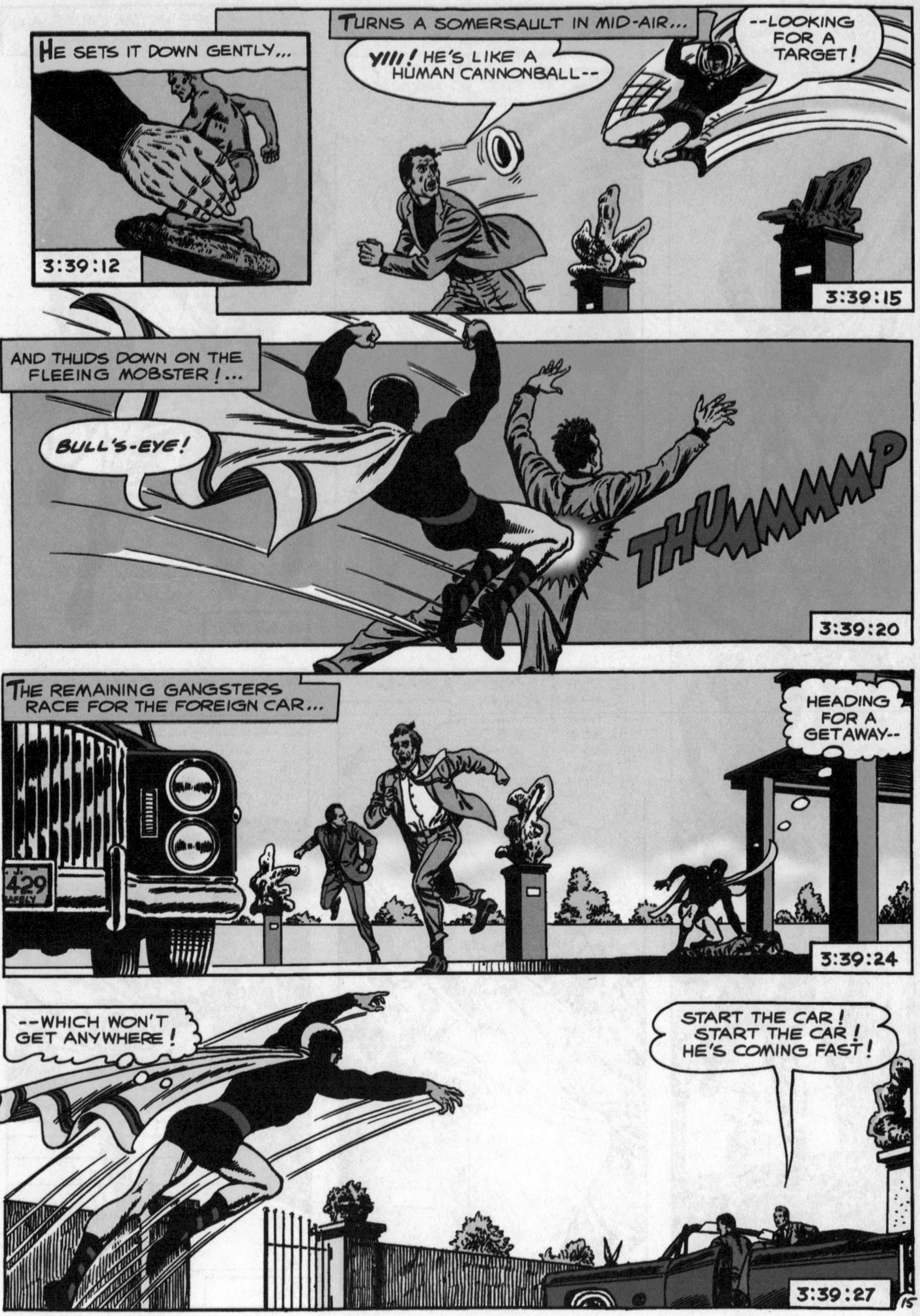
HE SETS IT DOWN GENTLY...
3:39:12
TURNS A SOMERSAULT IN MID-AIR...
YIII! HE'S LIKE A HUMAN CANNONBALL--
--LOOKING FOR A TARGET!
3:39:15
AND THUDS DOWN ON THE FLEEING MOBSTER!...
BULL'S-EYE!
THUMMMMP
3:39:20
THE REMAINING GANGSTERS RACE FOR THE FOREIGN CAR...
HEADING FOR A GETAWAY--
429
3:39:24
--WHICH WON'T GET ANYWHERE!
START THE CAR! START THE CAR! HE'S COMING FAST!
3:39:27
15

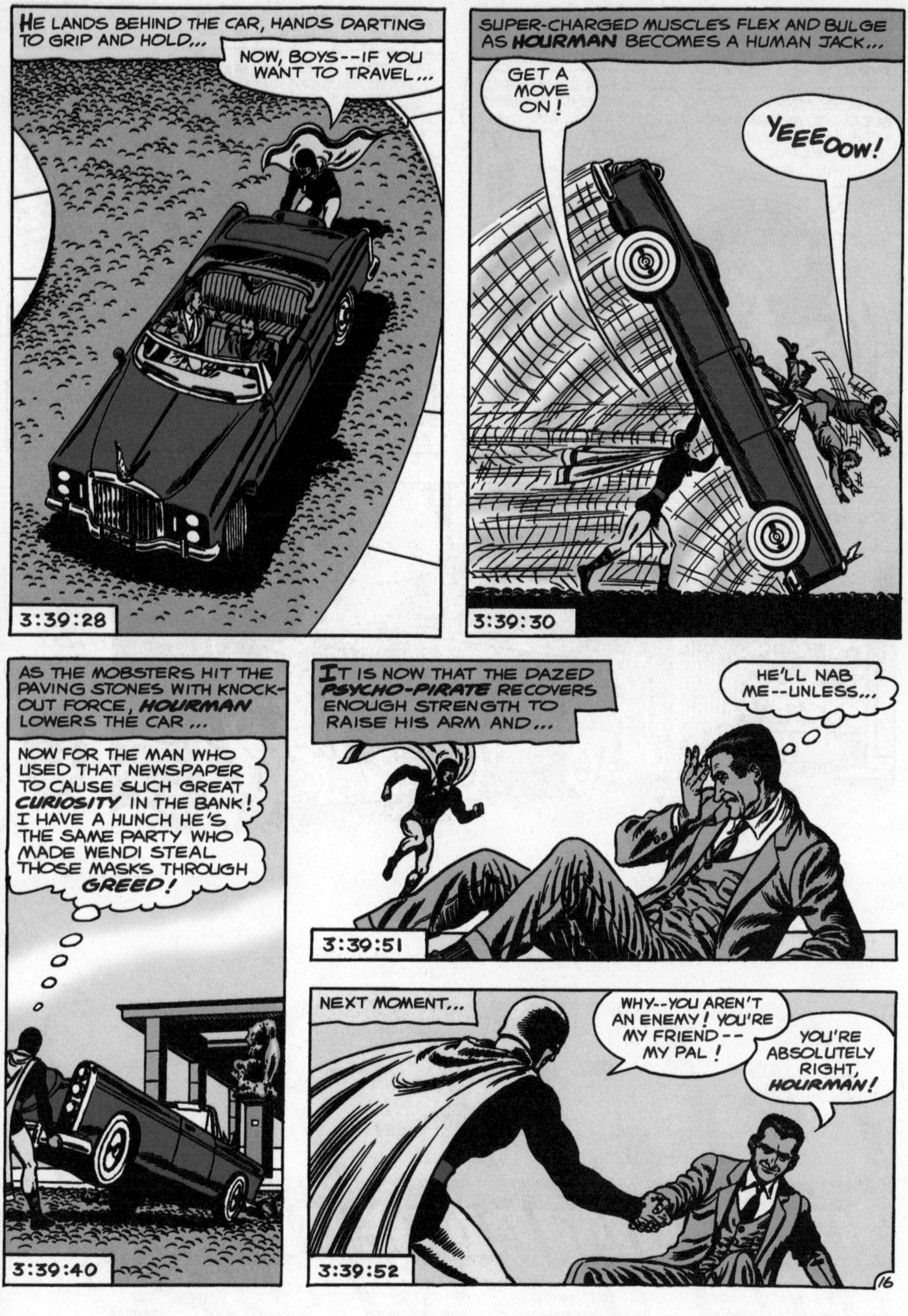

HE LANDS BEHIND THE CAR, HANDS DARTING TO GRIP AND HOLD...
NOW, BOYS--IF YOU WANT TO TRAVEL...
3:39:28
SUPER-CHARGED MUSCLES FLEX AND BULGE AS HOURMAN BECOMES A HUMAN JACK...
GET A MOVE ON!
YEEEOOW!
3:39:30
AS THE MOBSTERS HIT THE PAVING STONES WITH KNOCK-OUT FORCE, HOURMAN LOWERS THE CAR...
NOW FOR THE MAN WHO USED THAT NEWSPAPER TO CAUSE SUCH GREAT CURIOSITY IN THE BANK! I HAVE A HUNCH HE'S THE SAME PARTY WHO MADE WENDI STEAL THOSE MASKS THROUGH GREED!
3:39:40
IT IS NOW THAT THE DAZED PSYCHO-PIRATE RECOVERS ENOUGH STRENGTH TO RAISE HIS ARM AND...
HE'LL NAB ME--UNLESS...
3:39:51
NEXT MOMENT...
WHY--YOU AREN'T AN ENEMY! YOU'RE MY FRIEND--MY PAL!
YOU'RE ABSOLUTELY RIGHT, HOURMAN!
3:39:52
16

STORY CONTINUES ON NEXT PAGE FOLLOWING!

⑰

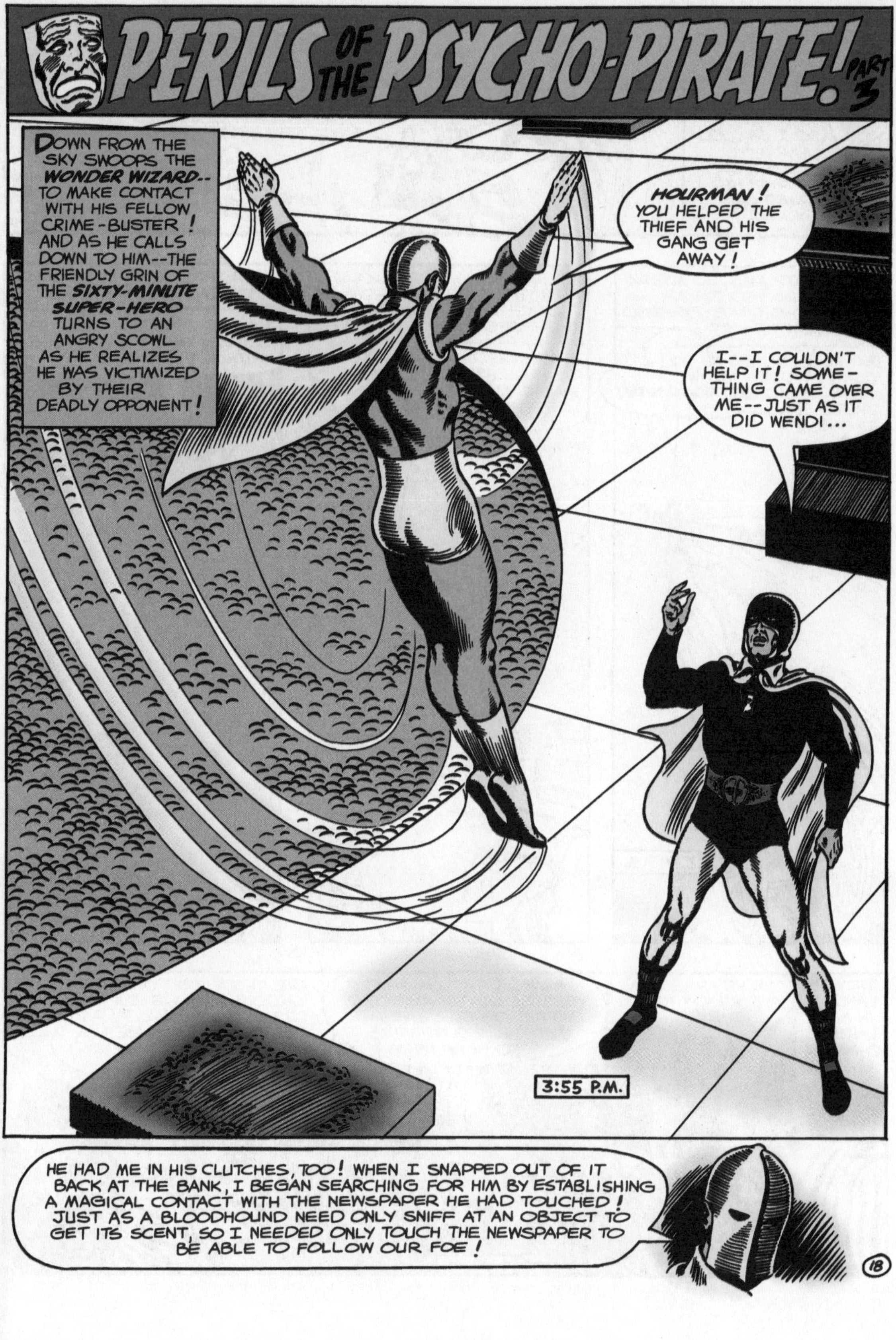
PERILS OF THE PSYCHO-PIRATE! PART 3
DOWN FROM THE SKY SWOOPS THE WONDER WIZARD-- TO MAKE CONTACT WITH HIS FELLOW CRIME-BUSTER! AND AS HE CALLS DOWN TO HIM--THE FRIENDLY GRIN OF THE SIXTY-MINUTE SUPER-HERO TURNS TO AN ANGRY SCOWL AS HE REALIZES HE WAS VICTIMIZED BY THEIR DEADLY OPPONENT!
HOURMAN! YOU HELPED THE THIEF AND HIS GANG GET AWAY!
I--I COULDN'T HELP IT! SOMETHING CAME OVER ME--JUST AS IT DID WENDI...
3:55 P.M.
HE HAD ME IN HIS CLUTCHES, TOO! WHEN I SNAPPED OUT OF IT BACK AT THE BANK, I BEGAN SEARCHING FOR HIM BY ESTABLISHING A MAGICAL CONTACT WITH THE NEWSPAPER HE HAD TOUCHED! JUST AS A BLOODHOUND NEED ONLY SNIFF AT AN OBJECT TO GET ITS SCENT, SO I NEEDED ONLY TOUCH THE NEWSPAPER TO BE ABLE TO FOLLOW OUR FOE!
18

"THOUGH MY MAGIC COULD NOT FOLLOW THE MASKS, IT COULD TRACK DOWN THE THIEF-- SO I SAW YOU LEAP INTO ACTION AND THE TRICK HE PLAYED ON YOU..."

I WON'T INTERFERE YET! I WANT TO LEARN WHERE HE HAS HIS HIDE-OUT SO WE CAN RECOVER HIS LOOT!

AFTER HE EXPLAINS, THE *MYSTIC MAGE* RISES INTO THE AIR, BRINGING HIS CRIME-FIGHTING COMPANION WITH HIM...

BUT WE DON'T KNOW WHERE TO FIND THE THIEF!

OH, YES WE DO! LOOK AT THE CLOUDS, *HOURMAN!*

3:59 P.M.

FOLLOWING A WISPY CLOUD PATH, THE BATTLERS FOR JUSTICE SPEED TOWARD THEIR DESTINATION...

I CONJURED UP THOSE CLOUDS TO TRAIL HIM-- USING THE MAGIC "SCENT" I TOOK OFF HIS NEWSPAPER!

4:03 P.M.

THEN THEY DROP DOWNWARD ABOVE A SEACOAST MANSION..

THESE WIZARDOUS DRILLS WILL SLIP US INSIDE THE HOUSE WITHOUT HARMING IT!

4:09 P.M.

THEY LAND IN A LARGE CHAMBER WHERE...

WE'RE ARMED AND READY FOR THEM!

HUH! I THOUGHT WE WERE GOING TO HAVE THE BATTLE OF OUR LIVES-- BUT THERE'S NOTHING TO FEAR HERE!

ARE THOSE ODD OBJECTS IN THE CROOKS' HANDS SUPPOSED TO BE-- *WEAPONS?!* A KNITTING NEEDLE! A PIZZA PIE! AN ELECTRIC FAN! A WATER PISTOL!

4:09:24

19

THOSE INNOCENT-LOOKING OBJECTS ARE DEADLIER WEAPONS THAN YOU MIGHT SUSPECT, *DOCTOR FATE!* FOR THE *PSYCHO-PIRATE* IS WELL PREPARED FOR YOU AND *HOURMAN!*

IN HIS PSYCHOLOGICAL LABORATORY HE HAS ALREADY DONNED HIS GARB AS THE *EMIR OF EMOTION* AND...

RIGHT AT THIS MOMENT HE IS OUTSIDE THE VERY CHAMBER IN WHICH YOU STAND--HURLING A BATTERY OF *PHOBIAS* AT YOU BOTH !...

I KNEW IT WOULDN'T BE LONG BEFORE THEY CAUGHT UP TO US--SO I'M ABOUT TO FILL THEM WITH SO MANY *PHOBIAS*-- THEY'LL BE TOO TERRIFIED TO ACT !

4:09:29

AS THEY HURTLE FORWARD--*DOCTOR FATE* AND *HOURMAN* FIND THAT THE INNOCENT OBJECTS ARE INDEED WEAPONS OF A DIABOLICAL NATURE...

EEE-YAH!

NO! NO! NO!!

4:09:34

DOCTOR FATE SUFFERS FROM *AEROPHOBIA,* A DREAD OF AIR CURRENTS-- WHILE *HOURMAN* IS AFFECTED BY *HYDROPHOBIA,* A FEAR OF WATER !

THEY TURN TO FLEE--ONLY TO DISCOVER THAT THE PIZZA PIE AND THE KNITTING NEEDLE ARE JUST AS ALARMING !...

I'M SO AFRAID-- I'M SHAKING !

¿GULP? I'VE GOT TO GET OUT OF HERE !

4:09:42

NOW *DOCTOR FATE* IS ATTACKED BY *SITOPHOBIA,* A FEAR OF FOOD-- WHILE HIS COMPANION IS STRICKEN BY *AICHMOPHOBIA,* THE FEAR OF POINTED OBJECTS !

20

As this mortal fear strikes deep into their individual hearts, each crime-fighter knows he must strike back--or perish! **DOCTOR FATE** lifts quivering fingers...

I CAN DO NOTHING AGAINST THE OBJECTS THAT CAUSE *MY* FEARS-- BUT PERHAPS I CAN HELP *HOURMAN!*

4:09:58

INSTANTLY THE WATER PISTOL AND THE KNITTING NEEDLE ARE MAGICALLY TRANSFORMED...

HUH? OUR WEAPONS-- TURNED INTO SMOKE!

TEAMWORK CAN HELP US HERE! THE GANG-LEADER DIDN'T RECKON ON THE FACT THAT WE COULD FIGHT AGAINST THOSE OBJECTS THAT CAUSED THE OTHER TO BE STRICKEN WITH FEAR!

4:09:59

BUT--EVEN AS HE SPRINGS, THE *TICK-TOCK THUNDER- BOLT* REALIZES THAT...

MY HOUR HAS PASSED! I'M A NORMAL HUMAN AGAIN--WITHOUT ANY SUPER- CHARGED POWERS!

4:10 P.M.

YET THE GRIM DETERMINATION OF THE CRIME-FIGHTER ENABLES HIM TO LAND A KNOCKOUT BLOW! ...

I'LL HAVE TO PLAYACT-- TO PREVENT THOSE THUGS FROM REALIZING MY POWERS HAVE LEFT ME!

4:10:02

THE *WONDER WIZARD* LEAPS TO KNOCK OUT THE GANGSTERS HARRYING HIS PARTNER...

WHILE *HOURMAN* HANDLES MY OPPONENTS, I'LL TAKE CARE OF HIS!

21

HARSH LAUGHTER FILLS THE AIR AS THE *PSYCHO-PIRATE* TOUCHES A HIDDEN CONTROL AND CAUSES THE GOLD MASKS TO BECOME AGLOW...

HA, HA! I'M NOT BEATEN YET! I WANTED TO GIVE MY BOYS A CHANCE TO GET EVEN--BUT IN CASE THEY FAILED, I STILL RESERVED A TRUMP CARD TO PLAY!

FROM THE GLOWING *MEDUSA MASKS* A DOZEN CONFLICTING EMOTIONS SLAM INTO *DOCTOR FATE* AND *HOURMAN!* THEY QUIVER UNDER A GAMUT OF SPINE-TINGLING EMOTIONS...

DOCTOR FATE, I'VE ALWAYS BEEN *JEALOUS* OF YOUR MAGICAL POWERS! I'M GOING TO PROVE MY ENERGY-CHARGED ABILITIES ARE BETTER THAN YOUR MAGIC!

A JEALOUS RAGE TWISTS THE AUREATE HELMET OF THE *WONDER WIZARD* AS HE ANSWERS *HOURMAN'S* ATTACK WITH A BLOW OF HIS OWN...

THIS IS ONLY THE STARTER--

IN MY BOOK, MAGIC OUTSPELLS ENERGY-POWER!

FROM *JEALOUSY*, THE MASKS BURN *MOCKERY* INTO EACH CRIME-FIGHTER...

HOW DO YOU HAVE THE GALL TO APPEAR IN PUBLIC WITH THAT RIDICULOUS-LOOKING UNIFORM!?

I DON'T KNOW HOW YOU EVER HAD THE NERVE TO TAKE YOUR OLD UNIFORM OUT OF MOTHBALLS!

AGAIN THEY LEAP AND STRUGGLE AS *HATE* OVERWHELMS THEM...

I'M GOING TO SEND YOU BACK INTO RETIREMENT, YOU HAS-BEEN!

WHEN I GET THROUGH BLASTING YOU WITH MY MAGIC, YOU'LL ONLY BE A MEMORY!

22

ONE AFTER ANOTHER, THE CRIME-FIGHTERS SUFFER THE EMOTIONS OF THE *MEDUSA MASKS*... UNTIL THEY BECOME EXHAUSTED, WORN OUT BY THEIR AWESOME EXPERIENCES...

AT LAST! YOU ARE UTTERLY HELPLESS! THE STRENGTH HAS BEEN DRAINED OUT OF YOU BY THE EMOTIONAL WRINGER I PUT YOU THROUGH!

TAUNTING HIS OPPONENTS, THE *PSYCHO-PIRATE* RAMS A FIST AGAINST *HOURMAN'S* JAW...

I DON'T NEED ANY HOCUS-POCUS POWERS TO KNOCK *YOU* OUT...

THOSE MASKS ROUSED UP YOUR EMOTIONS BY AN ELECTRICAL STIMULATION OF THE BODY'S EMOTIONAL CONTROL CENTERS, THE *HYPOTHALAMUS* AND THE *SEPTAL REGION* OF OF THE HUMAN BRAIN! NEUROPHYSIOLOGISTS HAVE ALREADY PROVED THIS TO BE A SCIENTIFIC FACT!*

*Editor's Note: BY THE EXPERIMENTS OF DR. C.W. SEM-JACOBSEN OF NORWAY, OF DR. ROBERT G. HEATH OF TULANE UNIVERSITY, AND DR. JOSE M. DELGADO OF YALE.

HE DRIVES AN UPPERCUT AGAINST THE JAW OF *DOCTOR FATE*...

THIS IS NO MAGIC ILLUSION STRIKING YOU, *DOCTOR FATE!*

BUT--TO THE INTENSE STUPEFACTION OF THE *EMIR OF EMOTIONS*--THE *WONDER WIZARD* RETURNS HIS BLOW!...

HUH?! YOU--YOU ARE NOT AFFECTED BY THE GOLDEN MASKS!

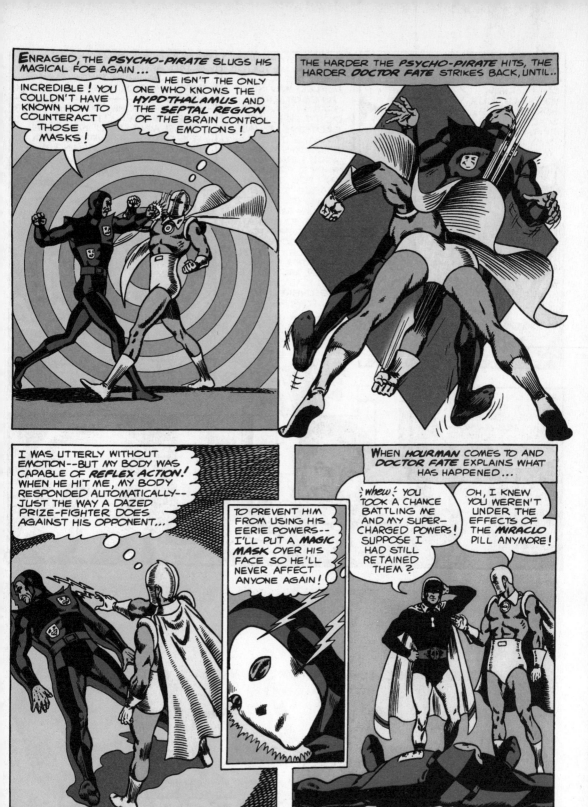

ENRAGED, THE *PSYCHO-PIRATE* SLUGS HIS MAGICAL FOE AGAIN...

INCREDIBLE! YOU COULDN'T HAVE KNOWN HOW TO COUNTERACT THOSE MASKS!

HE ISN'T THE ONLY ONE WHO KNOWS THE *HYPOTHALAMUS* AND THE *SEPTAL REGION* OF THE BRAIN CONTROL EMOTIONS!

THE HARDER THE *PSYCHO-PIRATE* HITS, THE HARDER *DOCTOR FATE* STRIKES BACK, UNTIL...

I WAS UTTERLY WITHOUT EMOTION--BUT MY BODY WAS CAPABLE OF *REFLEX ACTION!* WHEN HE HIT ME, MY BODY RESPONDED AUTOMATICALLY-- JUST THE WAY A DAZED PRIZE-FIGHTER DOES AGAINST HIS OPPONENT...

TO PREVENT HIM FROM USING HIS EERIE POWERS-- I'LL PUT A *MAGIC MASK* OVER HIS FACE SO HE'LL NEVER AFFECT ANYONE AGAIN!

WHEN *HOURMAN* COMES TO AND *DOCTOR FATE* EXPLAINS WHAT HAS HAPPENED...

¡WHEW! YOU TOOK A CHANCE BATTLING ME AND MY SUPER-CHARGED POWERS! SUPPOSE I HAD STILL RETAINED THEM?

OH, I KNEW YOU WEREN'T UNDER THE EFFECTS OF THE *MIRACLO* PILL ANYMORE!

24

I SAW THE SANDS OF YOUR HOUR-GLASS HAD RUN OUT! I KNEW YOU WERE YOUR NORMAL SELF, SO I "PULLED MY PUNCHES" IN MY FIGHT WITH YOU!

I SEE! YOU ACTED OUT A PART JUST AS I DID WHEN FIGHTING THOSE MOBSTERS-- AFTER I REALIZED MY POWERS HAD LEFT ME!

I TOOK MY ACTING CUES FROM YOU WHEN THE MASKS HURLED YOU INTO AN EMOTIONAL SPASM! SINCE I DIDN'T FEEL ANY EMOTIONS, I HAD TO FAKE THE EMOTIONS YOU WERE FEELING! WHEN I FOUGHT OUR FOE, I WAS UNABLE TO USE MAGIC BECAUSE I NEED MY EMOTIONAL FORCES TO OPERATE IT, SO I HAD TO DEPEND SOLELY ON MY REFLEX ACTIONS! WHEN THE GANG LEADER WAS KNOCKED OUT, I AUTOMATICALLY RECOVERED MY POWERS!

THE MASKED PSYCHO-PIRATE IS PUT BEHIND JAIL BARS--AND A JOYFUL REUNION TAKES PLACE BETWEEN REX TYLER AND WENDI HARRIS...

HONEY, NOW THAT YOUR NAME HAS BEEN CLEARED AND YOU'VE AGREED TO MARRY ME, IT'S ONLY FAIR THAT YOU SHOULD KNOW I'VE BEEN LEADING A DOUBLE LIFE! I AM ALSO-- HOURMAN!

IT'S TRUE, WENDI!

ALL I CARE ABOUT, REALLY, IS THAT YOU'RE GOING TO BE MY HUSBAND-- TWENTY-FOUR HOURS A DAY!

The END

25

CRISIS
ON MULTIPLE EARTHS
THE TEAM UPS

ORIGIN OF THE ORIGINAL PSYCHO-PIRATE

Charley Halstead, the original *Psycho-Pirate*, was twice pitted against the heroes of the *Justice Society of America*. The first of these battles took place just over "twenty years" ago. ("The Plunder of the Psycho-Pirate"—ALL-STAR COMICS No. 23.)

Halstead was a linotyper on the *Daily Courier*. Although considered a valued friend of publisher *Rex Morgan*, Halstead was *jealous* of his success. He grew to *hate* his employer, and was overcome by *greed*. Conceiving the idea of basing crimes on emotions, he secretly embarked on a career as a successful gang leader, calling himself the *Psycho-Pirate*, while helping Morgan crusade against his crooked alter ego in his Charley Halstead identity. Finally, made reckless through *conceit*, he sent challenges, through the *Courier*, to the *Justice Society*.

The *JSA's* active members at this time were: *Hawkman*, Chairman; *Dr. Mid-Nite; The Spectre; The Atom; Starman;* and *Johnny Thunder*.

One of the *Psycho-Pirate's* crimes was based on the *love* of a wealthy man for his daughter. While one of the gang kept the girl out late on a date, others gained possession of her handbag and used it to convince her father that they had kidnaped her. But they *really* kidnaped Shiera (*Hawkgirl*) Sanders in order to lure *Hawkman* into a trap. However, the *Flying Fury* escaped, and, instead of ransom money, the crooks got jail sentences.

Another plot involved stirring up rich men to *hate* each other, charging them $100,000 apiece for dueling lessons, and letting them fight it out. *Starman* intervened and exposed the scheme.

One of the *Psycho-Pirate's* most ambitious plans was to strike *fear* into the hearts of the inhabitants of a city by threatening to release deadly plague germs unless they paid a huge ransom. It was *Dr. Mid-Nite* who discovered the whole thing was a bluff—the gang had no such microbes!

A pair of safe manufacturers fell victim to their own *conceit* when they were asked to open one of their vaults, whose new owner, it was said, could not do so because it was so fool-proof. Only the caller was not the owner, but a thief. Furthermore, the crooks used *Johnny Thunder's* conceit to trap him in the vault. However, aided by the magical *Thunderbolt* he controlled, Johnny escaped and nabbed the outlaws.

There were two priceless idols—identical and the only ones of their kind. Each was owned by a wealthy collector who wanted both. One of the *Psycho-Pirate's* men made a deal with each of them to steal the other's idol. Then he pretended the police were after him, he had thrown away the stolen idol, and both he and the collector, trapped by his *greed*, would go to prison unless he could replace it with its mate. Both men fell for the story, and the swindler would have made off with both figurines if *The Spectre* had not caught up with him.

Meanwhile, at the *Courier*, Halstead embarked on a campaign to destroy Morgan through *despair*. He convinced him that his whole world was crumbling. Also, he lured *The Atom* into a trap by making him think his fellow *JSA-ers* had met defeat. But the *Mighty Mite* discovered the fraud—and the *Psycho-Pirate's* secret identity! To keep him quiet, Halstead shot him; but the wounded hero made his way back to the *Courier* and exposed him. Halstead went to prison.

However, two years later, the *Psycho-Pirate* was back. ("The Return of the Psycho-Pirate" —ALL-STAR No. 32.) By playing on a guard's emotions, he had lured him too near his cell door, overpowered him, and taken his keys. Then he and his cell-mate, Big Mike, escaped.

Big Mike, who had also been jailed by the *JSA*, wanted revenge. So, to lure the heroes into traps, he arranged for *Johnny Thunder*, the only member without a secret identity, to find a wallet containing plans for his and the *Psycho-Pirate's* crimes. Armed with this information, the six heroes swung into action. (*Green Lantern* and *The Flash* had replaced *Starman* and *The Spectre* as active members.)

Hawkman broke up a plot to use an opera star's *pride* to blackmail her. *Dr. Mid-Nite* stopped a plan to turn a man into a thief by appealing to his *ambition. Green Lantern* saved another man from turning dishonest through *envy. The Atom* kept a college student from innocently aiding crime by yielding to his *curiosity.* When the *Psycho-Pirate* planned to drug a boxing champ so he could collect big money by betting on a has-been noted for his *humility, Johnny Thunder* turned the tables, humiliating the *Master of Emotions.* And *The Flash* checked a scheme to steal a valuable invention by playing on the inventor's *anger.*

These things done, the *JSA* closed in on the *Psycho-Pirate's* hide-out and captured him. It was easy, for in the wallet planted by Big Mike was an identification card *filled out with the address of the hide-out!* Halstead and Mike were returned to their cell.

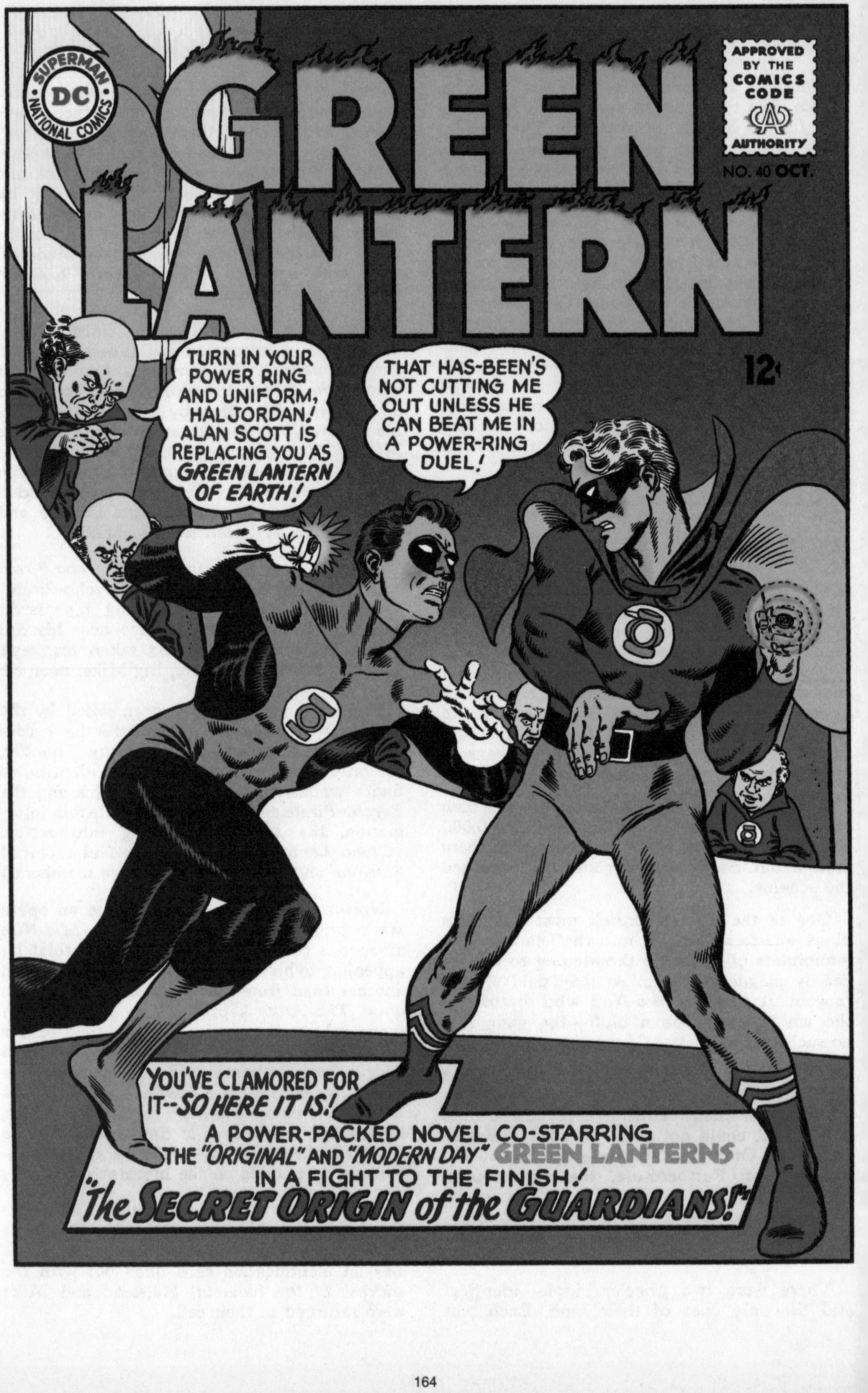
SUPERMAN DC NATIONAL COMICS
GREEN LANTERN
APPROVED BY THE COMICS CODE AUTHORITY
NO. 40 OCT.
12¢
TURN IN YOUR POWER RING AND UNIFORM, HAL JORDAN! ALAN SCOTT IS REPLACING YOU AS *GREEN LANTERN OF EARTH!*
THAT HAS-BEEN'S NOT CUTTING ME OUT UNLESS HE CAN BEAT ME IN A POWER-RING DUEL!
YOU'VE CLAMORED FOR IT--*SO HERE IT IS!*
A POWER-PACKED NOVEL CO-STARRING THE *"ORIGINAL"* AND *"MODERN DAY"* GREEN LANTERNS IN A FIGHT TO THE FINISH!
"The SECRET ORIGIN of the GUARDIANS!"

GREEN LANTERN

CO-STARRING the "ORIGINAL" GREEN LANTERN IN A FULL-LENGTH POWER-PACKED NOVEL!

I HOLD THE TRUMP CARD IN THIS BATTLE WITH MY RIVAL *GREEN LANTERN!* I CAN SAFEGUARD MYSELF WITH THIS *YELLOW* SHIELD FROM THE EFFECTS OF HIS *POWER RING*--WHILE HE HAS *NOTHING* TO PROTECT HIM FROM THE POWER OF *MY RING!*

THE UNIVERSE IS DOOMED UNLESS OUR *HAL JORDAN--GREEN LANTERN* CAN DEFEAT THE *ALAN SCOTT--GREEN LANTERN* FROM ANOTHER EARTH!

YES! THE VERY EXISTENCE OF OUR UNIVERSE ITSELF HUNG IN THE BALANCE AS TWO *GREEN-CLAD CRUSADERS*-- *HAL JORDAN* AND *ALAN SCOTT* (THE *GREEN LANTERN* OF *EARTH-TWO* AND OF ANOTHER, BYGONE ERA!) DUELLED WITH MIGHTY *POWER RINGS* IN A TITANIC BATTLE FROM WHICH ONLY *ONE* COULD EMERGE THE VICTOR! WHAT LAY BEHIND THIS SHOCKING, STARTLING COMBAT BETWEEN JUSTICE-LOVING RING-WEARERS? HOW DID IT ALL TIE IN WITH A FORBIDDEN EXPERIMENT TO SOLVE THE RIDDLE OF THE...

SECRET ORIGIN OF THE GUARDIANS!

Story by John Broome
Art by Gil Kane & Sid Greene

AT A "COME AS YOU WERE" PARTY GIVEN BY THE GOTHAM BROADCASTING COMPANY ON EARTH-TWO*...

...THAT'S ALAN SCOTT! HE'S NOW THE PRESIDENT OF GOTHAM BROADCASTING! BUT TWENTY YEARS AGO HE WAS A RADIO ANNOUNCER... SO FOR THE PARTY HE'S PLAYING THAT ROLE AGAIN!

WHAT A FORCEFUL-LOOKING MAN! YOU CAN TELL HE WAS BOUND TO REACH THE TOP!

*EDITOR'S NOTE: EARTH-TWO IS A CONVENIENT DESIGNATION FOR A PARALLEL EARTH IN ANOTHER DIMENSION -- WHERE LIFE, CUSTOMS, LANGUAGES -- EVEN SUPER-HEROES -- EVOLVED SIMILARLY TO THOSE ON EARTH-ONE!

AND THERE'S DOIBY DICKLES! HE'S MR. SCOTT'S MAN FRIDAY NOW! HE USED TO BE A CAB DRIVER -- AND TO FIT IN WITH THE NOSTALGIC SPIRIT OF THE OCCASION, HE TOOK MR. SCOTT HERE IN HIS FAMOUS TAXI CALLED GOITRUDE!

HOW CUTE!

AS THE PARTY BREAKS UP...

GOITRUDE AWAITS YOUSE -- WIT' "SOIVICE DAT DON'T MAKE YOUSE NOIVICE"!

HOW SWELL TO HEAR THAT OLD SLOGAN OF YOURS AGAIN, DOIBY!

TAXI STAND NO PARKING

IT WAS A GREAT IDEA -- RELIVING OUR ROLES OF TWENTY YEARS AGO, eh, DOIBY?

AH -- DEM WAS DA GOOD OLD DAYS, ALAN! YES SIRREE!

THEN, AS NOSTALGIC REMINISCENCES ARE RUDELY INTERRUPTED...

...AND WHAT LOOKS LIKE A SIZEABLE METEOR HAS BEEN SIGHTED OUT IN SPACE... HEADING DIRECTLY FOR GOTHAM CITY! WARNING...

I GET THE MESSAGE, DOIBY!

A DANGEROUS METEOR! WHATCHA WAITIN' FER, PAL?

2

IN THE BACK OF "GOITRUDE" A SWIFT TRANSFORMATION TAKES PLACE...

HURRY, LANTRIN! I T'INK I SEE IT COMIN' DIS WAY!

I'M ALL SET TO GO!

OUT OF THE STILL-ROLLING CAB CATAPULTS A UNIFORMED FIGURE THAT HAS THRILLED MANY A HEART...

THERE IT IS-- STREAKING IN VERY LOW! GOT TO BEAM MY RING ON IT BEFORE IT STRIKES--!

I'LL CATCH UP TO YOUSE, GL--IN CASE MY VALUABLE ASSISTRANCE IS NEEDED!

UNERRINGLY, THE OCCULT POWER BEAM MEETS ITS TARGET! BUT STRANGELY ENOUGH...

IT BLASTED RIGHT THROUGH MY BEAM AND VANISHED!

IN FACT, THE ONLY CRASHING SOUND TO BE HEARD IS...

eh? DOIBY MUST HAVE BEEN WATCHING ME-- AND NOT WHERE HE WAS GOING! HE'S SMACKED INTO A TREE--!

CRASH!

IT MUST HAVE BEEN ROTTEN! HE'S CRACKED IT--GOING TO FALL ON HIM!

YOICKS! GOITRUDE'S IN DANGER! DAT TREE--! HELP, LANTRIN!

CRAACK!

3

167

INSTANTLY, THE GREEN-CLAD CRUSADER RESPONDS TO THE APPEAL...

MY POWER BEAM-- THE TREE WAS DEFLECTED BY IT!

DOIBY, LOOK AT THAT!

HUH? LOOK AT WOT--?

THE TREE WAS DEFLECTED BY MY RING! DIDN'T YOU SEE IT?

IMPOSSIBLE, LANTRIN! YER POWER BEAM HAS NO EFFECT ON ANYTHING MADE O' WOOD -- AND DAT'S A FACK!

ON IMPULSE, GREEN LANTERN TRIES OUT HIS BEAM ON THE TREE ONCE AGAIN...

NO EFFECT, eh? WHAT DO YOU CALL THAT?

IT'S A COCKEYED WONDER, DAT'S WOT IT IS! I DON'T UNDERSTAND!

YOU KNOW WHAT I THINK, DOIBY? IT HAD SOMETHING TO DO WITH THAT METEOR! SOMEHOW, CONTACT WITH THAT METEOR HAS ELIMINATED THE WEAKNESS OF MY RING! IT HAS NO WEAKNESS ANY MORE! THIS IS TOO GOOD TO KEEP TO OURSELVES--

I'VE GOT TO TELL THE GREEN LANTERN OF EARTH-ONE ABOUT THIS! IF THAT METEOR REMOVED THE WEAKNESS OF MY RING, A SIMILAR METEOR-CONTACT ON HIS EARTH MIGHT REMOVE THE WEAKNESS OF HIS RING!*

*EDITOR'S NOTE: DUE TO NECESSARY IMPURITIES IN THE POWER BATTERY, THE EARTH-ONE POWER RING CANNOT AFFECT ANYTHING COLORED YELLOW!

4

GEE, DAT'S MIGHTY BIG OF YOUSE TO T'INK RIGHT AWAY OF HELPIN' YER FRIEND, DA OTHER *GREEN LANTRIN!*

I'M TAKING RIGHT OFF, DOIBY! SEE YOU LATER!

SOON, THE WONDER BEAM IS CLEAVING THE VIBRATORY BARRIER BETWEEN THE *TWO EARTHS*...

I ALWAYS GET A KICK OUT OF VISITING HAL JORDAN, MY COUNTERPART *GREEN LANTERN* ON *EARTH-ONE!* BUT ESPECIALLY NOW WHEN I HAVE EXCITING NEWS TO TELL HIM!

IN DUE COURSE, AT THE *FERRIS AIRCRAFT COMPANY* WHERE TEST PILOT HAL JORDAN IS AT WORK...

I'M GETTING A MENTAL MESSAGE--FROM *GREEN LANTERN OF EARTH-TWO!* HE'S ARRIVED HERE ON OUR EARTH--AND IS WAITING TO SEE ME JUST OUTSIDE THE COMPANY AREA!

IN A CORNER OF THE HANGAR, A SWIFT CHANGE TAKES PLACE--AND A SOLEMN OATH IS RENEWED...

IN BRIGHTEST DAY, IN BLACKEST NIGHT, NO EVIL SHALL ESCAPE MY SIGHT! LET THOSE WHO WORSHIP EVIL'S MIGHT BEWARE MY POWER-- *GREEN LANTERN'S* LIGHT!

SHORTLY, NEARBY, A WARM REUNION...

GOOD TO SEE YOU AGAIN, ALAN!

FINE TO SEE YOU, HAL! WAIT TILL YOU HEAR THE EXCITING NEWS THAT BROUGHT ME HERE!

...AND AS A RESULT OF THAT METEOR, MY RING NOW HAS POWER OVER *WOOD!* WATCH--I'LL RAISE *THAT* WOODEN CRATE--

FERRIS AIRCR

5

BUT THEN, ASTONISHINGLY...

I--I DON'T UNDERSTAND! I--I CAN'T BUDGE THE CRATE -- CAN'T AFFECT IT AT ALL! LOOKS LIKE I'VE MADE SOME KIND OF MISTAKE, HAL...!

I WAS *SURE* MY RING HAD POWER OVER WOOD -- BUT OBVIOUSLY IT DOESN'T HAVE -- ANY LONGER! SO MY VISIT HERE TO TRY AND HELP YOU WAS USELESS! I MIGHT AS WELL GET ON HOME --

NO, WAIT, ALAN! YOUR STORY HAS INTRIGUED ME...

AS *EARTH-ONE'S GREEN GLADIATOR* REFLECTS THOUGHTFULLY...

...A METEOR THAT COMES IN LOW,...AT AN ODD ANGLE! THEN IT SEEMS TO SHOOT RIGHT THROUGH YOUR POWER BEAM AND DIS- APPEAR...! AND AFTER THAT,... YOUR RING SUDDENLY HAS POWER OVER WOOD...WHICH NOW JUST AS SUDDENLY DOESN'T HAVE ANY *MORE*! THIS IS A BIT OF A *MYSTERY*!

ALAN, I HAVE A SUGGESTION! WHY NOT GET YOUR RING TO REVEAL TO US WHAT *REALLY* HAPPENED WHEN IT CON- TACTED THAT METEOR! IT MIGHT ENABLE US TO GET TO THE BOTTOM OF THIS STRANGE OCCURRENCE!

A GOOD IDEA, HAL! GUESS I SHOULD HAVE THOUGHT OF THAT MYSELF!

UNDER A MENTAL COMMAND, THE MYSTIC RING RESPONDS INSTANTLY...

TELL US WHAT REALLY HAPPENED WHEN I TRIED TO STOP THAT METEOR! LEAVE NO DETAILS OUT...!

TO BEGIN WITH....IT WAS *NOT* A METEOR...

"IT WAS REALLY A PACKET OF PURE ENERGY... THAT HAD BEEN CREATED *TEN BILLION YEARS* BEFORE! I KNOW THIS BECAUSE MY BEAM..."

"CONTACTED THE DISEMBODIED MIND, THE EXTRAORDINARY MIND, IN THE ENERGY PACKET, AND ABSORBED THE CONTENTS OF THAT MIND!"

6

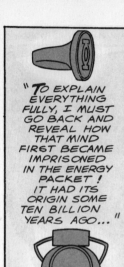

"TO EXPLAIN EVERYTHING FULLY, I MUST GO BACK AND REVEAL HOW THAT MIND FIRST BECAME IMPRISONED IN THE ENERGY PACKET! IT HAD ITS ORIGIN SOME TEN BILLION YEARS AGO..."

"AT WHICH TIME THERE DWELT ON THIS WORLD A RACE DIFFERENT FROM HUMANS WHO CALLED THEMSELVES **OANS**. THEY WERE IMMORTAL, NEVER NEEDED SLEEP OR REST..."

"THEY STRODE THE PLANET LIKE GIANTS..."

"THEIR TREMENDOUS NATURAL POWERS THEY EVINCED OFTEN AT THE EARLIEST AGE..."

LOOK! MY CHILD CAN ALREADY LIFT A GREAT BOULDER BY **MENTAL** FORCE!

VERY GOOD INDEED! MY SON COULD NOT DO THAT UNTIL HE WAS TWICE AS OLD!

"THE ADULTS AMONG THE **OANS** BUSIED THEM- SELVES IN AN ETERNAL STUDY OF NATURE..."

WE STILL DO NOT KNOW THE TRUE ESSENCE OF **LIGHT**! BUT SINCE WE ARE IMMORTAL, WE HAVE ENDLESS TIME TO EXAMINE THE PROBLEM AND ONE DAY PERHAPS WE SHALL SOLVE IT...

"GAMES AND SPORTS ROUNDED OUT THEIR DAY! TRULY IT WAS A KIND OF PARADISE THEY LIVED IN..."

"BUT THERE WAS ONE DISTURBING NOTE IN THIS HARMONY, THAT TROUBLED THE **OAN** ELDERS..."

7

"AMONG THEIR NUMBER WAS ONE NAMED *KRONA* WHOSE THOUGHTS WERE PRIMARILY CONCERNED WITH ONE THING ..."

BY THIS INSTRUMENT OF MY OWN DEVISING I SHALL PROBE THE BEGINNING OF ALL THINGS! NOTHING SHALL BE HIDDEN FROM ME!

KRONA, THERE IS A LEGEND OF TIME-LESS AGE AMONG US...

...THAT IF WE *EVER* LEARNED THE TRUTH ABOUT OUR SECRET ORIGINS, WE AND OUR UNIVERSE WOULD BE INSTANTLY DESTROYED!

BAH! SUCH LEGENDS ARE TALES ONLY FOOLS *WOULD* FEAR!

"DESPITE ALL PLEAS AND URGING, *KRONA* CONTINUED HIS CEASELESS LABORS, AND ONE DAY ..."

AN IMAGE FORMING--!? A SHADOW LIKE A GIANT HAND ... WITH SOMETHING ... A CLUSTER OF STARS IN IT--! I MUST GO BACK FURTHER-- FURTHER--!

"THEN..."

YAAH--!

CK RACK

"THE TERRIBLE COSMIC LIGHTNING BOLT SPLINTERED THE MACHINE! IT WOULD HAVE DE-STROYED *KRONA* TOO HAD HE NOT BEEN IMMORTAL!"

"BUT FROM THAT MOMENT ON, *EVIL* WAS LOOSED ON THE UNIVERSE! IT SWIFTLY SPREAD FROM WORLD TO WORLD WHERE INTELLIGENT CREATURES LIVED WHO HAD NOT THE GIFT OF IMMORTALITY LIKE THE *OANS* ..."

KILL... KILL!

"BROTHER KILLED BROTHER! HATRED AND VIOLENCE GREW, FLOURISHED! AND THE *OANS*, BY THEIR SUPER-MENTALITY, KNEW IT HAD ALL BEEN CAUSED BY *KRONA'S* INSATIABLE AMBITION!"

⑧

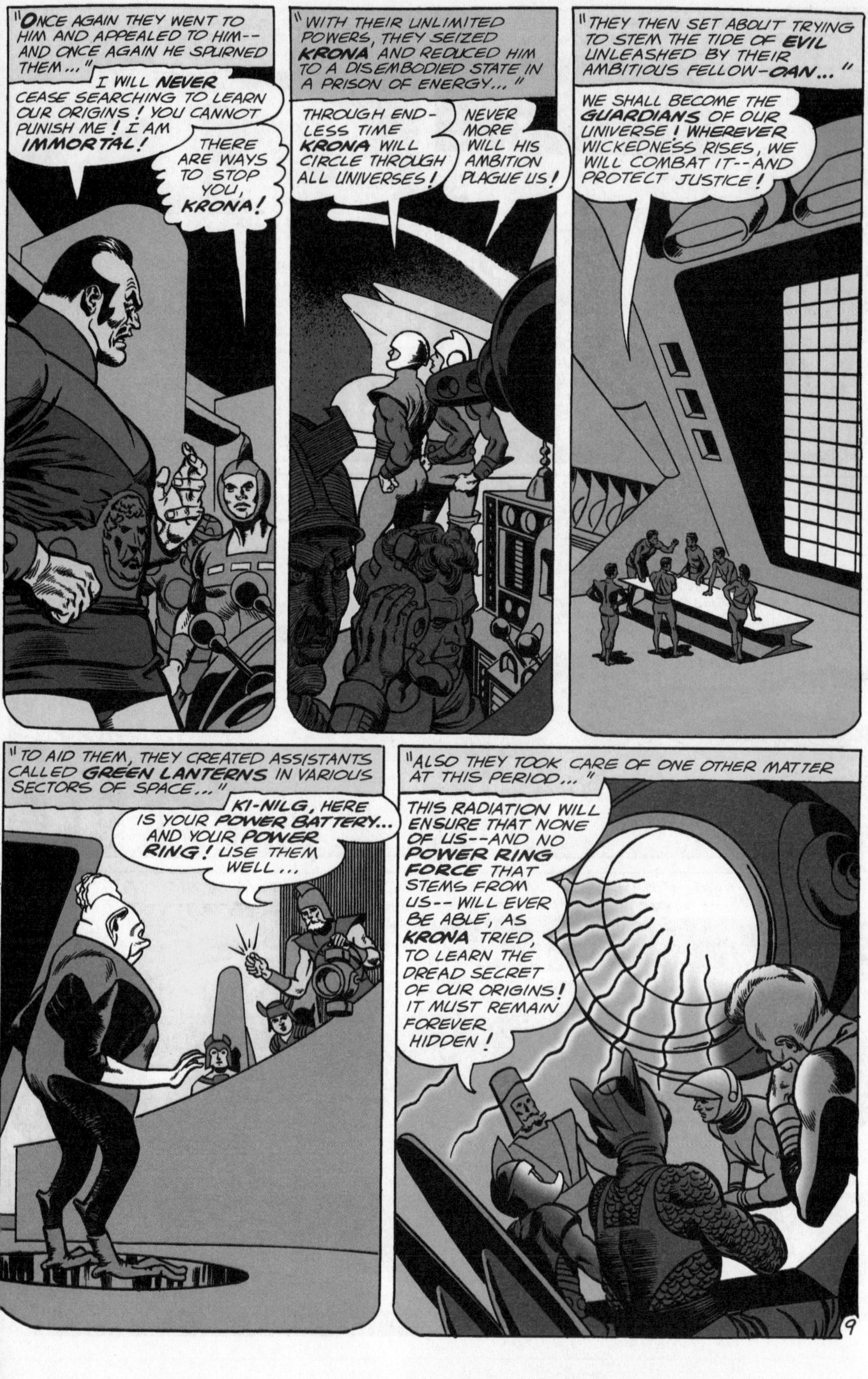
"ONCE AGAIN THEY WENT TO HIM AND APPEALED TO HIM-- AND ONCE AGAIN HE SPURNED THEM..."
I WILL NEVER CEASE SEARCHING TO LEARN OUR ORIGINS! YOU CANNOT PUNISH ME! I AM IMMORTAL!
THERE ARE WAYS TO STOP YOU, KRONA!
"WITH THEIR UNLIMITED POWERS, THEY SEIZED KRONA AND REDUCED HIM TO A DISEMBODIED STATE IN A PRISON OF ENERGY..."
THROUGH END-LESS TIME KRONA WILL CIRCLE THROUGH ALL UNIVERSES!
NEVER MORE WILL HIS AMBITION PLAGUE US!
"THEY THEN SET ABOUT TRYING TO STEM THE TIDE OF EVIL UNLEASHED BY THEIR AMBITIOUS FELLOW-OAN..."
WE SHALL BECOME THE GUARDIANS OF OUR UNIVERSE! WHEREVER WICKEDNESS RISES, WE WILL COMBAT IT--AND PROTECT JUSTICE!
"TO AID THEM, THEY CREATED ASSISTANTS CALLED GREEN LANTERNS IN VARIOUS SECTORS OF SPACE..."
KI-NILG, HERE IS YOUR POWER BATTERY... AND YOUR POWER RING! USE THEM WELL...
"ALSO THEY TOOK CARE OF ONE OTHER MATTER AT THIS PERIOD..."
THIS RADIATION WILL ENSURE THAT NONE OF US--AND NO POWER RING FORCE THAT STEMS FROM US-- WILL EVER BE ABLE, AS KRONA TRIED, TO LEARN THE DREAD SECRET OF OUR ORIGINS! IT MUST REMAIN FOREVER HIDDEN!
9

"AS THE EONS PASSED, THE *OANS* EVOLVED, AS A FORM OF AGING, INTO THE *GUARDIANS* AS YOU KNOW THEM NOW..."

"LONG BEFORE, THEY HAD FORGOTTEN *KRONA* TRAVELING THROUGH ENDLESS UNIVERSES IN HIS ENERGY-PRISON..."

"BUT *KRONA*, STILL ALIVE AND STILL POSSESSED OF HIS TREMENDOUS *MIND*, HAD NEVER GIVEN UP SCHEMING TO FREE HIMSELF!"

"STILL BATTLING EVIL AND AIDING ALL CREATURES OF GOOD WILL!"

"RECENTLY TRAVERSING THE UNIVERSE OF *EARTH-TWO*, HIS RESTLESS DIABOLIC MENTALITY DETECTED THE LONG HOPED-FOR OPPORTUNITY..."

ON THIS APPROACHING PLANET... A CRUSADER CALLED *GREEN LANTERN* WITH A *POWER RING* FILLED WITH *OCCULT ENERGY*! IT IS POSSIBLE... THERE IS A CHANCE... THAT I CAN MAKE USE OF HIM TO GAIN MY FREEDOM...

"BY SHEER MIND-FORCE, *KRONA* INCREASED THE HEAT IN THE ENERGY-PACKET UNTIL IT GLOWED LIKE A METEOR..."

WARNING! A METEOR FALLING FROM SPACE! IT WILL LAND IN *GOTHAM CITY*! WARNING!

MY SCHEME IS WORKING--!

"YOU, TOO, BELIEVED IT WAS A METEOR! YOU FLARED OUT MY BEAM TO STOP IT, TO PREVENT DAMAGE..."

"BUT WHAT YOU DIDN'T REALIZE WAS THAT AT THE MOMENT OF CONTACT..."

"...THE BODILESS IMMORTAL MIND OF *KRONA*--BY A PRODIGIOUS FEAT OF THE WILL--STRUGGLED FREE OF THE ENERGY-PACKET AND PASSED DOWN MY MYSTIC BEAM..."

AFTER TEN BILLION YEARS-- FREE!!

10

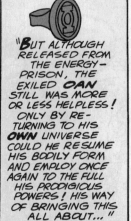

"*BUT ALTHOUGH RELEASED FROM THE ENERGY-PRISON, THE EXILED OAN STILL WAS MORE OR LESS HELPLESS! ONLY BY RETURNING TO HIS OWN UNIVERSE COULD HE RESUME HIS BODILY FORM AND EMPLOY ONCE AGAIN TO THE FULL HIS PRODIGIOUS POWERS! HIS WAY OF BRINGING THIS ALL ABOUT...*"

"*...WAS TO ENABLE YOU, ALAN SCOTT, TEMPORARILY TO HAVE CONTROL OVER WOODEN OBJECTS!*"

MY RING -- LIFTING THIS WOODEN FENCE --!

"*HE ANTICIPATED THAT YOU WOULD IMMEDIATELY THINK OF HELPING YOUR FRIEND, THE GREEN LANTERN OF EARTH-ONE..*"

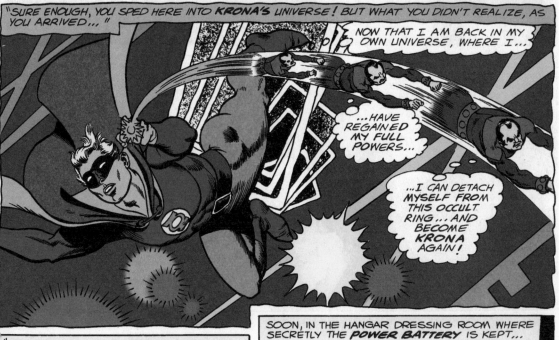

"*SURE ENOUGH, YOU SPED HERE INTO KRONA'S UNIVERSE! BUT WHAT YOU DIDN'T REALIZE, AS YOU ARRIVED...*"

NOW THAT I AM BACK IN MY OWN UNIVERSE, WHERE I...

...HAVE REGAINED MY FULL POWERS...

...I CAN DETACH MYSELF FROM THIS OCCULT RING... AND BECOME KRONA AGAIN!

"*I THEREUPON LOST CONTACT WITH HIM AND CAN GIVE NO MORE INFORMATION...*"

ALAN, THE FIRST THING I MUST DO IS NOTIFY THE GUARDIANS -- WARN THEM OF WHAT HAS HAPPENED! AFTER THAT I MUST FIND KRONA!

WE MUST FIND KRONA! AFTER ALL, I'M RESPONSIBLE FOR HIS BEING HERE!

SOON, IN THE HANGAR DRESSING ROOM WHERE SECRETLY THE POWER BATTERY IS KEPT...

I'VE CONTACTED THE GUARDIANS -- eh?

YES! WE ALREADY KNOW WHAT YOU WANT TO TELL US, GREEN LANTERN! WE TOO LISTENED IN ON THE ACCOUNT OF YOUR FRIEND'S RING! THE SITUATION IS GRAVE! IT REQUIRES EMERGENCY ACTION!

KRONA IS SOMEWHERE ON *EARTH!* BUT HE HAS SET UP MENTAL DEFENSES TO PREVENT OUR DISCOVERING HIS EXACT LOCATION! UNDOUBTEDLY HE WILL SEEK AGAIN TO PROBE THE FORBIDDEN SECRET OF OUR ORIGINS! THIS COULD RESULT...

...IN THE INSTANTANEOUS DESTRUCTION OF THE UNIVERSE! OUR CALCULATIONS SHOW THAT THE *FIRST RESULTS* OF HIS MAD EFFORTS WILL BE A TERRIBLE OUTPOURING OF EVIL IN HIS IMMEDIATE VICINITY! THAT MEANS...

...THAT YOUR *EARTH* IS IN THE UTMOST DANGER! WE SHALL ARRIVE THERE AS SOON AS POSSIBLE TO SET UP A TEMPORARY HEADQUARTERS! MEANWHILE, USE YOUR RING, DO ALL IN YOUR POWER TO AVERT DISASTER...

I UNDERSTAND!

WE UNDERSTAND, HAL! WE'RE TOGETHER IN THIS -- COME WHAT MAY!

CRISIS
ON MULTIPLE EARTHS
THE TEAM UPS

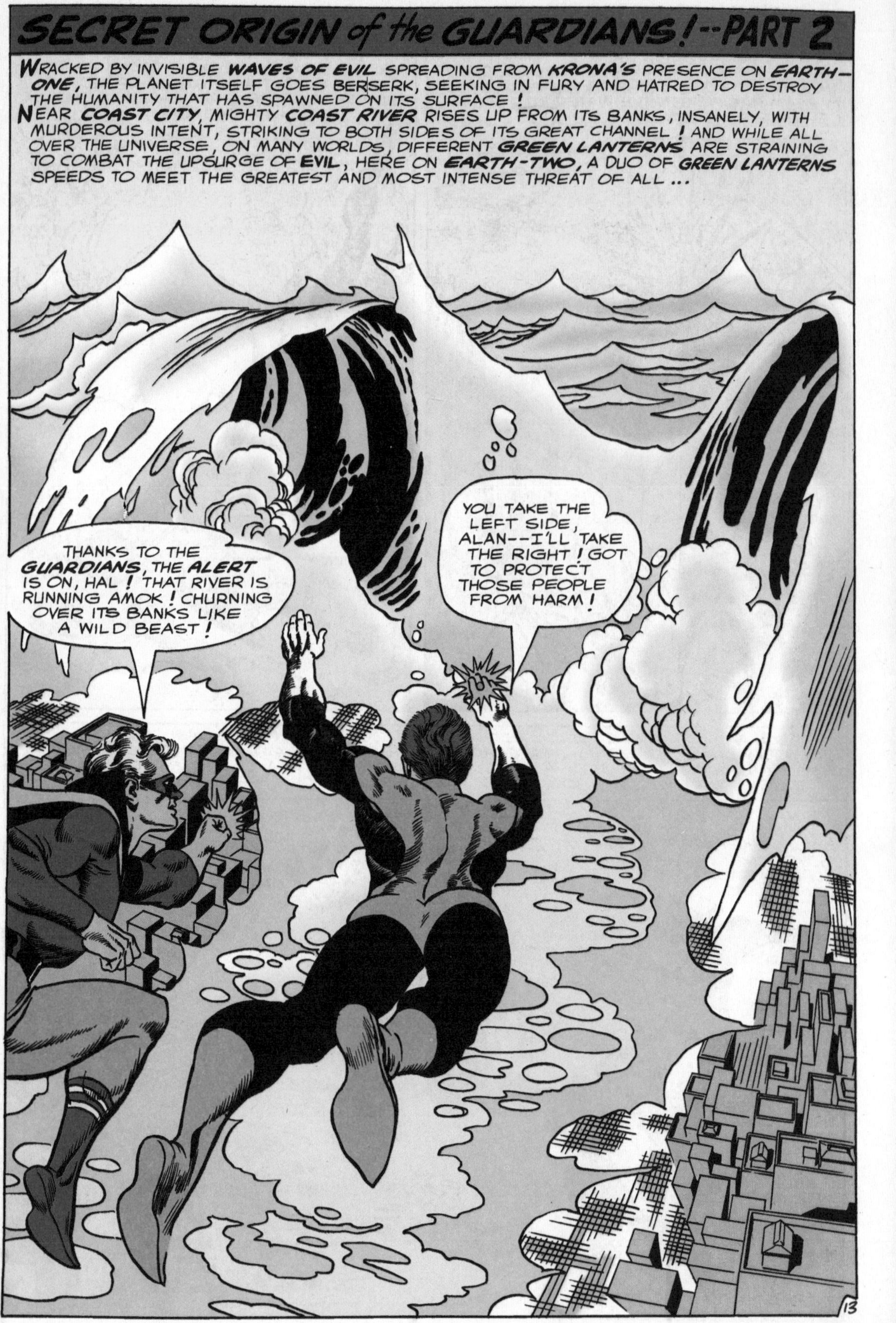
SECRET ORIGIN of the GUARDIANS! --PART 2
WRACKED BY INVISIBLE WAVES OF EVIL SPREADING FROM KRONA'S PRESENCE ON EARTH-ONE, THE PLANET ITSELF GOES BERSERK, SEEKING IN FURY AND HATRED TO DESTROY THE HUMANITY THAT HAS SPAWNED ON ITS SURFACE!
NEAR COAST CITY, MIGHTY COAST RIVER RISES UP FROM ITS BANKS, INSANELY, WITH MURDEROUS INTENT, STRIKING TO BOTH SIDES OF ITS GREAT CHANNEL! AND WHILE ALL OVER THE UNIVERSE, ON MANY WORLDS, DIFFERENT GREEN LANTERNS ARE STRAINING TO COMBAT THE UPSURGE OF EVIL, HERE ON EARTH-TWO, A DUO OF GREEN LANTERNS SPEEDS TO MEET THE GREATEST AND MOST INTENSE THREAT OF ALL...
THANKS TO THE GUARDIANS, THE ALERT IS ON, HAL! THAT RIVER IS RUNNING AMOK! CHURNING OVER ITS BANKS LIKE A WILD BEAST!
YOU TAKE THE LEFT SIDE, ALAN--I'LL TAKE THE RIGHT! GOT TO PROTECT THOSE PEOPLE FROM HARM!
13

AT ONCE THE VISITING *GREEN LANTERN* OF *EARTH-TWO* BURSTS INTO ACTION, TRAINING HIS MIGHTY RING AT THE RAGING WATERS...

WHILE ON THE OTHER SIDE OF THE RIVER...

WAVES LIKE ENORMOUS PINCERS--TRYING TO CRUSH THOSE PEOPLE! BUT MY BEAM HAS FROZEN THE WATER INTO SOLID ICE--STOPPED IT *COLD!*

MY RING IS CREATING HUGE ATOMIC OVENS INSIDE THE WAVES--TURNING THE WATER INTO STEAM--AS FAST AS IT COMES UP FROM ITS BED! THOSE PEOPLE ARE SAFE FOR THE TIME BEING--!

AND SOON AFTER, ANOTHER DREAD SPECTACLE ENGAGES THE TWIN RING-WIELDERS! FOR *MOUNT PACIFIC,* TOWERING OVER *COAST CITY,* HAS THRUST A HUGE TONGUE OF ITSELF UPWARD--LIKE THE TONGUE OF A HUGE SLAVERING WOLF!--AND A WEIGHT OF MILLIONS OF TONS OF EARTH WHIRLS TOWARD THE HELPLESS METROPOLIS--!

THE MOUNTAIN IS BENDING OVER--LIKE SOMETHING *ALIVE!* HURTLING TOWARD THE CITY!

IT'S SPROUTED LIKE A GIGANTIC ONION-- AND THE TOP PART ELONGATED-- WHIRLING-- LIKE A HUGE WHIP--TOWARD THOSE BUILD-INGS! AT IT, ALAN, WITH FULL POWER!

14

AS TWIN GREEN BEAMS SWIFTLY FORM COLOSSAL IMPLEMENTS TO ATTACK THE HUGE "WHIP" AND HALT ITS MAD THRUST AT HUMANITY...

ALAN HAS FORMED AN ENORMOUS *SAW* WITH HIS RING -- SLICING THROUGH THE MENACE --!

HAL'S BEAM HAS CREATED A MAMMOTH RIVETING MACHINE -- JOLTING THE "TONGUE" TO PIECES --!

DEFEATED, THE MOUNTAIN SEEMS TO WITHDRAW INTO ITSELF, AS IF TO LICK ITS WOUNDS ...

WE BEAT IT! THE MOUNTAIN IS SHRINKING BACK --!

MOTHER NATURE'S NOT CALLING IT QUITS YET, ALAN! LOOK -- THAT *CLOUD*!

ANGRY CLOUDS, FLOATING TOGETHER, HAVE FORMED AN AERIAL WHIRLPOOL, REVOLVING AT INCREDIBLE SPEED,...

THE TORNADO-LIKE CLOUD -- WHIPPING UP TERRIFIC WINDS!

IF IT STRIKES THE CITY, IT WILL LEVEL IT IN MOMENTS --!

INSTANTLY, THE GREEN-CLAD SENTINELS ARE ON THE MOVE, SEEDING THE WHIRLING CLOUD WITH *SILVER IODIDE* CRYSTALS FORMED BY THEIR REMARKABLE RINGS...

THE CLOUD MATTER IS CON- DENSING AROUND THE SILVER IODIDE CRYSTALS CREATED BY OUR BEAMS AND TURNING INTO *RAIN*!

THE RAIN IS FALLING IN TORRENTS -- BUT AT LEAST IT WON'T HARM ANYONE THIS WAY!

15

179

THEN, SUDDENLY...

ALAN! ONE OF THE *GUARDIANS* -- APPEARING BEFORE US!

PAY HEED! WE HAVE ARRIVED ON THIS PLANET AND HAVE SET UP A TEMPORARY HEADQUARTERS! YOU MUST JOIN US AT ONCE -- TO PLAN OUR BATTLE AGAINST *KRONA!*

YOU NEED NO LONGER FEAR THE OUTPOURING OF EVIL! OUR PRESENCES HERE ARE ENOUGH TO HOLD IN CHECK THE WAVES OF EVIL CAUSED BY *KRONA!* FOLLOW MY IMAGE -- IT WILL LEAD YOU TO US!

SOON, AN UNEXPECTED DEVELOPMENT AT THE *GUARDIANS'* TEMPORARY HEADQUARTERS, AN UNUSED COURTROOM IN *COAST CITY*...

TURN IN YOUR *POWER RING* AND *UNIFORM,* HAL JORDAN! ALAN SCOTT IS REPLACING YOU AS *GREEN LANTERN* OF EARTH!

WHAT?!

I'VE DONE EVERYTHING YOU'VE EVER ASKED ME! I'VE NEVER SHIRKED A DUTY! I'VE SUFFERED AND FOUGHT -- AND NOW YOU SUDDENLY TAKE AWAY MY STATUS AS *GREEN LANTERN* -- AND GIVE IT TO *ALAN SCOTT?* WHY?

WHY?

WHY?

16

SECRET ORIGIN of the GUARDIANS! --PART 3

HAL JORDAN DISPOSED AS **GREEN LANTERN**--! WHAT COULD ACCOUNT FOR THIS SHOCK-ING SWITCH ON THE PART OF THE **GUARDIANS**? TO UNDERSTAND, LET US ONCE AGAIN TURN BACK THE CLOCK A SHORT WHILE--TO THE INCREDIBLE **KRONA**, BLACK SHEEP OF THE IMMORTAL **OAN** RACE, INTENT ON HIS REVENGE AGAINST HIS FELLOW **OANS**-- NOW KNOWN AS THE **GUARDIANS** -- IN A CAVE OUTSIDE **COAST CITY** WHERE HE HAS SET UP A FANTASTIC WORKSHOP...

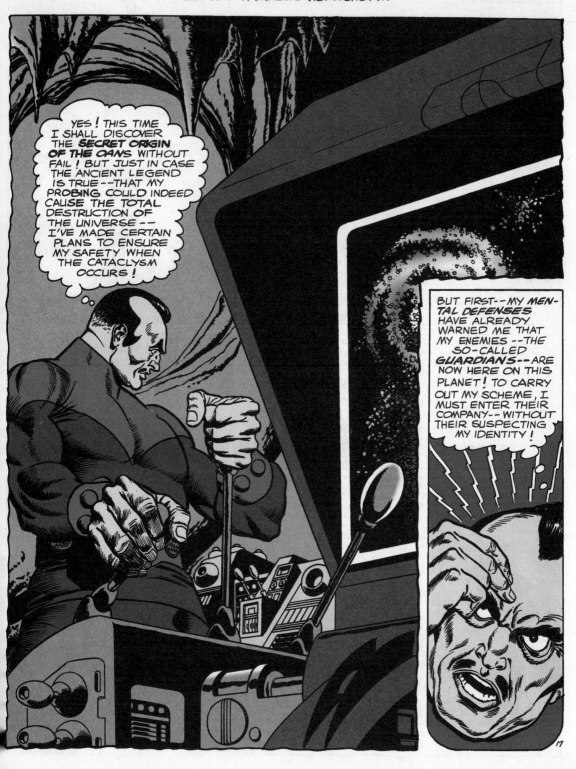

YES! THIS TIME I SHALL DISCOVER THE **SECRET ORIGIN OF THE OANS** WITHOUT FAIL! BUT JUST IN CASE THE ANCIENT LEGEND IS TRUE--THAT MY PROBING COULD INDEED CAUSE THE TOTAL DESTRUCTION OF THE UNIVERSE -- I'VE MADE CERTAIN PLANS TO ENSURE MY SAFETY WHEN THE CATACLYSM OCCURS!

BUT FIRST-- MY **MENTAL DEFENSES** HAVE ALREADY WARNED ME THAT MY ENEMIES --THE SO-CALLED **GUARDIANS**--ARE NOW HERE ON THIS PLANET! TO CARRY OUT MY SCHEME, I MUST ENTER THEIR COMPANY-- WITHOUT THEIR SUSPECTING MY IDENTITY!

USING HIS STUPENDOUS MENTAL CONTROL OVER MATTER, THE RENEGADE *OAN* REDUCED HIMSELF ONCE MORE TO AN ENERGY STATE, AND...

IT WAS EASY ENOUGH TO LOCATE THESE TWO *GREEN LANTERNS*... BY TUNING IN ON THE SPECIAL VIBRATIONS GIVEN OFF BY THEIR *POWER BEAMS!*...

THEN, AT BLINDING SPEED, INVISIBLY, A STARTLING EVENT OCCURRED...

I'M TAKING OVER THE BODY OF THE ONE CALLED *ALAN SCOTT!* I HAVE URGENT NEED FOR HIS BODY!... AT THE SAME TIME I'M EJECTING HIS MIND-- FOR WHICH I HAVE NO NEED...!

THUS *KRONA* GAINED HIS INITIAL OBJECTIVE: CLOSE PROXIMITY TO THE GUARDIANS WITHOUT AROUSING THEIR SUSPICIONS...

FROM THIS SHORT DISTANCE... I'M ABLE TO CAST AN UNBREAKABLE SPELL OVER THE *GUARDIANS!* FROM NOW ON, THEY'LL DO WHAT *I* MENTALLY COMMAND THEM--!

THUS IT WAS UNDER THE EVIL *OAN'S* SINISTER INFLUENCE THAT THE *PROTECTORS OF THE UNIVERSE* ISSUED THEIR STARTLING ORDER...

TURN IN YOUR *POWER RING* AND *UNIFORM*, HAL JORDAN! ALAN SCOTT IS REPLACING YOU AS *GREEN LANTERN OF EARTH!*

WHAT?!

BUT NOW TO PICK UP OUR NARRATIVE AGAIN FROM THE POINT WHERE WE LEFT IT...

AS A STUNNED HAL JORDAN REACTS VIOLENTLY...

NOTHING DOING! THE ONLY WAY I'LL QUIT IS IF SCOTT CAN BEAT ME IN A *GREEN LANTERN* DUEL! AND I'M CHALLENGING HIM TO TAKE ME ON RIGHT NOW!

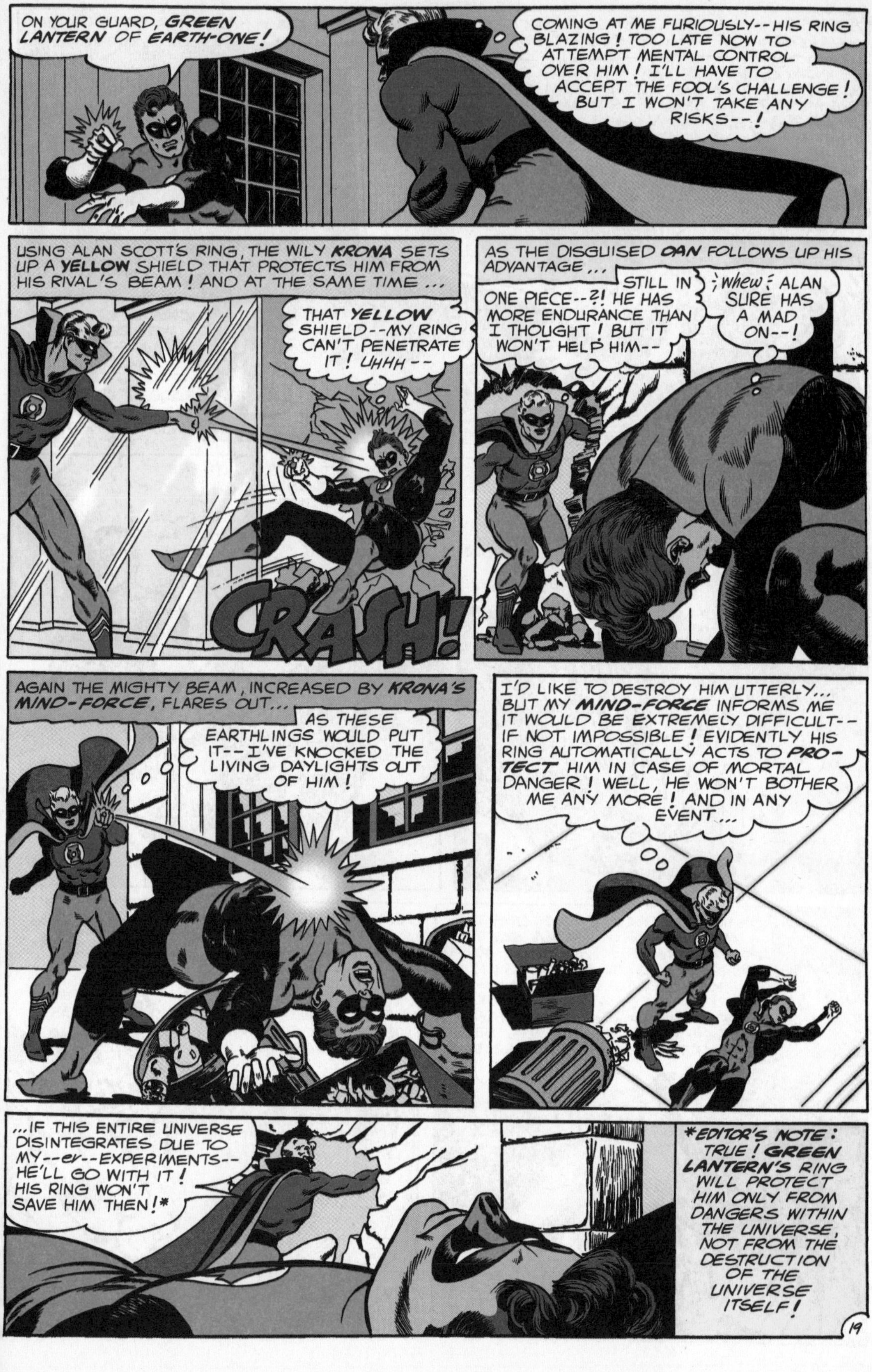
ON YOUR GUARD, GREEN LANTERN OF EARTH-ONE!
COMING AT ME FURIOUSLY--HIS RING BLAZING! TOO LATE NOW TO ATTEMPT MENTAL CONTROL OVER HIM! I'LL HAVE TO ACCEPT THE FOOL'S CHALLENGE! BUT I WON'T TAKE ANY RISKS--!
USING ALAN SCOTT'S RING, THE WILY KRONA SETS UP A YELLOW SHIELD THAT PROTECTS HIM FROM HIS RIVAL'S BEAM! AND AT THE SAME TIME...
THAT YELLOW SHIELD--MY RING CAN'T PENETRATE IT! UHHH--
CRASH!
AS THE DISGUISED OAN FOLLOWS UP HIS ADVANTAGE...
STILL IN ONE PIECE--?! HE HAS MORE ENDURANCE THAN I THOUGHT! BUT IT WON'T HELP HIM--
;whew; ALAN SURE HAS A MAD ON--!
AGAIN THE MIGHTY BEAM, INCREASED BY KRONA'S MIND-FORCE, FLARES OUT...
AS THESE EARTHLINGS WOULD PUT IT--I'VE KNOCKED THE LIVING DAYLIGHTS OUT OF HIM!
I'D LIKE TO DESTROY HIM UTTERLY... BUT MY MIND-FORCE INFORMS ME IT WOULD BE EXTREMELY DIFFICULT--IF NOT IMPOSSIBLE! EVIDENTLY HIS RING AUTOMATICALLY ACTS TO PROTECT HIM IN CASE OF MORTAL DANGER! WELL, HE WON'T BOTHER ME ANY MORE! AND IN ANY EVENT...
...IF THIS ENTIRE UNIVERSE DISINTEGRATES DUE TO MY--er--EXPERIMENTS--HE'LL GO WITH IT! HIS RING WON'T SAVE HIM THEN!*
*EDITOR'S NOTE: TRUE! GREEN LANTERN'S RING WILL PROTECT HIM ONLY FROM DANGERS WITHIN THE UNIVERSE, NOT FROM THE DESTRUCTION OF THE UNIVERSE ITSELF!
19

AND SOON, IN THE CAVE OUTSIDE *COAST CITY* WHERE THE *EVIL OAN* HAS TRANSPORTED HIS *GUARDIAN* CAPTIVES BY MIND-POWER...

WE KNOW NOW IT IS THE MIND OF *KRONA* THAT HAS US IN THRALL!

YES! BUT WE ARE HELPLESS TO BREAK LOOSE FROM THE EVIL SPELL HE MANAGED TO THROW OVER US WHILE IN DISGUISE--!

NOW, MY FELLOW *OANS*, YOU SHALL WITNESS MY ULTIMATE TRIUMPH..! NOT ONLY WILL I EXPOSE OUR *SECRET ORIGIN*-- BUT I SHALL DO IT RIGHT IN FRONT OF YOUR EYES!

THAT WAY, MY PLEASURE IN BREAKING THE ONE GREAT FORBIDDEN RULE OF OUR RACE WILL BE INFINITELY INCREASED-- BY YOUR TERROR AND FEAR WHEN IT HAPPENS!

THEN...

BUT FIRST... TO RE-ENTER MY OWN BODY...

...THERE IS NO LONGER ANY REASON...

...FOR DIS-GUISING MYSELF!

BY MENTAL FORCE I HAVE CREATED A *DUPLICATE* OF *ALAN SCOTT'S POWER RING*! THIS IS OF *VITAL IMPORTANCE* IN MY PLANS! IT IS THE KEY DEVICE I MUST USE TO SPIRIT MYSELF AWAY FROM HARM-- IN CASE OUR ANCIENT LEGEND REALLY COMES TRUE-- AND THIS UNIVERSE STARTS TO DISINTEGRATE!

FOR YOU SEE, THIS *POWER RING* IS *NOT* OF *THIS* UNIVERSE--AND WILL *NOT* BE AFFECTED BY ITS COLLAPSE! IT WILL AUTOMATICALLY BEAR ME TO SAFETY--TO THE UNIVERSE OF *EARTH-TWO!* CUNNING--AM I NOT?

20

THEN, BEFORE THE HORRIFIED EYES OF THE *GUARDIANS*, POWERLESS TO MOVE...TO INTER-FERE WITH THEIR EX-COLLEAGUE'S SINISTER PLAN...

THIS TIME NO COSMIC LIGHTNING BOLT WILL HALT MY ATTEMPT! I HAVE SHIELDED MY WORK-SHOP HERE FROM ANY SUCH ACCIDENT!

THERE..! AGAIN...THE FORMLESS HAND-LIKE CLOUD...THE STARRY NEBULA!... BUT I MUST GO BACK FURTHER...TO THE BEGINNING...TO OUR VERY ORIGIN!...

MEANWHILE...

...HAL...WAKE UP...YOU MUST LISTEN TO ME...!

ALAN SCOTT...CON-TACTING ME TELE-PATHICALLY..!

QUESTINGLY, THE *POWER BEAM* FLARES OUT AND...

ALAN!

KRONA TOOK OVER MY BODY! AND HE'S TAKEN CONTROL OF THE *GUARDIANS* TOO! I'VE BEEN SEARCHING FOR YOU! LISTEN--THERE'S HARDLY ANY TIME LEFT--

AS THE BODILESS HERO REVEALS TO HIS COMRADE-IN-ARMS THE DUPLICITY OF *KRONA* AND ALL THAT HAS OCCURRED...

I KNOW ALL THIS, HAL, BECAUSE IN THIS DISEMBODIED STATE MY MIND HAS WIDE TELEPATHIC POWERS--! YOU MUST STOP *KRONA*!

ALAN'S WARNING--GIVING ME STRENGTH TO CARRY ON THE FIGHT AGAINST *KRONA*! I SURE COULD USE HIS HELP!

SUMMONING UP ALL MY WILL POWER, ALAN--TO COMMAND MY RING TO ABSORB YOUR MIND INTO MY OWN BRAIN--! THAT WAY WE CAN BATTLE *KRONA* TOGETHER!

I'LL GUIDE YOU TO HIM!

AS THE DOUBLE-MINDED *GREEN LANTERN* FLIES OFF TO CONTACT *KRONA*...

FANTASTIC LIGHTNING--! THE SKY GROWING DARK--!

HURRY! DOOMSDAY IS ALMOST UPON US!

2I

As a timely arrival interrupts the **EVIL OAN'S** hour of triumph...

IN ANOTHER MOMENT I'LL KNOW THE SECRET-- eh? THAT **GREEN LANTERN** AGAIN-- BLUNDERING IN ON ME!

AT HIM, HAL!

HERE GOES, ALAN--!

Bah! IT IS ALMOST **TOO** EASY TO DEFEAT HIM! A MERE MATTER OF INSTANTLY ERECTING A YELLOW BARRIER BEFORE ME-- THAT HIS POWER BEAM CANNOT PIERCE--

--WHILE AT THE SAME INSTANT I SHOOT A BURST OF THIS RING'S OVERWHELMING POWER AT HIM-- **UH**--

OUR PLAN'S WORKING!

To HIS STUNNED AMAZEMENT, THINGS DON'T GO QUITE ACCORDING TO PLAN FOR **KRONA**...

WE'VE SENT HIM REELING! PRESS ON, HAL-- DON'T GIVE HIM TIME TO **RECOVER**!

HOW CAN I MISS-- WITH ALAN ROOTING ME ON!

BUT EVEN THOUGH STRICKEN, THE **EVIL OAN** IS STILL PLENTY DANGEROUS...

A COSMIC LIGHTNING BOLT WILL FLATTEN HIM--!

SOMETHING COMING FROM HIS **MIND**-- WITH TREMENDOUS POWERS!

22

AGAIN THE GRIM GLADIATOR IS HURLED BACKWARD...

HAL! HAL!

RELAX, PAL--HE HASN'T WON YET! LISTEN-- WHEN I GIVE THE SIGNAL-- ADD *YOUR* WILL POWER TO MINE! GIVE IT ALL YOU'VE GOT!

THEN, AS THE STEEL-LIKE STRENGTH OF WILL OF BOTH HEROES COMBINES WITH SHATTERING EFFECT AGAINST THEIR FOE...

WE'VE KNOCKED HIM DOWN! WEAKENED HIM-- DAZED HIM!

WHAM!

AT THAT INSTANT, WITH *KRONA'S* CONCENTRATION BROKEN, HIS OMNIPOTENT ENEMIES, THE *GUARDIANS*, BURST LOOSE FROM THRALL...

FIRST WE DESTROY THE DIABOLIC DEVICE THAT THREATENED OUR FORBIDDEN SECRET...

CRACK

THEN WE DEAL WITH YOU, *KRONA*--!

I'M WEAK...IN YOUR POWER...BUT I *STILL* DEFY YOU!

YOUR DEFIANCE CANNOT HELP YOU NOW!

SHORTLY... WE HAVE ONCE AGAIN REDUCED *KRONA* TO AN ENERGY-FORM! BUT THIS TIME WE HAVE SENT HIM OFF ON AN ORBIT THAT WILL *NEVER* IN- TERSECT ANY PLANET OR STAR! NEVER AGAIN WILL HE BE ABLE TO FREE HIMSELF--OR THREATEN ANY UNIVERSE!

23

LATER, AFTER THE GUARDIANS HAVE RETURNED TO OA AND GREEN LANTERN'S RING HAS REPLACED ALAN SCOTT'S MIND IN HIS OWN BODY...
THE IDEA OF SWITCHING POWER RINGS--SO THAT I HAD ON THE RING FROM YOUR BODY INSTEAD OF MY OWN--WAS AN INSPIRATION, ALAN!
YES, IT GAVE US THE ADVANTAGE OF SURPRISE, HAL--WHEN MY RING'S BEAM PIERCED KRONA'S YELLOW ENERGY—SHIELD!
THAT TRICK SURE SAVED THE DAY! BUT--WHOSE IDEA WAS IT, YOURS OR MINE? YOU KNOW, I CAN'T RECALL--!
WHAT DIFFERENCE DOES IT MAKE? WE WERE BOTH IN THE SAME BRAIN!
SO I GUESS WE CAN BOTH TAKE THE CREDIT! AND NOW, I'VE GOT TO GET BACK TO MY OWN EARTH! SO LONG, HAL!
'BY, ALAN! THANKS--THANKS FOR THE TERRIFIC TEAM-WORK!
AS A WEARY GREEN LANTERN OF EARTH--DRAWS A DEEP BREATH...
THE SUN IS SHINING NOW--AND ALL IS PEACEFUL! HOW BEAUTIFUL EVERYTHING IS NOW THAT THE MENACE IS OVER! I CAN ONLY HOPE IT STAYS THAT WAY--AND THAT KRONA NEVER GETS LOOSE TO SPREAD EVIL AND TERROR AGAIN..!
The End
24

CRISIS ON MULTIPLE EARTHS THE TEAM UPS

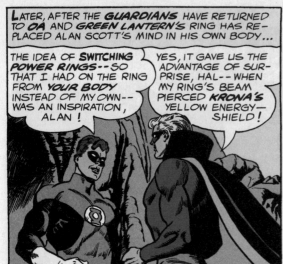

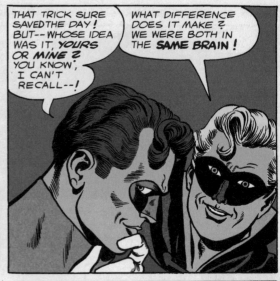

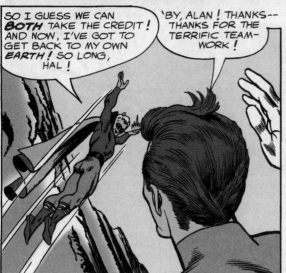

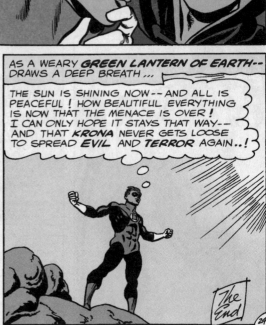

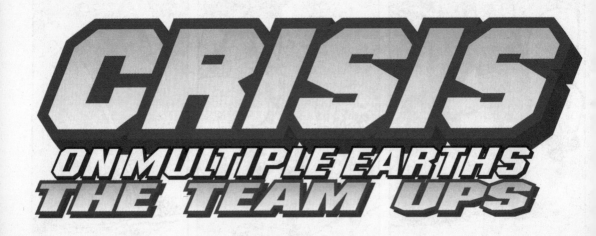

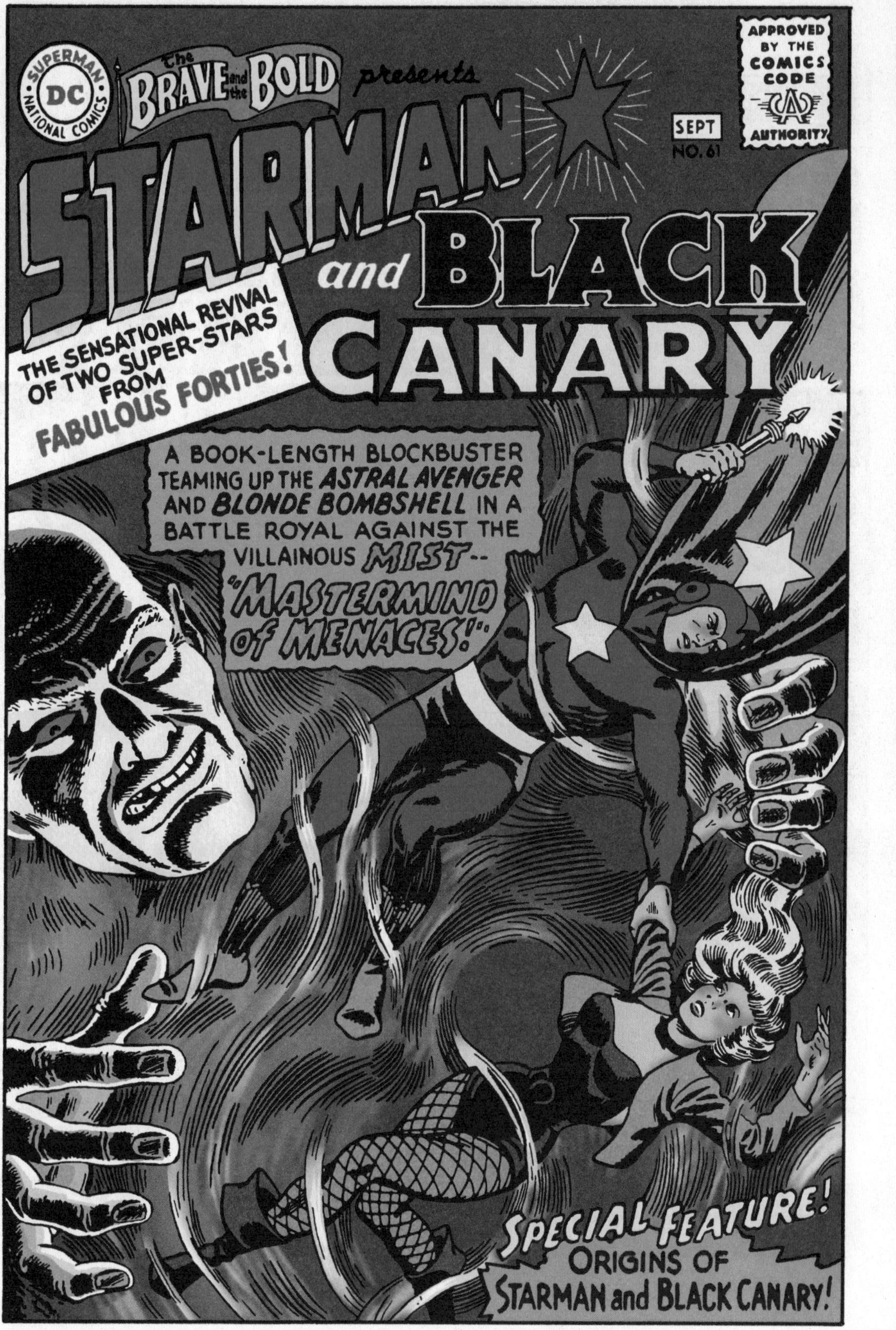
SUPERMAN DC NATIONAL COMICS
The BRAVE and the BOLD presents
APPROVED BY THE COMICS CODE AUTHORITY
SEPT NO. 61
STARMAN and BLACK CANARY
THE SENSATIONAL REVIVAL OF TWO SUPER-STARS FROM FABULOUS FORTIES!
A BOOK-LENGTH BLOCKBUSTER TEAMING UP THE ASTRAL AVENGER AND BLONDE BOMBSHELL IN A BATTLE ROYAL AGAINST THE VILLAINOUS MIST-- "MASTERMIND of MENACES!"
SPECIAL FEATURE! ORIGINS OF STARMAN and BLACK CANARY!

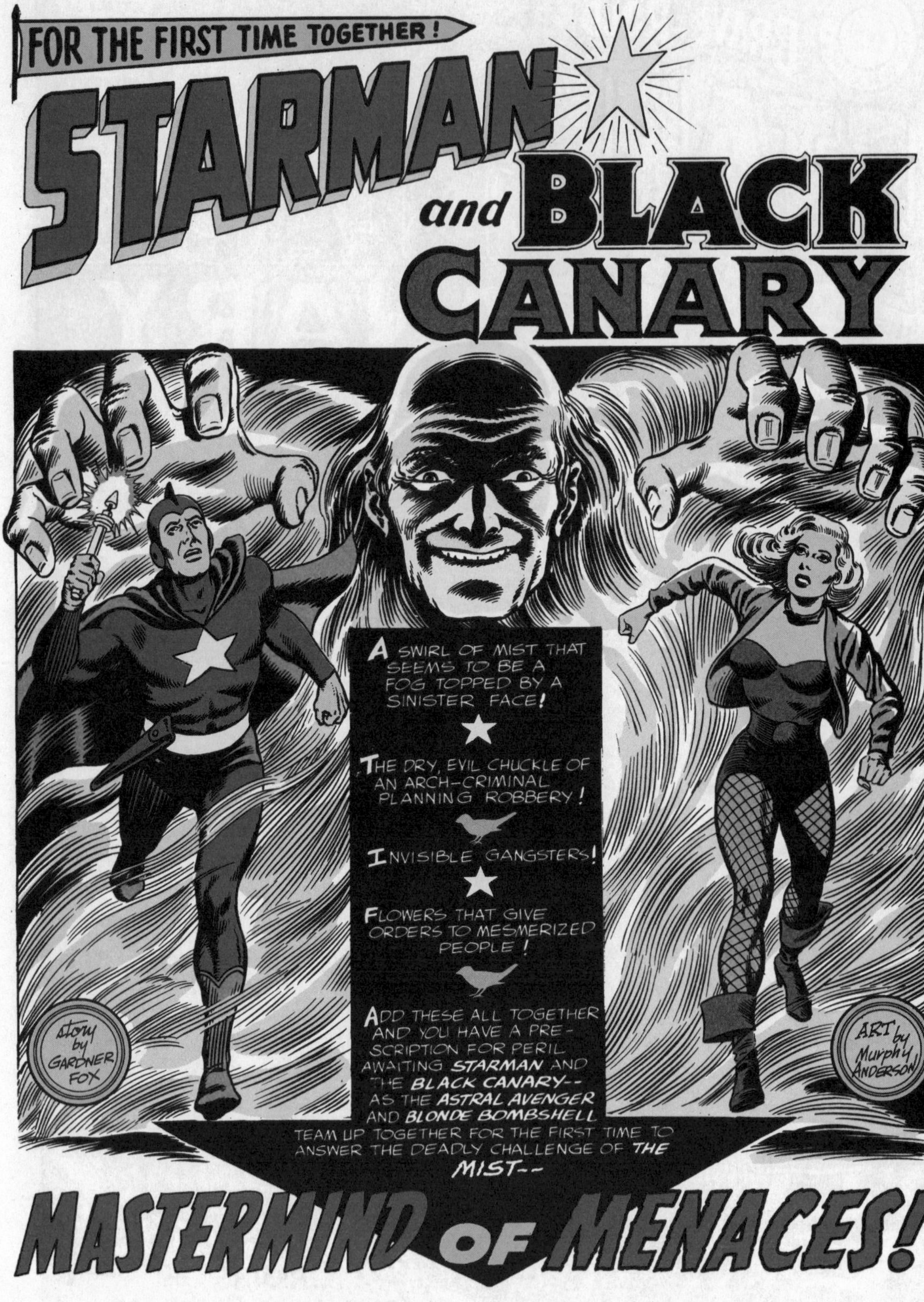
FOR THE FIRST TIME TOGETHER!
STARMAN and BLACK CANARY
A SWIRL OF MIST THAT SEEMS TO BE A FOG TOPPED BY A SINISTER FACE!
THE DRY, EVIL CHUCKLE OF AN ARCH-CRIMINAL PLANNING ROBBERY!
INVISIBLE GANGSTERS!
FLOWERS THAT GIVE ORDERS TO MESMERIZED PEOPLE!
ADD THESE ALL TOGETHER AND YOU HAVE A PRE-SCRIPTION FOR PERIL AWAITING STARMAN AND THE BLACK CANARY-- AS THE ASTRAL AVENGER AND BLONDE BOMBSHELL TEAM UP TOGETHER FOR THE FIRST TIME TO ANSWER THE DEADLY CHALLENGE OF THE MIST--
story by GARDNER FOX
ART by Murphy ANDERSON
MASTERMIND OF MENACES!

RETIRED FINANCIER ALAN MORELAND HAS A STANDING ORDER WITH THE *DRAKE FLOWER SHOPPE* TO DELIVER A BOUQUET EVERY SATURDAY...

DURING THE COURSE OF THE EVENING, THE FLOWER PETALS BEGIN MOVING TO AND FRO-- VIBRATING--SETTING UP SOUND WAVES IN THE ROOM ...

ALAN MORELAND! HEAR AND OBEY! OPEN THE DOOR OF YOUR WALL SAFE AND REMOVE ITS CONTENTS!

NONE BUT THE ENTRANCED ALAN MORELAND HEARS THE HYPNOTIC FLOWERS, BUT HE WILL BE UNABLE TO REMEMBER WHAT IT WAS THAT CAUSED HIM TO "ROB" HIMSELF! IT IS THE LATEST IN THE SERIES OF CLUELESS CRIMES THAT HAS BAFFLED THE POLICE OF *PARK CITY*...

LATER, IN ANOTHER PART OF *PARK CITY*, INSIDE THE LAVISH *DRAKE FLOWER SHOPPE*, LARRY LANCE, HEAD OF A PRIVATE EYE AGENCY, MAKES A HURRIED CALL ON HIS WIFE, *DINAH DRAKE LANCE*...

JUST DROPPED IN TO SAY HELLO, HONEY-- AND SO LONG, SWEETHEART ! THERE'S BEEN ANOTHER ONE OF THOSE MYSTERIOUS ROBBERIES-- AND I'VE GOT TO CHECK IT OUT!

GOOD CLUE-HUNTING, DARLING !

A FEW MINUTES LATER, ANOTHER VISITOR...

TED ! TED KNIGHT !

DINAH, YOU DOLL ! I'M IN *PARK CITY* TO LOOK OVER SOME OF MY BUSINESS INTERESTS-- NONE OF WHICH WILL BE HALF AS INTERESTING AS SPENDING AN EVENING WITH MY FRIENDS, THE *LANCES*!

TED (*STARMAN*) KNIGHT GIVES THE GIRL HE KNOWS TO BE THE *BLACK CANARY* A FRIENDLY KISS...

I HEAR YOUR HUSBAND DOES ALL THE CRIME-CHASING, THESE DAYS !

WELL, I *AM* IN SEMI-RETIREMENT-- BUT SPEAKING OF EVENING-SPENDING, I INSIST YOU HAVE SUPPER WITH LARRY AND ME SOON AS I CLOSE UP SHOP!

GOOD DEAL ! THAT'LL GIVE ME A CHANCE TO DO SOME RESEARCH AT THE OBSERVATORY...

②

DINAH BREAKS OFF A FLOWER FROM A BUNCH SHE IS PRE-PARING FOR DELIVERY AND...

WEAR THIS FLOWER AS A REMINDER TO KEEP THAT DATE--

HA! AS IF I'D LET IT SLIP MY MIND!

TED KNIGHT'S FAME AS AN AMATEUR ASTRONOMER GAINS HIM ADMITTANCE TO THE *PARK CITY ASTRONOMICAL OBSERVATORY*..

THE STARS ARE REALLY BRIGHT TONIGHT. VIEWING CONDITIONS ARE PERFECT FOR MY NEEDS.

FOR A LONG TIME NOW, I'VE BEEN WORKING TO IMPROVE MY *COSMIC ROD*. THE RECENT DISCOVERY OF "*QUASARS*" AND THE FANTASTIC ENERGIES THEY GIVE OFF * HAS CONVINCED ME THEY CAN ADD TO MY EFFECTIVE-NESS AS *STARMAN* !

*Editor's Note: QUASARS -- OR QUASI-STELLAR STARS -- IS THE NAME GIVEN TO GIGANTIC FIERY OBJECTS AS LARGE AS A MILLION SUNS, THAT BURN AT *100 TIMES THE BRIGHT-NESS OF OUR ENTIRE GALAXY!* THEY ARE TEN BILLION LIGHT YEARS FROM EARTH.

THE STEADY HUM AND THROB OF THE MOTORS THAT DRIVE THE TELE-SCOPIC TUBE ON ITS DECLINATION AXIS AND THE MOUNT OF ITS POLAR AXIS FILL THE AIR AS HE WORKS...

THEN THE FLOWER IN HIS BUTTONHOLE GLIMMERS LIKE MIST AND ...

THERE'S SOMETHING WRONG ! THE STARS HAVE SUDDENLY DIS-APPEARED ! NOBODY ELSE IN HERE SEEMS TO BE BOTHERED THAT WAY ! IT'S JUST *MY* EYES THAT HAVE BEEN AFFECTED ! BUT WHY ?

(3

DEEPLY TROUBLED--FOR HE CAN SEE EVERYTHING PERFECTLY EXCEPT FOR THE BLOTTED-OUT STARS-- HE STRIDES BACK TOWARD THE DRAKE FLOWER SHOPPE...

ODD! NOW I HEAR A RINGING IN MY EARS AND... *HUH*?

GO TO YOUR WALL SAFE, CHARLES PRENTICE...

HE HALTS IN ASTONISHMENT, JAW DROPPING....

--OPEN THE SAFE! REMOVE THE CASH INSIDE AND PUT IT IN A PLAIN PAPER BAG--

FLOWER-- VIBRATING --PRODUCING SOUND SENSATIONS! I SEEM TO HAVE INTERCEPTED A SOUND-CRIME-WAVE!...

HE BREAKS INTO A RUN AS...

TAKE THE CASH IN THE BAG TO THE CORNER OF FIFTH STREET AND JEFFERSON BOULEVARD! LEAVE IT UNDER A BUSH--

FIFTH AND JEFFERSON! THAT'S NOT FAR FROM HERE!

ONLY THE TREES AND BUSHES WITNESS THE CHANGE THAT COMES OVER THE BUSINESS-MAN AS HE SHEDS HIS STREET CLOTHES TO BECOME--

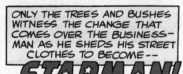

STARMAN!

MOMENTS LATER, THE *ASTRAL AVENGER* WATCHES CHARLES PRENTICE DROP A PAPER BAG--

I'VE BEEN TOO LONG IN THE *STARMAN* BUSINESS NOT TO BE PREPARED FOR ANY EMERGENCY!

--THEN SEES, AFTER A FEW MINUTES' WAIT, THREE MEN APPROACH AND ONE MAN REACH FOR THAT BAG!...

4

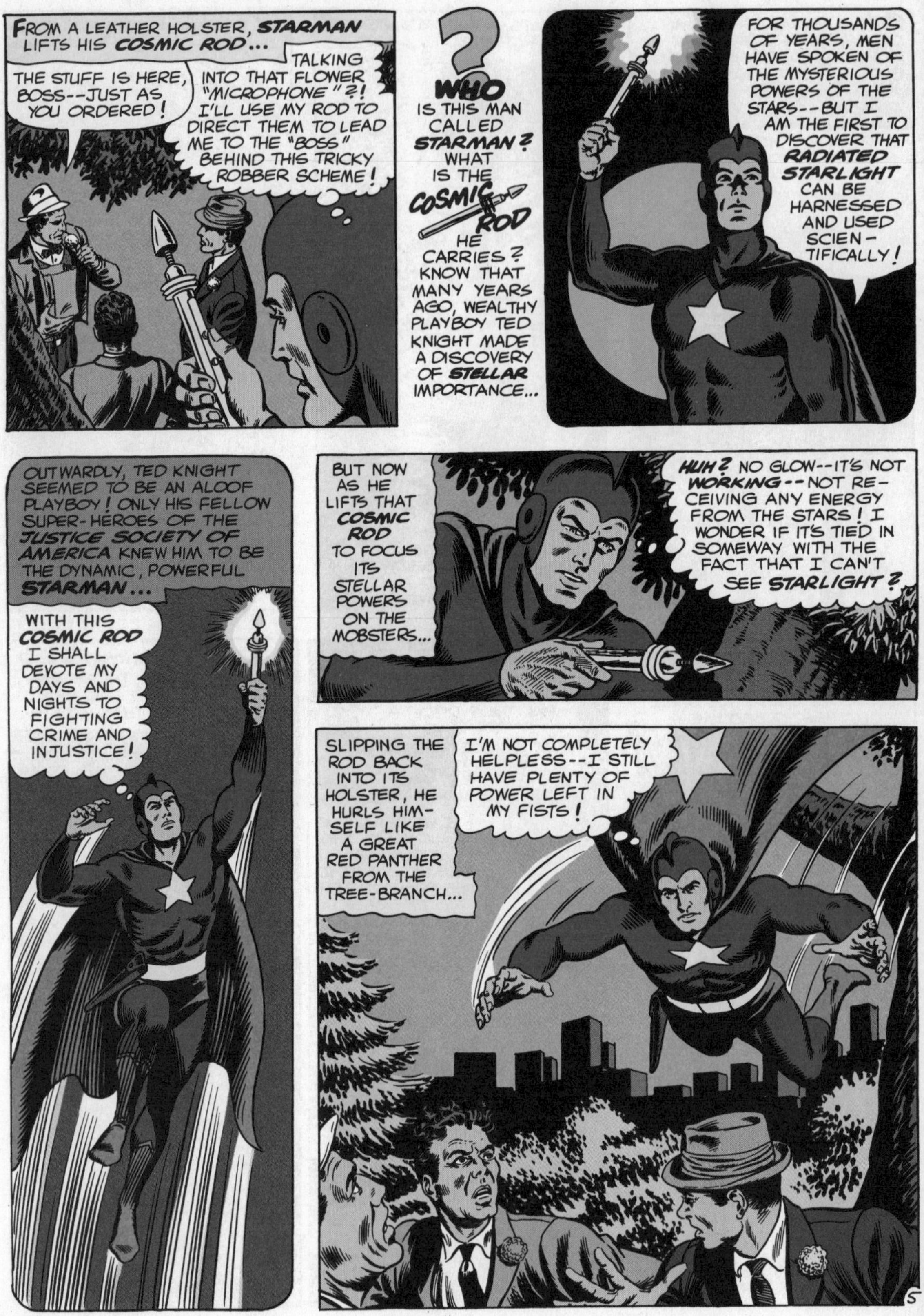
FROM A LEATHER HOLSTER, STARMAN LIFTS HIS COSMIC ROD...
THE STUFF IS HERE, BOSS--JUST AS YOU ORDERED!
TALKING INTO THAT FLOWER "MICROPHONE"?! I'LL USE MY ROD TO DIRECT THEM TO LEAD ME TO THE "BOSS" BEHIND THIS TRICKY ROBBER SCHEME!
? WHO IS THIS MAN CALLED STARMAN? WHAT IS THE COSMIC ROD HE CARRIES? KNOW THAT MANY YEARS AGO, WEALTHY PLAYBOY TED KNIGHT MADE A DISCOVERY OF STELLAR IMPORTANCE...
FOR THOUSANDS OF YEARS, MEN HAVE SPOKEN OF THE MYSTERIOUS POWERS OF THE STARS--BUT I AM THE FIRST TO DISCOVER THAT RADIATED STARLIGHT CAN BE HARNESSED AND USED SCIEN-TIFICALLY!
OUTWARDLY, TED KNIGHT SEEMED TO BE AN ALOOF PLAYBOY! ONLY HIS FELLOW SUPER-HEROES OF THE JUSTICE SOCIETY OF AMERICA KNEW HIM TO BE THE DYNAMIC, POWERFUL STARMAN...
WITH THIS COSMIC ROD I SHALL DEVOTE MY DAYS AND NIGHTS TO FIGHTING CRIME AND INJUSTICE!
BUT NOW AS HE LIFTS THAT COSMIC ROD TO FOCUS ITS STELLAR POWERS ON THE MOBSTERS...
HUH? NO GLOW--IT'S NOT WORKING--NOT RE-CEIVING ANY ENERGY FROM THE STARS! I WONDER IF IT'S TIED IN SOMEWAY WITH THE FACT THAT I CAN'T SEE STARLIGHT?
SLIPPING THE ROD BACK INTO ITS HOLSTER, HE HURLS HIM-SELF LIKE A GREAT RED PANTHER FROM THE TREE-BRANCH...
I'M NOT COMPLETELY HELPLESS--I STILL HAVE PLENTY OF POWER LEFT IN MY FISTS!
5

LIKE A LIVING BOMB HE SMASHES INTO THE GANGSTERS, CATAPULTING THEM TOWARD THE GROUND...

THE *COUNTDOWN* HAS BEGUN...

ON A KNEE AND A TOE, HIS FIST RAMS OUT...

THREE--!

ZOK!

HE RISES TO HIS FEET, BRINGING HIS OTHER FIST UP WITH HIM--INTO THE "JAW-Y" TARGET OF A SECOND MOBSTER...

TWO--!

BUT THE THIRD THUG-- MADE FRANTIC BY THE PILE-DRIVING BLOWS OF THE *ASTRAL AVENGER*-- SWINGS INTO ACTION...

WACK!

COUNT-DOWN-- HOLDING !

SHAKING OFF THE EFFECTS FROM HIS ATTACK, THE FIRST MOBSTER JOINS THE BENCH-SWINGER....

EACH OF US GRAB AN ARM--

--AND PULL IN OPPOSITE DIRECTIONS!

6

DRAWING ON HIS RESERVE STRENGTH, *STARMAN* LUNGES FORWARD, CARRYING THE GANGSTERS WITH HIM....

GOT ONE CHANCE TO DISLODGE THEM--BY JARRING THEM LOOSE!

LIKE A FULLBACK HITTING THE LINE, HE DRIVES A SHOULDER INTO A TREE BOLE-- SIMULTANEOUSLY WHIPPING HIS ARMS AROUND ON EITHER SIDE OF THAT THICK TRUNK...

THUMMMP!

I CAN'T HANG ON!

HIS PERFECTLY CONDITIONED BODY QUICKLY RECOVERING FROM THAT BLASTING BLOW, *STARMAN* WHIRLS AND HURLS HIMSELF THROUGH THE AIR, TO GRIP AND LIFT A GANGSTER...

UP YOU GO!

SLAMMING HIM FLAT UPON THE GROUND, HE DIVES OVER HIM TOWARD THE REMAINING MOBSTER STRUGGLING TO HIS FEET...

NOW TO *ZERO* OFF MY DELAYED COUNTDOWN --

SUDDENLY, FROM THE FLOWER IN THE MOBSTER'S JACKET COMES A HIGH-PITCHED SERIES OF EAR-SPLITTING FREQUENCIES...

THOSE SOUNDS -- STRIKING INTO MY VERY BRAIN -- BLACKING ME OUT!

KKKNEEEE

HA! I KNEW THE BOSS WOULDN'T FAIL US!

7

BY THE TIME THE SOUNDS DIE AWAY, AND A SHAKEN *STARMAN* STAGGERS FROM THE SCENE...

THEY'RE GONE! WHILE I WAS BEING BATTERED BY THOSE SOUND-WAVES, THEY MADE THEIR GETAWAY-- AND I LOST MY CHANCE TO TRACK DOWN THEIR "BOSS"!

ELSEWHERE IN THE CITY, AN OLD FOE-- *THE MIST*-- IS GLOATING OVER *STARMAN'S* DEFEAT...

MY LONG-TIME ENEMY-- BACK AGAIN! *Ah*, IT SEEMS LIKE OLD TIMES PITTING MY INGENIOUS CRIMINAL MIND AND POWERS AGAINST *STARMAN'S* STAR-POWERED STUNTS!

YES, THIS IS *THE MIST!* THE MASTER OF THAT *INVISO-SOLUTION* WHICH ENABLES HIM TO MAKE ANY OBJECT WITH WHICH IT IS COATED-- DISAPPEAR FROM VIEW!

EVEN THE VERY CLOAK HE WEARS SEEMS TO BE A *MIST* OUT OF WHICH HIS HEAD PROTRUDES...

WITH THIS SAME SOLUTION HE HAS LEARNED TO TRANSMIT HYPNOTIC INFLUENCES TO VICTIMS HE CHOOSES TO ROB...

JUST AS I SENT SOUND-SHOCK WAVES TO THE FLOWER WORN BY MY HIRELING -- WHO WAS PROTECTED AGAINST IT--TO KNOCK OUT *STARMAN!* WHAT PUZZLES ME IS, HOW DID *STARMAN* GET WISE TO MY LATEST RACKET? I MUST ASK MY MEN WHEN THEY ARRIVE!

CRISIS
ON MULTIPLE EARTHS
THE TEAM UPS

MASTERMIND OF MENACES!

PART 2

WE GOT THE CASH, *MIST*, EVEN IF *STARMAN* DID STUMBLE ONTO OUR RACKET!

STARMAN PUT UP A WHALE OF A BATTLE-- BUT WHAT GETS ME IS WHY HE DIDN'T USE HIS *COSMIC ROD* AGAINST US!

WHAT'S THAT? *STARMAN* DIDN'T USE HIS FAMOUS POWER-GIMMICK? VERRRY INTERESTING! COULD BE THAT HE WAS *UNABLE* TO USE HIS WEAPON!

AS HIS GANG MEMBERS MAKE THEIR REPORT AND TURN OVER THE LOOT OF THEIR LATEST *"CLUELESS CRIME", THE MIST* REFLECTS WITH THAT COLD, CLEVER BRAIN THAT HAS MADE HIM SO AWE-SOME AN ANTAGONIST IN THE PAST!

TOO OFTEN HAS HE FOUGHT THE *ASTRAL AVENGER*-- AND BEEN DEFEATED BY HIM!-- NOT TO UNDERSTAND THAT HE MUST TAKE ADVANTAGE OF ANY BIT OF INFORMATION THAT MAY HELP HIM GAIN A VICTORY OVER HIS LONGSTANDING FOE!

HAD I KNOWN HE COULDN'T COUNTERATTACK WITH HIS *COSMIC ROD*, I'D HAVE FOLLOWED UP THAT FLORAL SOUND-WAVE BLAST I HURLED AT HIM WITH EVEN MORE DESTRUCTIVE ONES!

BUT I HAVE NO TIME AT THE MOMENT TO CONCERN MYSELF ABOUT *STARMAN*! I MUST LISTEN IN ON DINAH DRAKE'S REPORT OF WHAT SELECT CUSTOMERS SHE IS DE-LIVERING FLOWERS TO ON THE MORROW!

9

AT THIS MOMENT, IN THE *DRAKE FLOWER SHOPPE* OFFICE ...

HI, HONEY! DID YOU COME UP WITH ANYTHING ON THOSE MYSTERIOUS ROBBERIES?

I SURE DID! I FOUND OUT WHO'S ONE OF THE KEY CULPRITS -- A WOMAN! A *VERY PRETTY* WOMAN, I MIGHT ADD!

OH, REALLY! WELL, DON'T KEEP ME IN SUSPENSE! WHO IS SHE?

WHY-- NONE OTHER THAN *YOU!*

M-ME?? YOU MUST BE KIDDING--!

I KID YOU NOT, DOLL! GET THIS-- THE ONE COMMON DENOMINATOR IN THE ROBBERIES HAS BEEN THE FLOWERS *YOU* SENT TO EVERY ONE OF THOSE PLACES JUST BEFORE THEY WERE ROBBED!

MY FLOWERS HAD *NOTHING* TO DO WITH IT-- THEY *COULDN'T* HAVE!

OH, *YES* THEY DID, DINAH! THIS FLOWER YOU GAVE ME HAD A DIRECT BEARING ON A ROBBERY-- AS A *TALKING FLOWER* ...

IT INSTRUCTED A MAN NAMED CHARLES PRENTICE TO TAKE CASH FROM HIS SAFE, PUT IT IN A BAG AND DELIVER IT TO *FIFTH AND JEFFERSON!* I WENT THERE -- AND WHEN MY *COSMIC ROD* WOULDN'T WORK, HAD TO WADE IN WITH MY FISTS!

10

AS HE TELLS HIS STORY, THE *ASTRAL AVENGER* DISPLAYS HIS *COSMIC ROD,* WHICH TO HIS ASTONISHMENT...

IT'S GLOWING WITH STELLAR ENERGY! I'M IN BUSINESS AGAIN!

YOU TWO WAIT IN HERE WHILE I LOCK UP! THEN WE'LL GO INTO A DEEP HUDDLE ON HOW TO HANDLE THIS INCREDIBLE AFFAIR!

HI, *STARMAN!* FIRST CHANCE I'VE BEEN ABLE TO CUT IN WITH THE BIG HELLO! ...

SOME MOMENTS LATER, LARRY AND *STARMAN* STIFFEN IN SURPRISE--AS AN ODD CHANGE COMES OVER DINAH DRAKE LANCE...

LEAVE MY OFFICE AT ONCE! I HAVE PRIVATE BUSINESS TO ATTEND TO!

QUICKLY, LARRY-- OBEY HER!

AS THEY LEAVE THE PRIVATE OFFICE...

SOMETHING IS OBVIOUSLY WRONG-- SHE SEEMS TO BE IN A TRANCE!

BUT I WANT TO *SEE* WHAT SHE INTENDS DOING! IT'LL GIVE US SOME IDEA OF WHAT IS GOING ON!

AS SOON AS THE OFFICE DOOR IS LOCKED, THE *COSMIC ROD* LIFTS AND FOCUSES! AS IT GLOWS TO FULL POWER, THE SOLID WALL BE-TWEEN THE MEN AND DINAH BECOMES TRANSPARENT...

GOOD GOSH! DINAH'S SPEAKING TO THOSE FLOWERS!

I AM ALONE--AND AM REPORTING AS ORDERED! FOLLOWING ARE THE WEALTHY CUSTOMERS WHO ORDERED FLOWERS DELIVERED TOMORROW--

IN ANOTHER PART OF TOWN, *THE MIST* GLOATS TRIUMPHANTLY...

--THE VAN TALLERS, THE BURTONS, THE PARK YACHT CLUB! THESE ARE THEIR ADDRESSES...

THIS IS RICH! I HAVE SPIES--SPECIALLY TREATED FLOWERS--IN THE ENEMY CAMP! I HEARD *STARMAN* TELLING WHAT HAP-PENED TO HIM--AND NOW MRS. LANCE IS GIVING ME HER REGULAR REPORT...

NONE OF THEM SUSPECTS THAT I SEND A DIFFERENT MAN EACH DAY TO THE FLOWER SHOP, WHO SECRETLY SPRAYS THE PLACE WHILE CONSIDERING WHAT FLOWERS TO PURCHASE! I ONLY CONCERN MYSELF WITH THE FLORAL DELIVERIES TO THE HOMES OF PEOPLE WORTH ROBBING!

THE SPECIAL SPRAY CAUSES THE FLOWERS TO VIBRATE TO CERTAIN ULTRA-FREQUENCIES, JUST AS DOES A TELEPHONE TRANSMITTER, TRANSLATING THOSE FREQUENCIES INTO THE SOUND OF MY HYPNOTIC VOICE--WHICH I BEAM DIRECTLY AT MY VICTIMS' HOMES!

FROM WHAT I OVERHEARD *STARMAN* SAY IN DINAH'S OFFICE, IT'S EVIDENT THAT HE--AND THE FLOWER SHE GAVE HIM--WERE IN LINE WITH MY BEAMING VOICE TO THE PRENTICE PLACE! BUT BEST OF ALL--

--I NOW KNOW WHY HIS *COSMIC ROD* DIDN'T WORK! THE FREQUENCIES GIVEN OFF BY HIS FLOWER--COMBINED WITH THE MOTOR NOISES IN THE OBSERVATORY-- RESULTED IN STARLIGHT NOT REACHING HIM FOR A BRIEF TIME!

THE ARCH-CRIMINAL HANDS A TAPE RECORDER TO ONE OF HIS THUGS...

SNEAK INTO THAT OBSERVATORY AND RECORD THOSE SOUNDS! BY COMBINING THE SOUNDS WITH MY ULTRA-FREQUENCIES, I'LL BE ABLE TO *PERMANENTLY* CUT OFF THE RADIO-ENERGY FROM THE STARS ON WHICH *STARMAN'S COSMIC ROD* OPERATES!

NOW--WHEN *STARMAN* AND I CLASH AGAIN--THE WEAPONS WILL BE STACKED IN MY FAVOR!

MEANTIME, DINAH OPENS THE DOOR OF HER PRIVATE OFFICE...

HUH? THEY DON'T WANT ME TO SPEAK--

WE'VE GOT TO TALK TO DINAH--WHERE THOSE FLOWERS CAN'T "LISTEN IN"!

IN A BACK ROOM, MATTERS ARE EXPLAINED TO THE DISMAYED FLOWER STORE OWNER...

SO! SOMEONE'S BEEN USING ME AS A DUPE! WELL, HE WON'T GET AWAY WITH IT! I'M TAKING AN ACTIVE PART IN THIS CASE-- AS THE *BLACK CANARY!*

12

IN HER SPECIAL DRESSING ROOM, ANGRY FINGERS LIFT AND FIT THE DARK FABRIC OF HER COSTUME OVER THE FLUSHED GIRL...

THE NERVE OF THAT GUY--WHOEVER HE IS! USING ME AND MY FLOWERS TO HELP HIM ROB!

A BLONDE WIG IS FITTED OVER HER BLACK HAIR AND NOW SHE IS READY TO FACE THE WORLD AS THE CRIME-BUSTING **BLACK CANARY...**

YOU GAVE THE CROOK THREE ADDRESSES, HONEY! I SUGGEST WE EACH GO TO ONE AND NAB THEM!

GOOD IDEA, LARRY--WITH ONE ADDITION! **YOU** WILL GO THERE ONLY TO WATCH AND OBSERVE--AND THEN **FOLLOW** THE ROBBERS TO THEIR HIDE-OUT!

BLACK CANARY'S RIGHT! WE MUST FIND THE MASTERMIND BEHIND ALL THIS--BY HAVING ONE OF US FOLLOW THE MOBSTERS!

BUT WHY ELECT **ME?** I'M A PRETTY GOOD CROOK-CATCHER, YOU KNOW!

DEAR, YOU'RE AN EXPERIENCED DETECTIVE--A CRACKERJACK AT SHADOWING PEOPLE WITHOUT THEIR KNOWING IT!

SURE--THE RIGHT MAN FOR THE RIGHT JOB! WITH YOUR DETECTIVE GIMMICKS, YOU CAN CONTACT US AND PINPOINT THE HIDE-OUT'S LOCATION!

FLATTERY SURE GOT YOU SOMEWHERE! WHAT CAN I SAY BUT--**OKAY!**

HERE'S AN ADDRESS FOR EACH OF YOU! I'LL TAKE THE **VAN TALLER** HOUSE! LARRY, YOU GO TO THE **BURTONS'!** STARMAN, I'M PUTTING THE YACHT CLUB INTO YOUR KEEPING!

JUST AS I'M PUTTING THIS **MINIATURE COSMIC ROD** INTO YOURS, **BLACK CANARY!**

I WANT YOU TO USE IT AS A SECRET WEAPON AGAINST OUR FOE--IF MY REGULAR ONE FAILS TO WORK AGAIN, AS I SUSPECT! IT DRAWS ITS POWER FROM **QUASARS,** THE GREATEST KNOWN SOURCE OF ENERGY IN THE UNIVERSE! I'VE BEEN WORKING ON IT FOR SOME MONTHS--FINALLY FINISHING IT TODAY AT THE OBSERVATORY...

NEXT DAY, AFTER THE SPRAYED FLOWERS HAVE BEEN DELIVERED...

FREDA VAN TALLER, GATHER ALL YOUR EMERALDS AND LEAVE THEM ON YOUR VANITY TABLE! OPEN A DOWNSTAIRS WINDOW-- THEN LEAVE THE HOUSE FOR AN HOUR.

A FEW MINUTES AFTER THE WEALTHY WOMAN HAS LEFT HER HOME...

LET'S GO! SHE DID JUST WHAT *THE MIST* TOLD HER TO...

DON'T THEY ALWAYS? HE'S COME UP WITH THE NEATEST ROBBERY SCHEME OF ALL TIME!

IN THE BEDROOM ABOVE, INVISIBLE FINGERS LIFT AND DISPLAY GREEN FIRE IN THE SHAPE OF COSTLY EMERALDS...

MAN, WHEN IT COMES TO GREEN STUFF, I'LL TAKE EMERALDS OVER BUCKS ANY TIME!

BELOW, A *BLONDE BOMBSHELL* LEAPS THROUGH THE OPEN WINDOW...

I DIDN'T SEE ANYONE COME IN BUT I KNOW SOMEONE'S HERE --

FROM THE AMULET ABOUT HER THROAT, *BLACK CANARY* REMOVES A PELLET OF REDDISH POWDER AND BREAKS IT IN HER PALM...

I HEAR FOOTSTEPS AND VOICES UPSTAIRS! IT WAS GOOD OF *STARMAN* TO LET ME HAVE THAT *TINY COSMIC ROD* -- BUT I HAVE WAYS OF MY OWN FOR DEALING WITH INVISIBLE CROOKS!

MOMENTS LATER, PURSED LIPS BLOW A RED CLOUD INTO THE BEDROOM...

WHOOOSSSHH!

14

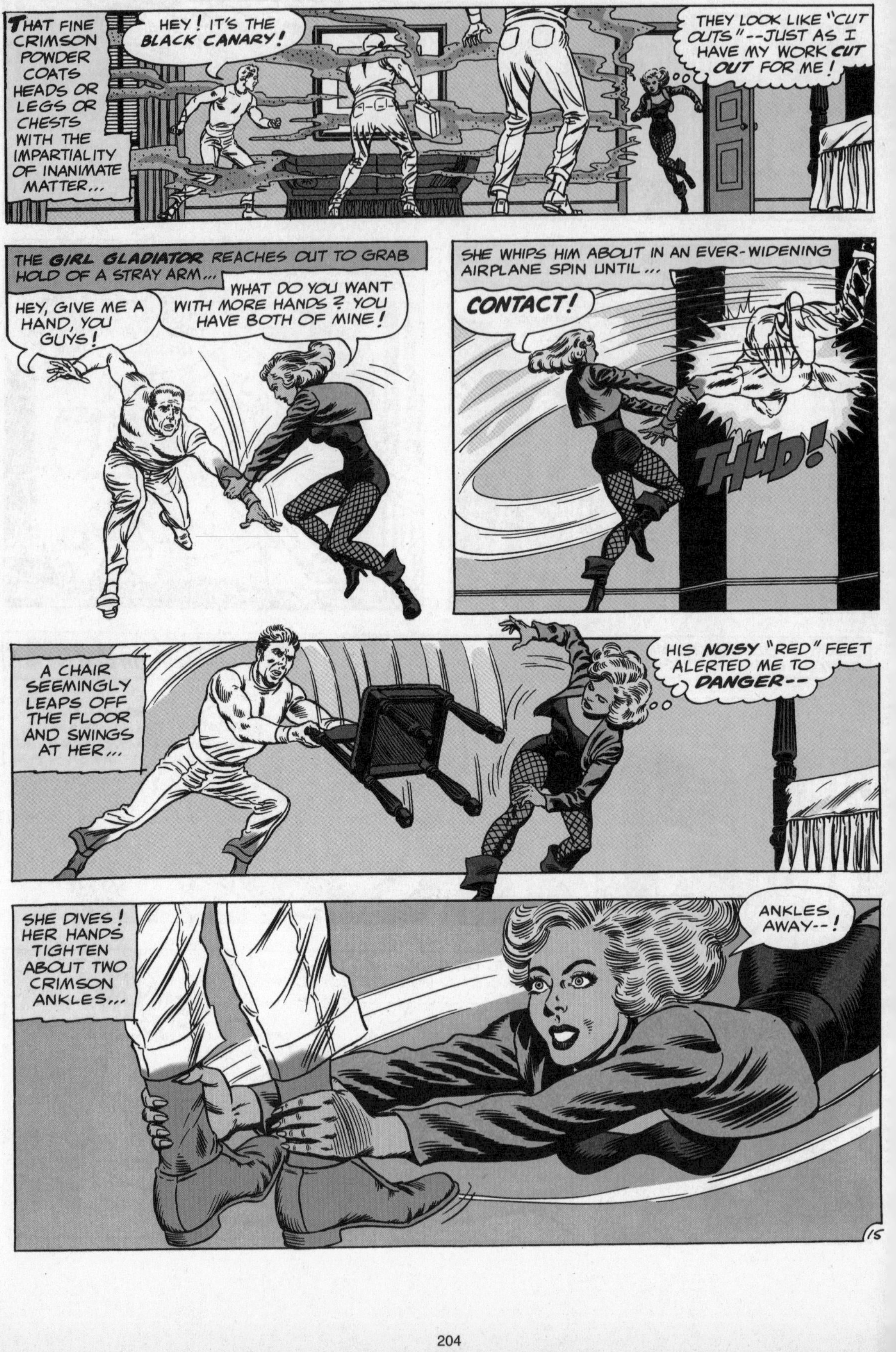
THAT FINE CRIMSON POWDER COATS HEADS OR LEGS OR CHESTS WITH THE IMPARTIALITY OF INANIMATE MATTER...
HEY! IT'S THE BLACK CANARY!
THEY LOOK LIKE "CUT OUTS"--JUST AS I HAVE MY WORK CUT OUT FOR ME!
THE GIRL GLADIATOR REACHES OUT TO GRAB HOLD OF A STRAY ARM...
HEY, GIVE ME A HAND, YOU GUYS!
WHAT DO YOU WANT WITH MORE HANDS? YOU HAVE BOTH OF MINE!
SHE WHIPS HIM ABOUT IN AN EVER-WIDENING AIRPLANE SPIN UNTIL...
CONTACT!
THUD!
A CHAIR SEEMINGLY LEAPS OFF THE FLOOR AND SWINGS AT HER...
HIS NOISY "RED" FEET ALERTED ME TO DANGER--
SHE DIVES! HER HANDS TIGHTEN ABOUT TWO CRIMSON ANKLES...
ANKLES AWAY--!
15

A DRESSING TABLE AND CHAIR EXPLODE IN A SPRAY OF SPLINTERS AS...

BEFORE THE *BLACK CANARY* CAN GET SET FOR HER NEXT FOE, A HURLED LAMP KNOCKS HER BACKWARD...

THAT *CHESTY* ONE CAUGHT ME BY SURPRISE! BUT AT LEAST HE DID ME THE FAVOR OF KNOCKING ME INTO THAT STRONG BEAM OF SUNLIGHT!

INSPIRATION ILLUMINES THE KEEN MIND AND QUICK WITS OF THE *GIRL GLADIATOR* AS SHE WHIPS OUT A TINY MIRROR FROM HER CANARY AMULET AND...

C-CAN'T SEE!

THE SUNLIGHT I'M AIMING AT HIM IS REFLECTING OFF HIS EYES!

UPWARD SHE ERUPTS--LIKE AN ANGRY GEYSER! HER DETERMINED FISTS MAKE CONTACT A FEW INCHES BELOW THOSE SUN-DAZZLED ORBS...

TARGET-- JAW!

THEN SHE BORROWS SOME DUSTING POWDER FROM FREDA VAN TALLER AND...

TAKE A POWDER, BOYS-- SO I CAN SEE WHO I'M GOING TO TAKE TO JAIL!

16

ACROSS *PARK CITY,* IN ITS *FASHIONABLE* YACHT CLUB...

REMOVE THE CHARITY RECEIPTS FROM THE CASH BOX AND PLACE THEM IN THE MODEL VIKING SHIP! PUT THE SHIP IN THE WATER...

AS THE *MESMERIZED* ATTENDANT DOES AS COMMANDED, A STRONG BREEZE CARRIES THE VESSEL OUTWARD INTO THE HARBOR...

OUT OF A PARTLY CLOUDY SKY DROPS A HELI-COPTER TOWARD THE LONGSHIP, JUST AS *STARMAN* HURTLES UPWARD FROM THE HARBOR WATERS...

WITH THE PROTECTION OF MY *COSMIC ROD,* I'VE BEEN SHADOWING THE SHIP MODEL *UNDERWATER* -- EXPECTING SOME SUCH DEVELOPMENT AS THIS *!*

AS THE ROD GLOWS MORE BRIGHTLY, THE PROPELLERS LIFT UPWARD OFF THE 'COPTER...

YIII! WE'LL FALL!

NOT BEFORE WE GET *STARMAN!*

17

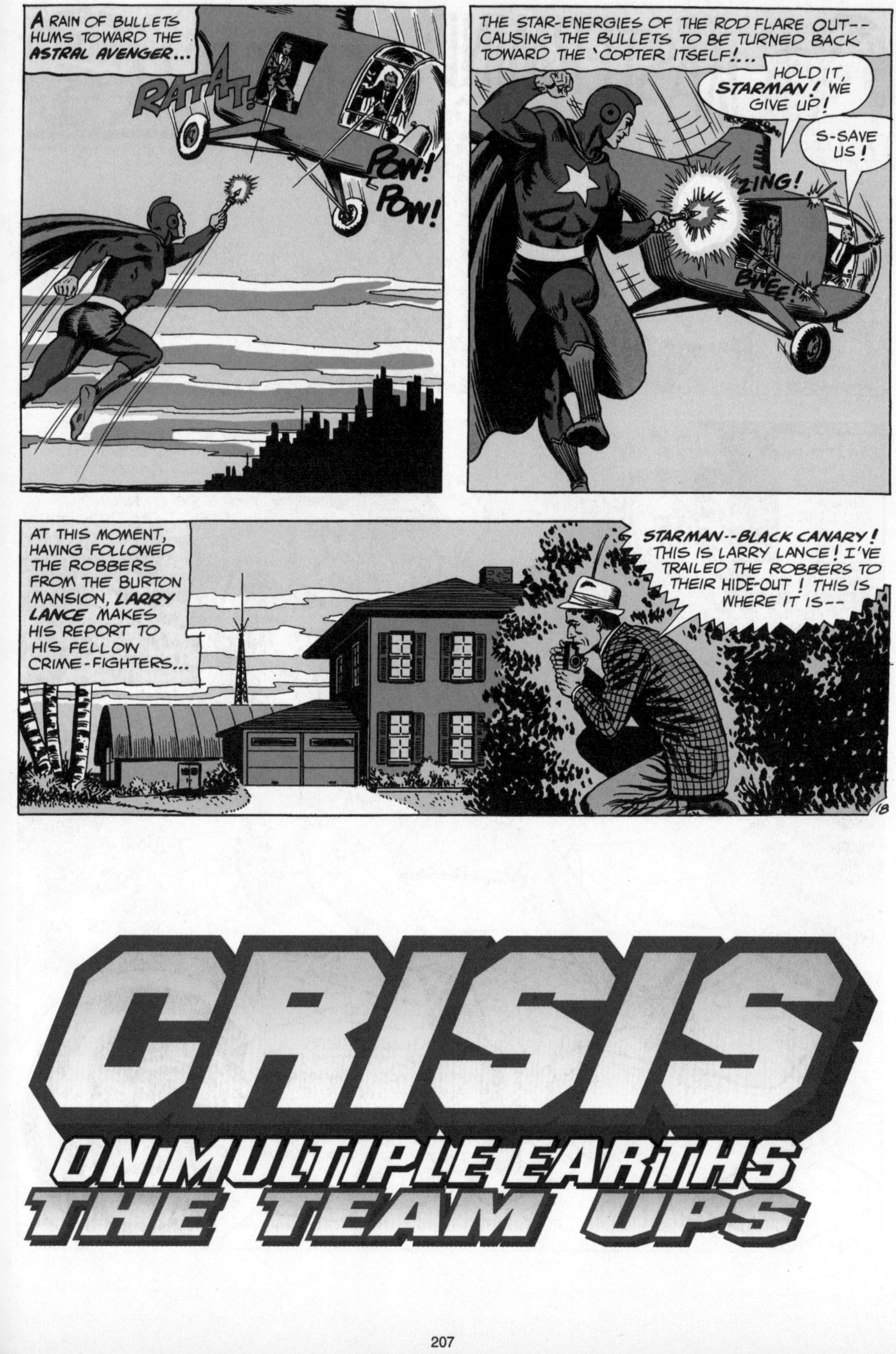
A RAIN OF BULLETS HUMS TOWARD THE ASTRAL AVENGER...
RATATAT!
POW! POW!
THE STAR-ENERGIES OF THE ROD FLARE OUT-- CAUSING THE BULLETS TO BE TURNED BACK TOWARD THE 'COPTER ITSELF!...
HOLD IT, STARMAN! WE GIVE UP!
S-SAVE US!
ZING!
BWEE!
AT THIS MOMENT, HAVING FOLLOWED THE ROBBERS FROM THE BURTON MANSION, LARRY LANCE MAKES HIS REPORT TO HIS FELLOW CRIME-FIGHTERS...
STARMAN--BLACK CANARY! THIS IS LARRY LANCE! I'VE TRAILED THE ROBBERS TO THEIR HIDE-OUT! THIS IS WHERE IT IS--
18

CRISIS ON MULTIPLE EARTHS THE TEAM UPS

As LARRY LANCE'S VOICE is TRANSMITTED to STARMAN AND THE BLACK CANARY, IT IS HEARD BY THE MIST INSIDE HIS LABORATORY-- VIA HIS FLORAL "MICRO-PHONES"!...

LARRY LANCE DIDN'T REALIZE HIS VOICE WOULD BE PICKED UP BY MY SPECIALLY-TREATED BUSHES OUTSIDE THIS BUILDING! GO GET HIM, YOU MEN! I WANT HIM OUT OF THE WAY WHEN STARMAN AND BLACK CANARY GET HERE!

GRAB HIM! HOLD HIM!

THEY WON'T HOLD ME LONG! AT LEAST THEY DON'T KNOW THE BLACK CANARY AND STARMAN ARE ON THEIR WAY HERE TO ROUND UP THE REST OF THIS GANG!

AN ATTACK BY THREE INVISIBLE THUGS-- AND LARRY LANCE GOES DOWN, STRIKING OUT BRAVELY BUT WITH FUTILE FISTS AS...

I HAVE SOME VERY SPECIAL WEAPONS PRE-PARED FOR STARMAN! AND ALSO FOR THE DARING LADY, THE BLACK CANARY! LANCE HAS BECKONED THEM INTO A TRAP FROM WHICH THERE IS NO ESCAPE!

FIRST ON THE SCENE IS THE *ASTRAL AVENGER*-- TO BE GREETED BY THE WILD LAUGHTER OF...

THE MIST!?

THE SURPRISE PARTY IS GOING TO BE ON *YOU*, STARMAN!

OUT FROM A WALL DART GIGANTIC FLOWERS-- SPRAYED WITH *THE MIST'S* SPECIAL SOLUTION! AT THE SAME TIME, TAPE-RECORDED SOUNDS OF THE ASTRONOMICAL OBSERVATORY FILL THE AIR...

MY ROD STOPPED GLOWING--!

SCREEEEK KK-KRREEEK

OF COURSE! BE- CAUSE STARLIGHT AND ITS ENERGIES ARE PREVENTED FROM REACHING YOU! YOUR *COSMIC WEAPON* IS POWERLESS TO STOP MY INVISIBLE GANG!

BATTERED BY A FLORAL FLOOD OF HIGH-FREQUENCY WAVES, ENCOMPASSED BY THE TAPE-RECORDED SOUNDS, *STARMAN* PLUMMETS INTO A TOOLBENCH...

GET HIM!

INVISIBLE GANGSTERS RUSH THE CRIME-FIGHTER! HIS FIST LASHES OUT--LANDS HARD ON AN UN- SEEN FACE--EVEN AS HE IS OVERCOME BY THE SHEER WEIGHT OF NUMBERS...

Panel 1 caption: AS STARMAN GOES DOWN, THE BLONDE BOMBSHELL CRASHES INTO THE BIG ROOM...

YOU'RE NEXT, BLACK CANARY-- AND YOU'LL BE EASIER TO TAKE THAN STARMAN!

STARMAN'S COSMIC ROD-- DEACTIVATED! NOW I SEE WHY HE ARMED ME WITH THAT MINIATURE ROD--

CRASH!

Panel 2 caption: INVISIBLE MEN LEAP AT HER-- AND GRAB EMPTY AIR AS SHE RISES UPWARD LIKE A ROCKET...

HUH? YOU AIN'T SUPER-POWERED! WHERE'D YOU LATCH ON TO THAT TRICK?

THAT'S ONLY THE BEGINNING OF THE TRICKS I'LL SHOW THAT MIST-FIT WITH MY HAND-CONCEALED WEAPON!

THUD! WHACK!

Panel 3 caption: FROM HER CLENCHED FINGERS A BEAM OF ENERGY STABS OUT...

AH! THERE THEY ARE! THE QUASARS FROM WHICH THIS TINY ROD GETS ITS POWERS ARE TOO POTENT FOR THE MIST TO OVERCOME AS HE DID STARMAN'S!

Panel 4 caption: HER FIST-- AIDED BY THE STRIKING POWER OF THE TINY STAR SCEPTRE-- LANDS WITH JARRING IMPACT...

SEE A FEW STARS ON ME, FELLA!

THWAK!

Panel 5 caption: A GRAVITY TUG FROM THE STAR-ROD AND SCIENTIFIC INSTRUMENTS ARE YANKED LOOSE...

HEY, WHAT'S WITH THE REST OF YOU GUYS? GET IN HERE AND LEND A HAND!

21

AT HIS CRY, THE REMAINING GANGSTERS RACE INTO THE ROOM--JUST AS THE *GIRL GLADIATOR* MANEUVERS THE SCIENTIFIC EQUIPMENT TOGETHER...

THEIR VOICES ARE TELLING ME WHERE THEY ARE!

WHAT'S SHE UP TO?

BEATS ME--I COULD NEVER FIGURE OUT A DAME!

A CONGLOMERATION OF INSTRUMENTS DROPS ON THE SURPRISED CRIMINALS...

IN AGONIZED DESPAIR, *THE MIST* SEES THE *BLACK CANARY* DESTROY HIS WONDER FLOWERS...

I'VE GOT TO STOP HER BEFORE *STARMAN* REGAINS CONSCIOUSNESS! HIS *COSMIC ROD* WILL START WORKING AGAIN WITH THOSE FLOWERS DESTROYED!

LEAPING TO A CONTROL STUD, THE *MIST* PRESSES IT--SHOOTING PELLETS FROM HIDDEN COMPRESSED-AIR GUNS...

MY LAST REMAINING GIMMICK--BUT IT'S *SUREFIRE!*

GOT TO DRIVE THEM AWAY FROM ME-- BY SHIELDING MYSELF!

22

INEXPERIENCED IN THE USE OF THE *COSMIC ROD*, A SINGLE PELLET PENETRATES HER FAULTY SHIELD AND...

OHHH-- ONE OF THEM GRAZED ME...

AS *STARMAN* STIRS, A COUPLE OF REVIVED MOBSTERS LEAP TOWARD THE *BLACK CANARY*...

BLACK CANARY-- IN DANGER!

RECOVERING HIS *COSMIC ROD,* HE THROWS A BUBBLE OF ENERGY AROUND THE FALLEN GIRL AS...

BY DESTROYING THE FLOWERS, *BLACK CANARY* ENABLED THE STAR-ENERGIES TO RECHARGE MY WEAPON!

THUMP!

WHAPP!

HALF-MAD WITH DESPAIR, *THE MIST* LEAPS FORWARD LIKE A MAN POSSESSED! HIS DESPERATE FINGERS REACH OUT TO WREST THE ROD AWAY FROM *STARMAN*...

BUT BEFORE HE CAN LAY A HAND ON IT, *STARMAN'S* FREE HAND LASHES OUT...

JUST LIKE OLD TIMES, *MIST!* YOU'RE MY PRISONER! AS SOON AS I *DE-MIST* YOU, I'M TAKING YOU IN!

THUD!

23

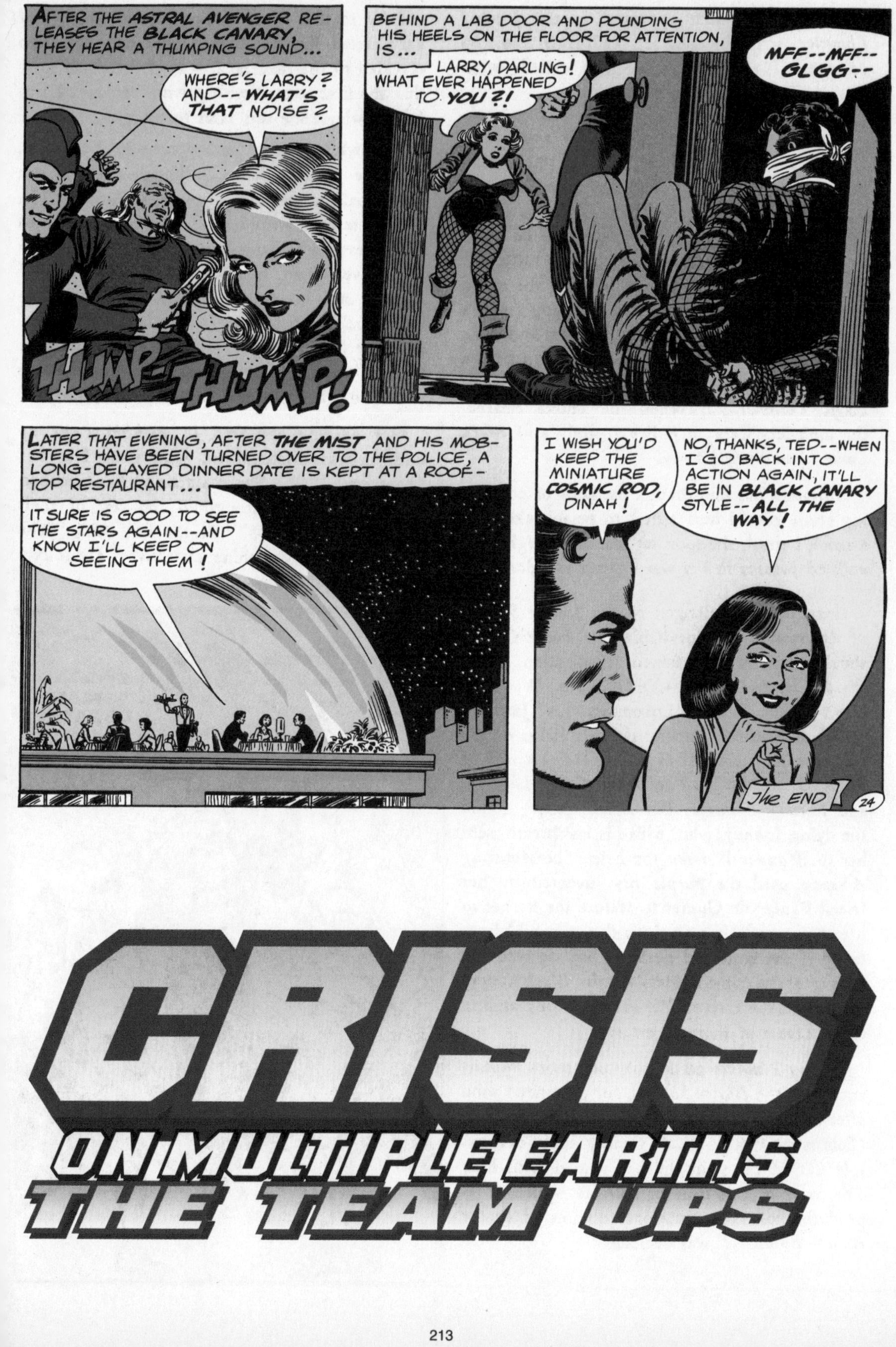
AFTER THE ASTRAL AVENGER RELEASES THE BLACK CANARY, THEY HEAR A THUMPING SOUND...
WHERE'S LARRY? AND-- WHAT'S THAT NOISE?
THUMP-THUMP!
BEHIND A LAB DOOR AND POUNDING HIS HEELS ON THE FLOOR FOR ATTENTION, IS...
LARRY, DARLING! WHAT EVER HAPPENED TO YOU?!
MFF--MFF-- GLGG--
LATER THAT EVENING, AFTER THE MIST AND HIS MOBSTERS HAVE BEEN TURNED OVER TO THE POLICE, A LONG-DELAYED DINNER DATE IS KEPT AT A ROOF-TOP RESTAURANT...
IT SURE IS GOOD TO SEE THE STARS AGAIN--AND KNOW I'LL KEEP ON SEEING THEM!
I WISH YOU'D KEEP THE MINIATURE COSMIC ROD, DINAH!
NO, THANKS, TED--WHEN I GO BACK INTO ACTION AGAIN, IT'LL BE IN BLACK CANARY STYLE--ALL THE WAY!
The END
24

CRISIS ON MULTIPLE EARTHS
THE TEAM UPS

THE ORIGIN OF BLACK CANARY

Black Canary first appeared in the *Johnny Thunder* strip in FLASH COMICS No. 86 (August, 1947.) The story was called—what else?—"The Black Canary."

The *Blonde Bombshell* originally acted as a sort of female *Robin Hood*, preying upon criminals by stealing their ill-gotten gains. In this first adventure, she tricked *Johnny Thunder* into swiping a mask of a special design to be worn by guests at a party given by a big-time racketeer. Gaining entry to his home by wearing the mask, *Black Canary* was about to rob the gang leader's safe when she was surprised by her host and some of his underlings. *Johnny*, always one to help a damsel in distress, came to her rescue with his magic *Thunderbolt*. When the smoke cleared, the mobsters were in police custody and *Black Canary* had slipped away.

Although her unorthodox methods of combating crime caused her at first to be mistaken for a crook herself, she soon set matters straight and enlisted *Johnny* in her war against evil-doers.

Since *Johnny* belonged to the *Justice Society of America*, it was inevitable that *Black Canary* should encounter that famed organization, which she did in ALL-STAR COMICS No. 38 ("History's Crime Wave," December, 1947-January, 1948.) A madman impersonating villains of the past actually succeeded in killing *Hawkman, The Flash, Dr. Mid-Nite, The Atom, Green Lantern,* and *Johnny Thunder.* But *Black Canary* found the dying *Johnny*, who, with his last breath, sent her to *Wonder Woman* for help. The *Amazing Amazon* used the *purple ray* invented by her friend Paula von Gunter to restore the heroes to life. But even this marvelous device would have failed if the costumed heroines had delayed too long after the crime-fighters' deaths. *Black Canary* then aided the revived *JSA-ers* in putting an end to the career of their adversary.

Johnny Thunder made only one more appearance with the *Justice Society*, for he retired soon afterward. So it was that, in FLASH No. 92, (February, 1948,) *Black Canary* took over as sole star of the strip she had shared with him. The cover of this issue of FLASH, which is reproduced below, was the only one on which the *Blonde Bombshell* was depicted.

Prior to this, *Black Canary's* secret identity of dark-haired florist Dinah Drake had not been revealed to the readers. It was in this same story that she first teamed with private detective Larry Lance, whom she was later to marry.

Meanwhile, *Black Canary* continued to work with the *Justice Society*, although she was not yet officially a member. Then, in ALL-STAR No. 41, she teamed with *The Harlequin*, a costumed "villainess" who later was revealed as a police undercover agent, to thwart the schemes of *The Wizard* and his fellow *Injustice Society* members, *The Fiddler, The Icicle, The Sportsmaster,* and *The Huntress,* in "The Case of the Patriotic Crimes." *Black Canary's* work on this case was rewarded when she was inducted into the *JSA*.

Our heroine appeared in FLASH right up until it was discontinued, with issue No. 104 (February, 1949.) She maintained her membership in the *JSA* throughout the rest of their adventures in ALL-STAR, the last being "The Mystery of the Vanishing Detectives" (issue No. 57, February-March, 1951).

HOURMAN

STORY BY GARDNER FOX

ART BY DICK DILLIN & SID GREENE

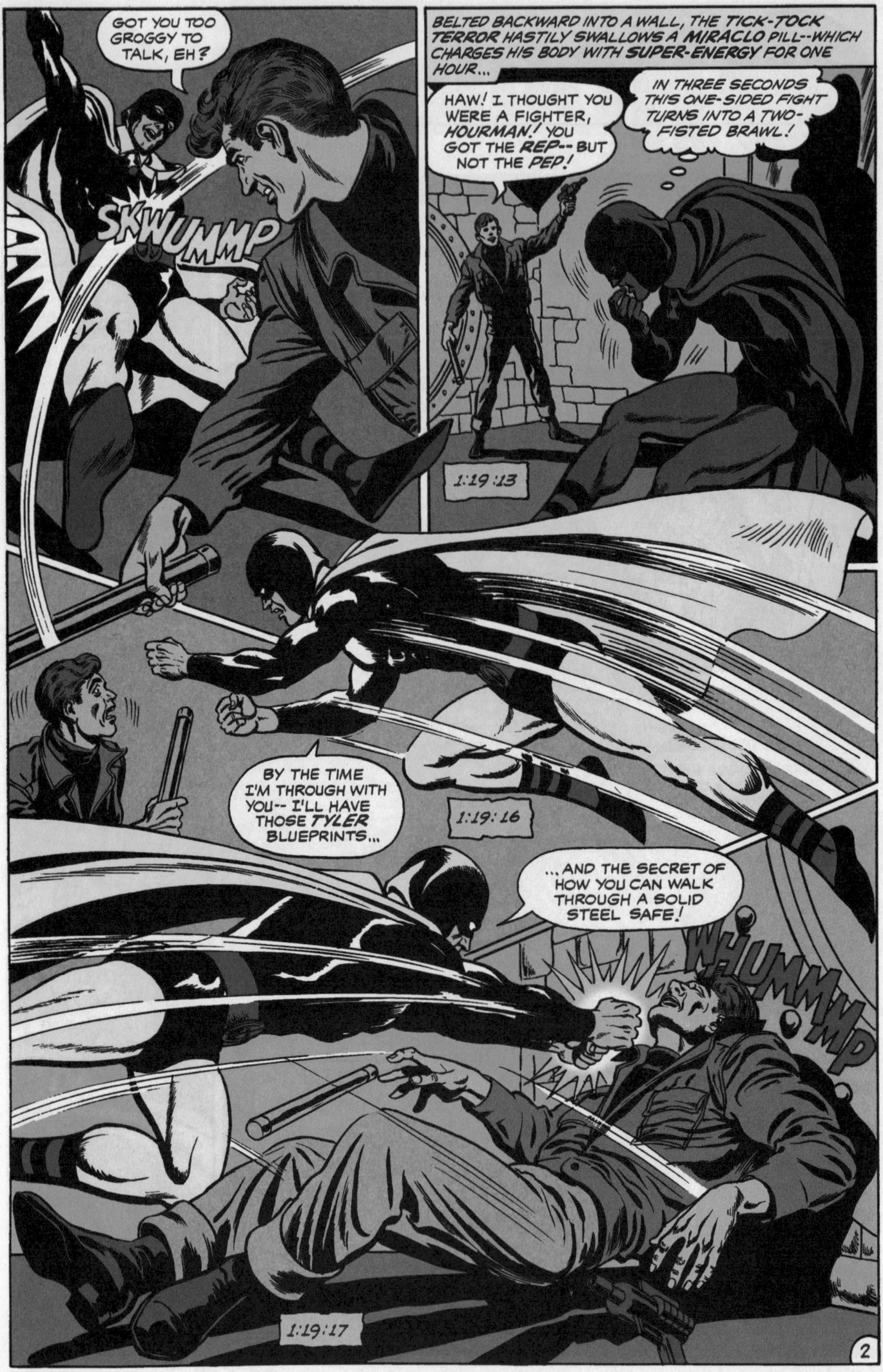

GOT YOU TOO GROGGY TO TALK, EH?
SKWUMMP
BELTED BACKWARD INTO A WALL, THE TICK-TOCK TERROR HASTILY SWALLOWS A MIRACLO PILL--WHICH CHARGES HIS BODY WITH SUPER-ENERGY FOR ONE HOUR...
HAW! I THOUGHT YOU WERE A FIGHTER, HOURMAN! YOU GOT THE REP-- BUT NOT THE PEP!
IN THREE SECONDS THIS ONE-SIDED FIGHT TURNS INTO A TWO-FISTED BRAWL!
1:19:13
BY THE TIME I'M THROUGH WITH YOU-- I'LL HAVE THOSE TYLER BLUEPRINTS...
1:19:16
...AND THE SECRET OF HOW YOU CAN WALK THROUGH A SOLID STEEL SAFE!
WHUMMMMP
1:19:17
2

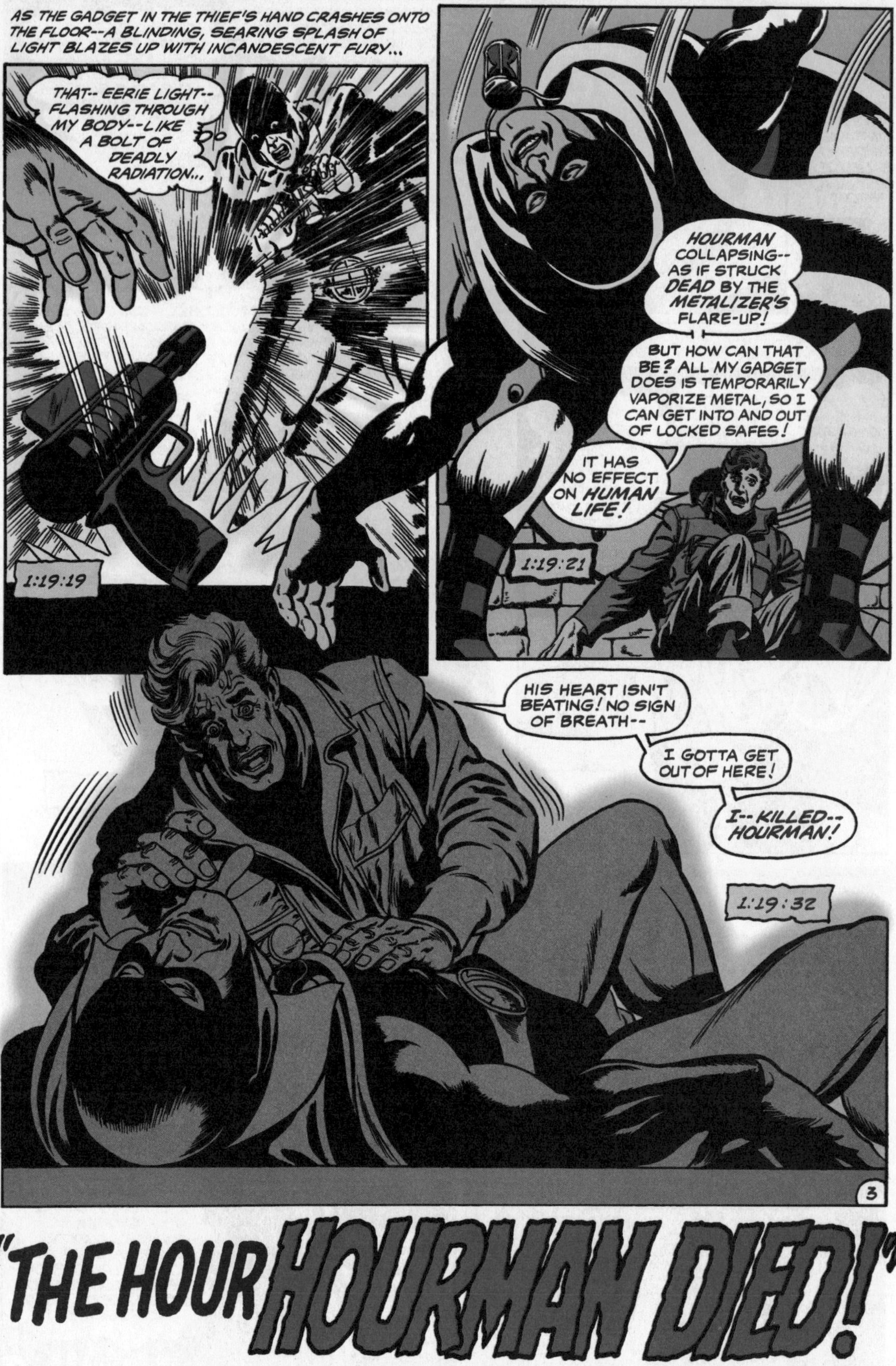
AS THE GADGET IN THE THIEF'S HAND CRASHES ONTO THE FLOOR--A BLINDING, SEARING SPLASH OF LIGHT BLAZES UP WITH INCANDESCENT FURY...
THAT-- EERIE LIGHT-- FLASHING THROUGH MY BODY--LIKE A BOLT OF DEADLY RADIATION...
1:19:19
HOURMAN COLLAPSING-- AS IF STRUCK DEAD BY THE METALIZER'S FLARE-UP!
BUT HOW CAN THAT BE? ALL MY GADGET DOES IS TEMPORARILY VAPORIZE METAL, SO I CAN GET INTO AND OUT OF LOCKED SAFES!
IT HAS NO EFFECT ON HUMAN LIFE!
1:19:21
HIS HEART ISN'T BEATING! NO SIGN OF BREATH--
I GOTTA GET OUT OF HERE!
I--KILLED-- HOURMAN!
1:19:32
3

"THE HOUR HOURMAN DIED!"

FOR ALMOST HALF AN HOUR AFTER THE FLEEING FOOTSTEPS OF TRICKY DICK ARNOLD HAVE FADED OUT, THERE IS DEAD SILENCE IN THE VAULT ROOM...

I HEARD HIM SAY I WAS DEAD-- AND YET, THOUGH MY HEART AND LUNGS ARE STILLED...

I STILL FEEL A CRUDE SEMBLANCE OF LIFE... MAINTAINED BY THE MIRACLO SUPER-ENERGY WITHIN MY BODY!

1:48:56

TAKING A FOLLOW-UP MIRACLO PILL WOULD HAVE NO EFFECT ON ME AT ALL! ONLY BY DISCOVERING THE NATURE OF THE RADIATION THAT KILLED ME--THEN NEUTRALIZING IT... CAN I HOPE TO BRING THIS DEAD BODY OF MINE--BACK TO REAL LIFE!

SLOWLY--HALTINGLY--THAT WHICH WAS HOURMAN RISES TO ITS FEET...

IT ISN'T HUMAN LIFE I HAVE-- BUT THE ENERGIZED REACTIONS OF A-- ROBOT!

A SYNTHETIC LIFE THAT WILL FADE AWAY WHEN THE MIRACLO-CHARGE WEARS OFF-- EXACTLY 29 MINUTES, 55 SECONDS FROM NOW!

1:49:18

I CAN FEEL MY SUPER-CHARGED SENSES TUNING IN ON THE RADIATION THAT DOOMED ME-- STILL LINGERING IN THE LETHAL WEAPON AND ON THE STOLEN BLUE-PRINT TUBE!

CAN'T WASTE A SINGLE SECOND! GOT TO GAIN POSSESSION OF THEM--ANALYZE THE RADIATION...

1:49:23

FAR AHEAD OF THE TICK-TOCK THUNDERBOLT, TRICKY DICK ARNOLD KEEPS HIS FOOT PRESSED DOWN HARD ON THE ACCELERATOR OF HIS GETAWAY CAR...

WHEN A SUPER-HERO LIKE HOURMAN IS KILLED, THE LAW GOES ALL OUT TO CATCH HIS MURDERER!

TO SAY NOTHING OF THE JUSTICE SOCIETY!

TOLL   TOLL

ONE THING'S FOR SURE! IF THEY CATCH UP TO ME THEY'RE NOT GONNA FIND ANY EVIDENCE ON ME! I'M GETTING RID OF THE METALIZER AND TYLER BLUE-PRINTS!

TO START OVER SOMEWHERE ELSE, I'LL NEED A STAKE! IT'LL TAKE ONLY A COUPLE OF EXTRA MINUTES TO GO TO MY HIDE-OUT, PICK UP THE LOOT OF MY OTHER METALIZER ROBBERIES...

4

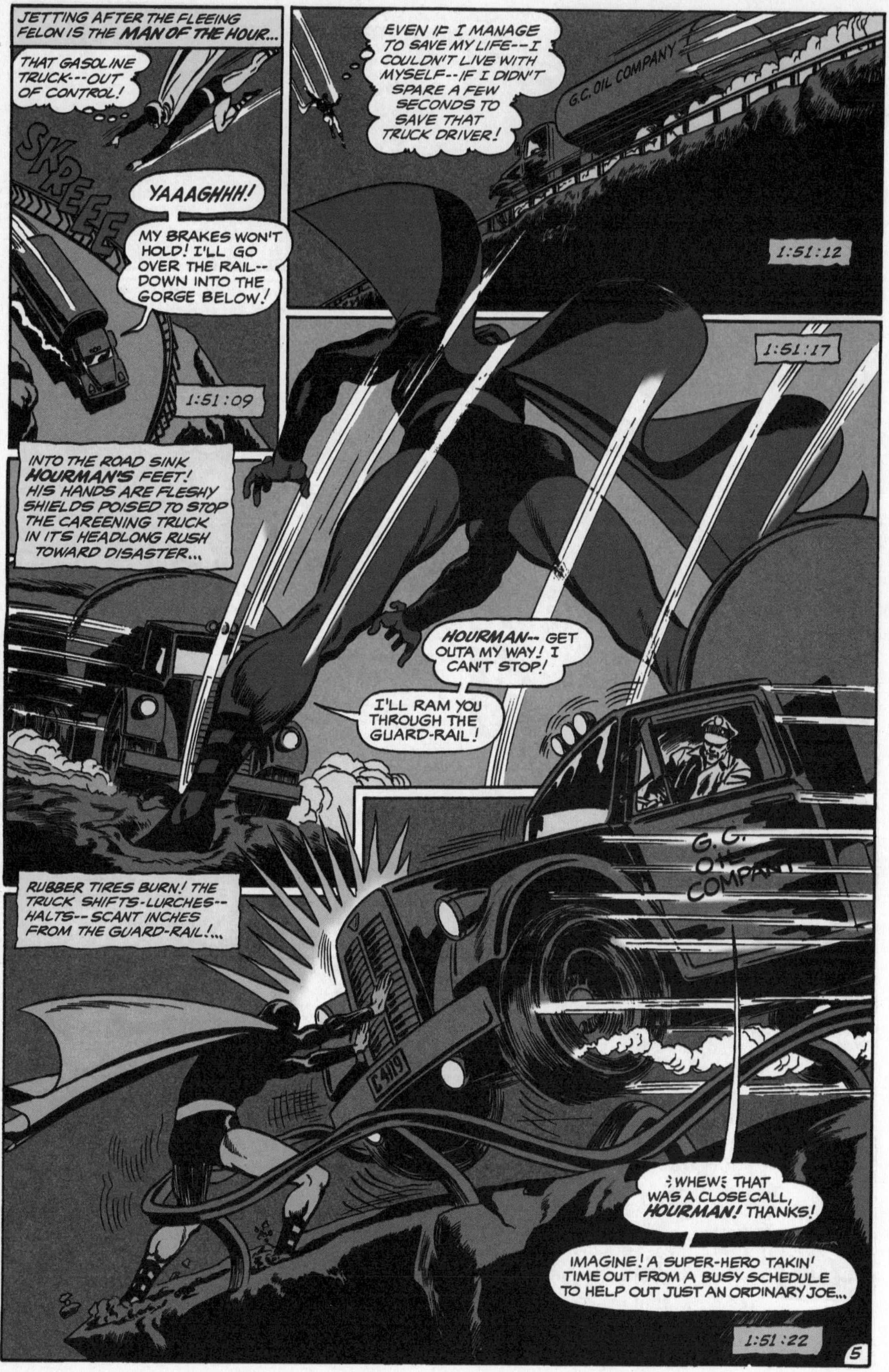
JETTING AFTER THE FLEEING FELON IS THE MAN OF THE HOUR...
THAT GASOLINE TRUCK---OUT OF CONTROL!
SKREEEE
YAAAGHHH!
MY BRAKES WON'T HOLD! I'LL GO OVER THE RAIL--DOWN INTO THE GORGE BELOW!
1:51:09
EVEN IF I MANAGE TO SAVE MY LIFE--I COULDN'T LIVE WITH MYSELF--IF I DIDN'T SPARE A FEW SECONDS TO SAVE THAT TRUCK DRIVER!
G.C. OIL COMPANY
1:51:12
1:51:17
INTO THE ROAD SINK HOURMAN'S FEET! HIS HANDS ARE FLESHY SHIELDS POISED TO STOP THE CAREENING TRUCK IN IT'S HEADLONG RUSH TOWARD DISASTER...
HOURMAN-- GET OUTA MY WAY! I CAN'T STOP!
I'LL RAM YOU THROUGH THE GUARD-RAIL!
RUBBER TIRES BURN! THE TRUCK SHIFTS-LURCHES--HALTS--SCANT INCHES FROM THE GUARD-RAIL!...
G.C. OIL COMPANY
C4119
WHEW! THAT WAS A CLOSE CALL, HOURMAN! THANKS!
IMAGINE! A SUPER-HERO TAKIN' TIME OUT FROM A BUSY SCHEDULE TO HELP OUT JUST AN ORDINARY JOE...
1:51:22
5

EH? THE RADIATION-TRAIL'S STOPPED SHORT--AT THE SURFACE OF THIS RIVER!

IT MUST MEAN MY KILLER'S UNLOADED HIS GADGET AND STOLEN BLUEPRINTS BELOW!

1:54:49

THERE THEY ARE! THE WATER'S PREVENTING THEM FROM GIVING OFF THEIR RADIATIONS!

MAYBE OUT IN THE OPEN AIR THEY'LL RADIATE AGAIN...

1:56:03

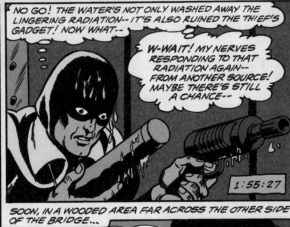

NO GO! THE WATER'S NOT ONLY WASHED AWAY THE LINGERING RADIATION--IT'S ALSO RUINED THE THIEF'S GADGET! NOW WHAT--

W-WAIT! MY NERVES RESPONDING TO THAT RADIATION AGAIN--FROM ANOTHER SOURCE! MAYBE THERE'S STILL A CHANCE--

1:55:27

SOON, IN A WOODED AREA FAR ACROSS THE OTHER SIDE OF THE BRIDGE...

SOMETHING HE'S CARRYING IN THE CAR--EMITTING THE RADIATION!

PROBABLY SOME IRRADIATED LOOT HE STOLE WITH THE HELP OF HIS GADGET...

1:59:49

GOT TO RUSH THIS MONEY TO MY LAB FOR ANALYSIS--COME UP WITH AN ANTIDOTE!

HOURMAN?! B-BUT I LEFT YOU FOR D-DEAD...!

KRAKK

1:59:56

6

THOUGH UNNERVED BY THE APPEARANCE OF THE MAN HE THINKS HE HAD MURDERED, ARNOLD BOLTS INTO FRENZIED COUNTER-ACTION...

I WENT TO A LOTTA TROUBLE STEALING THAT MONEY--AND NO DEAD MAN'S GHOST IS GONNA SPIRIT IT AWAY FROM ME!

HEY! I HIT *SOLID FLESH!* WH-WHAT KINDA GHOST ARE YOU, ANYWAY!

2:00:00

UNGUIDED, THE CAR CAREENS OFF THE ROAD, AND...

DROP IT, HOURMAN! DROP THE BREAD!

NOT WHEN IT'S MY BREAD--OF LIFE...

KA-R4ASH

2:00:07

WITHIN THREE SECONDS, THE TWO FOES ARE LEAPING AT ONE ANOTHER...

SANDS OF TIME RUNNING OUT ON ME...

THIS SPOOK'S NOT RUNNING OFF WITH MY DOUGH...

2:00:10

PHWA AAHAMMM

2:00:12

WITH THE SUPER-POWERED FIST SCORING THE DECISIVE BLOW...

2:00:14

7

IN A LABORATORY OF THE TYLER CHEMICAL COMPANY, 13 MINUTES, 31 SECONDS LATER...

I'M GETTING A CLEAR READING ON THE IRRADIATED MONEY...

HOURMAN-- EXPERIMENT-ING WITH MY LOOT...

NORMALLY, THAT RADIATION BLAST WOULD HAVE NO EFFECT ON HUMAN LIFE-- BUT WHEN COMBINED WITH THE MIRACLO ENERGY IN MY BODY, IT HAD A LETHAL REACTION ON ME...

2:13:45

WHA--?

HANDS OFF MY MONEY! I DON'T KNOW HOW TO KNOCK OUT A GHOST--

BUT I'M SURE GONNA GIVE IT A GOOD TRY!

GWUMP

2:13:48

I HOPE YOU'RE GETTING MORE OF A BANG OUTA THIS THAN I AM, HOURMAN!

BANG

BANG BANG

2:13:59

WITH A BURST OF SUPER-CHARGED ENERGY, THE TICK-TOCK TERROR CRASHES THE BACK OF HIS HEAD ONTO HIS ATTACKER'S FOREHEAD...

I'LL BE DEAD ON MY FEET IF I KEEP WASTING ANY MORE VALUABLE TIME WITH THIS THUG...

KWHAAAK

2:14:06

WHILE HE SLEEPS OFF THAT PUNCH, IT'S GOING TO TAKE ME A HECTIC FIVE MINUTES TO PREPARE THE RADIATION ANTIDOTE...

CLUNK

2:14:10

8

EVEN AS THE LAST GRAINS OF SAND TRICKLE DOWN THROUGH HIS HOUR GLASS, HOURMAN GULPS DOWN HIS LIFE-RESTORING CONCOCTION...
2:19:10
9
SHORTLY, AS HE TAKES HIS PRISONER TO POLICE HEADQUARTERS...
POLICE
WHAT GRIPES ME IS--IF I DIDN'T GET THAT MONEY FOR A STAKE--YOU'D NEVER HAVE CAUGHT UP WITH ME!
YES--YOUR STAKE TURNED OUT TO BE YOUR MISTAKE!
THE END

CRISIS ON MULTIPLE EARTHS THE TEAM UPS

MURPHY ANDERSON

Heavily influenced by artists Lou Fine and Will Eisner, Murphy Anderson entered the comics arena in 1944 as an artist for Fiction House. In 1950, he began his life-long association with DC Comics, pulling double duty as both a full illustrator and as an inker over other artists' pencil work. Though he inked only a few of Mike Sekowsky's first Justice League pages, Anderson continued his work on JUSTICE LEAGUE OF AMERICA covers for several years thereafter.

JOHN BROOME

Though he was well versed in all genres, John Broome was best known for the science-fiction-oriented writing he produced during his long career in comics, both under his own name and under the oft-used pen names of "John Osgood" and "Edgar Ray Merrit." Recruited from the sci-fi pulps in the early 1940s by DC editor Julie Schwartz, Broome adapted his skills effortlessly from prose to illustrated fiction.

Throughout the '40s, '50s and '60s, Broome penned a myriad of features for Schwartz, including the Justice Society of America, Captain Comet, Detective Chimp, and the Atomic Knights. Today, comics historians are most familiar with his work on the Silver Age FLASH and GREEN LANTERN, the two series that best gave him the opportunity to exercise his greatest strength: imbuing even the most straitlaced super-heroes with a whimsical sense of humor and strong, solid characterization.

John Broome retired from comic books in 1970 to travel the world and to teach English in Japan. He passed away in 1999.

DICK DILLIN

Born in Watertown, New York in 1929, Richard (Dick) Dillin graduated from Syracuse University and spent some years in the field of commercial illustration before embarking on a career in comics. Best remembered for his almost 12-year-long run on JUSTICE LEAGUE OF AMERICA, Dillin also had a decades-long association with the character Blackhawk both at Quality Comics and DC. It can safely be said that during the 1960s and '70s there was not a single DCU character that the prolific artist didn't draw at one time or another. Dillin passed away in 1980.

GARDNER FOX

Probably the single most imaginative and productive writer in the Golden Age of comics, Gardner Fox created or co-created dozens of long-running features, among them Flash, Hawkman, Sandman, and Dr. Fate. Working with editor Sheldon Mayer, and later with Julie Schwartz, Fox also penned the adventures of the Justice Society of America, comics' first super-team, during the 1940s. Following the late 1950s revival of the super-hero genre, Fox—again under Schwartz's guidance—assembled Earth's Mightiest Heroes once more and scripted an unbroken 65-issue run of JUSTICE LEAGUE OF AMERICA. Though Fox produced thousands of other scripts and wrote over 100 books, it is perhaps this body of work for which he is best known. Fox passed away in 1986.

JOE GIELLA

Born in 1928, Joe Giella began his art career in the 1940s and came to DC in 1951. Though an accomplished penciller, Giella made his name at DC as a talented and versatile inker. He worked only occasionally on JUSTICE LEAGUE OF AMERICA until 1969, at which point he teamed with penciller Dick Dillin for a landmark tenure of four years. He currently illustrates the *Mary Worth* comic strip.

SID GREENE

Brought to JUSTICE LEAGUE OF AMERICA to replace the retired Bernard Sachs, Sid Greene was one of editor Julie Schwartz's most prolific artists. He added a new crispness to Mike Sekowsky's pencils for three years until his retirement in 1969. Greene died in 1972.

CARMINE INFANTINO

The man most closely associated with the Silver Age Flash, Carmine Infantino began working in comics in the mid-1940s as the artist on such features as Green Lantern, Black Canary, Ghost Patrol...and the original Golden Age Flash. Infantino lent his unique style to a variety of superhero, supernatural, and Western features throughout the 1950s until he was tapped to pencil the 1956 revival of the Flash. While continuing to pencil the FLASH series, he also provided the art for other strips, including Batman, Elongated Man, and Adam Strange. Infantino became DC's editorial director in 1967 and, later, publisher before returning to freelancing in 1976, since which time he has pencilled and inked numerous features, including the Batman newspaper strip, GREEN LANTERN CORPS, and DANGER TRAIL.

GIL KANE

Born in 1926, Kane and his family moved from their native Latvia to New York City when Kane was three. By the time he'd reached his late teens, Kane, an artistic prodigy, had left his mark on every major comics publisher of the day, including MLJ, Prize, Quality, Marvel – and DC, for whom he produced Wildcat, Johnny Thunder, and a plethora of Western, science-fiction and true-crime tales. In 1959, he joined with John Broome to revive the Golden Age hero Green Lantern, in the process totally revamping the look of the strip and giving the Emerald Gladiator the trademark sleek, streamlined costume he wears to this day.

Over the years, Gil Kane's work has come to stand as the textbook definition of dynamic drawing. A master of style, Kane imbued each of his drawings with an unequaled sense of power and motion. Though Kane continued to illustrate GREEN LANTERN throughout the 1960s, he lent pencil and pen to many other series as well, such as Marvel Comics' *Amazing Spider-Man* and *Captain America* and Tower's *T.H.U.N.D.E.R. Agents*. Gil Kane passed away in 2000.

JULIUS SCHWARTZ

More than any other editor, Julie Schwartz, (1915-2004) helped shape the face of the comic-book medium as we know it today. Hired as a DC editor in 1944, Schwartz brought an inventiveness and dedication to the craft of storytelling that soon made him a legend in his own right. His true legacy, however, came to flower in the 1950s and early 1960s, when, together with Gardner Fox, John Broome, Carmine Infantino, and others, he revived and revitalized the all-but-abandoned super-hero genre, transforming such nearly forgotten heroes as The Flash and Green Lantern into the superstars that formed the Justice League. Without that timely infusion of energy, comic books might well have gone the way of the penny postcard, the automat and the drive-in movie – faded icons of a bygone era.

Biographical material researched and written by Mark Waid.